Outsiders Inside

Notions of diaspora are central to contemporary debates about 'race', ethnicity, identity and nationalism. Yet the Irish diaspora, one of the oldest and largest, is often excluded on the grounds of 'whiteness'. Irish diasporic women are 'invisible', yet their experiences illustrate the complexities of racial and ethnic entanglements in the histories of both the United States and Britain.

Outsiders Inside explores the themes of displacement and the meanings of home for these women and their descendants. This work juxtaposes the visibility of Irish women in the United States with their marginalization in Britain. Bronwen Walter challenges linear notions of migration and assimilation by demonstrating that two forms of identification can be held simultaneously. By exploring the life stories of Irish women living in Britain in the 1990s, she traces the inextricable links between gender, ethnicity and place in these diasporic identities.

In an age when the 'Celtic Tiger' economy and the Northern Ireland peace process are rapidly changing global perceptions of Irishness, this book reminds us that gender and race remain powerful subtexts. *Outsiders Inside* moves the empirical study of the Irish diaspora out of the 'ghetto' of Irish Studies and into the mainstream, challenging theorists and policy-makers to pay attention to the issue of white diversity.

Bronwen Walter is Reader in Social and Cultural Geography at Anglia Polytechnic University, Cambridge. She is a leading researcher of the Irish in Britain.

Gender, Racism, Ethnicity
Series editors:
Kum-Kum Bhavnani, *University of California at Santa Barbara*
Avtar Brah, *University of London*
Gail Lewis, *The Open University*
Ann Phoenix, *University of London*

Gender, Racism, Ethnicity is a series whose main concern is to promote rigorous feminist analysis of the intersections between gender, racism, ethnicity, class and sexuality within the contexts of imperialism, colonialism and neo-colonialism. Intended to contribute new perspectives to current debates and to introduce fresh analysis, it will provide valuable teaching texts for undergraduates, lecturers and researchers in anthropology, women's studies, cultural studies and sociology.

Other titles in the series:

White Women, Race Matters
Ruth Frankenberg

Fear of the Dark
Lola Young

Gendering Orientalism
Reina Lewis

Cartographies of Diaspora
Avtar Brah

'Other Kinds of Dreams'
Julia Sudbury

Against Purity
Irene Gedalof

Gender and International Migration in Europe
Eleonore Kofman, Annie Phizacklea, Parvati Raghuram and Rosemary Sales

Outsiders Inside

Whiteness, place and Irish women

Bronwen Walter

London and New York

First published 2001 by Routledge
11 New Fetter Lane, London EC4P 4EE

Simultaneously published in the USA and Canada
by Routledge
29 West 35th Street, New York, NY 10001

Routledge is an imprint of the Taylor & Francis Group

© 2001 Bronwen Walter

Typeset in Baskerville and Gill Sans by
Curran Publishing Services Ltd, Norwich
Printed and bound in Great Britain by
Biddles, Guildford and King's Lynn

British Library Cataloguing in Publication Data
A catalogue record for this book is available from the British
Library.

Library of Congress Cataloging in Publication Data

Walter, Bronwen.
    Outsiders inside: Whiteness, place and Irish women / Bronwen
Walter.
        p. cm.
    Includes bibiographical references and index.
    1. Women--Great Britain--Identity. 2. Women immigrants--Great
Britain--Social conditions. 3. Women--Ireland--Identity. 4. Irish--
Cultural assimilation--Great Britain. 5. Race awareness--Great
Britain. 6. Irish American women--Social conditions.

HQ1593.W35 2000
305.48'89162041--dc21
                                                        s00-035313

ISBN 0-415-12398-4 (pbk)
ISBN 0-415-12397-6 (hbk)

To my mother, Jane, and in memory of my father, Sam (Goronwy)

Contents

Plates

Figures

Acknowledgements

There are two people without whom this book would probably never have been started and certainly never finished. One is my research collaborator and friend Mary J. Hickman for whose intellectual generosity and political acuteness I am always extremely grateful. The other is John, who believed that the project could be completed and helped me carve a space in an overcrowded life to write the final chapters, as well as providing sustenance of every kind at the right moments. They both read drafts and offered invaluable advice. I am also very grateful to Gail Lewis for her patience, advice and determination to include Irish women in this series.

I would like to thank Anglia Polytechnic University for giving me research time and my wise and supportive colleagues in Geography and Women's Studies, particularly Maureen Fitzgerald, Maureen Fordham, Penelope Kenrick, Sarah Monk, and Shirley Prendergast. I also want to express my appreciation to my 'home from home', the Irish Studies Centre at the University of North London, especially for the cheerful and unstinting work of Sarah Morgan. I would like to acknowledge the contribution of Irish community workers in London whose tenacity I admire and from whom I have learned a great deal, especially Angie Birtill, John Brennan, Tom Connor, Sean Hutton and Seamus Taylor. I am also indebted to groups of students taking part in the module 'Irish women and migration' who constantly produced new insights from the life stories they collected, much to their surprise.

I am especially grateful to the anonymous women in Bolton who allowed me to ask questions about their lives and to Alan

Grattan for helping me to meet some of them. I want to thank Lois Rutherford for taking the photograph for Plate 2.1, and for her welcoming hospitality in Arlington, Massachusetts. Over the years I have enjoyed friendly and helpful service from Anglia Polytechnic University Library, Cambridge University Library and Bolton Public Library. The graphs and diagrams were drawn by Jackie Taylor.

I acknowledge support from Economic and Social Research Council (ESRC) Research Grant R000234790 in 1993–4 for 'Hidden Irishwomen: gender and migration to Britain 1951–1991'. I would also like to thank ONS for allowing the use of the Office for National Statistics (ONS) Longitudinal Study, and members of the Longitudinal Study (LS) User Support Programme at the Centre for Longitudinal Studies (CLS), Institute of Education, for assistance with accessing the data. The views expressed in this publication are not necessarily those of the ONS or CLS. The samples of anonymised records have been provided by the Census Microdata Unit (CMU) at the University of Manchester with the support of ESRC/Joint Information Systems Committee (JISC). Figure 2.2, from *Harper's New Monthly Magazine* vol.12 no. 69, February 1856, is reproduced by permission of The British Library. The extract from the *Boston Globe* on pp. 43–4 is reproduced with kind permission of the *Boston Globe*.

This is a good place to record my gratitude to family and friends who have shared eating, drinking and laughs, which restored my wellbeing when the enjoyably permeable but dangerously elastic boundaries between work and play became stretched, especially Jane, Merry, Eva, Keith, Jackie, Frank, Glenda and Alan. Finally, special thanks to Ben and Angharad for the pleasure as well as the freedom to write which their passionate absorptions in their own lives now give me.

Introduction

This is a story of diaspora. It highlights a population of migrants and their descendents, whose lives remain largely hidden although their labour has been strongly in demand. When I tell you that they are women, you will find this situation unexceptional. Working women have never been fully recognised in the West and migrants are even more marginal. But this group of women has also been rendered invisible because of the specific political context in which they have moved. This is the troubled relationship between Britain and Ireland, which continues to have wide-ranging and largely unacknowledged ramifications within the two countries and well beyond them. One way in which this history has been submerged, and separated from the broader histories of colonialism, has been through the homogenising notion of 'whiteness'.

Over seventy million people world-wide, more than half of them women, claim an Irish identity, but of these only five million live on the island of Ireland. The scattering of Irish people has been on an extraordinary scale in the wake of the catastrophe of the Famine in the 1840s. They and their descendents have become embedded in two of the largest industrial economies in the nineteenth and twentieth centuries, those of Britain and the United States, in ways that have hardly begun to be recognised.

The roles of women are especially invisible, yet women have been the most mobile part of this population. Their economic ties to the land in Ireland were shaken loose by the Famine and they became available to fill the massive gaps in rapidly-industrialising labour forces elsewhere. They were especially in demand for the most menial work of servants, a role which indigenous women left behind as soon as higher status employment became available.

Over 80 per cent of Irish-born women in both the United States and Britain were recorded as domestic servants well into the twentieth century. They are still substantially overrepresented in these areas of work in Britain, as were 1980s 'illegals' in the United States. The huge contribution of Irish women to domestic service links them to key processes in western industrialisation, including constructions of white middle-class masculinity through the cult of domesticity, and the constructions of whiteness in both the United States and Britain.

Irish women have also been strongly in demand in other sectors, notably in the textile industry in the second half of the nineteenth century and early twentieth century and more recently in health care. More than a quarter of all Irish-born women working in Britain since 1945 have been nurses. Their patterns of migration and employment show a striking resemblance to those of African-Caribbean women, who also left as independent migrants and in larger numbers than men in the post-war period. But these parallels are rarely drawn because the condition of migrancy is subordinated to that of black/white difference.

The absence of migrant Irish women from public discourse has been matched by a resounding silence in academic study. Women's place in Irish society has increasingly been recognised since the 1980s but emigrant women have been left almost entirely off the agenda. When Anna Brady's *Women in Ireland: An Annotated Bibliography* was published in 1988 it included over 2,300 entries: only eight were on emigration. Since then there has been a flowering of publications on women in Ireland (see for example Luddy and Murphy 1990; Smyth 1993; Luddy 1995; Hoff and Coulter 1995; Byrne and Leonard 1997; Bradley and Valliulis 1997; O'Connor 1998; Sales 1997). With a few notable exceptions this has not been matched by research on emigration from Ireland (Kelly and Nic Giolla Choille 1990; Mac Laughlin 1997; Ni Laoire 1999) or, until more recently, on women in the diaspora (see Akenson 1995).

This absence is especially marked in work on the Irish in Britain. John Jackson's (1963) classic work, still the only full-length treatment spanning the nineteenth and twentieth centuries, invariably writes of migrants as 'he', and indeed describes men's lives for the most part. In part this reflects the norms of the 1960s when Jackson was writing, but more recent works, which are primarily concerned with the nineteenth century, still pay little attention to women.

Their unmarked style is implicitly masculine and the content emphasises the public worlds of politics and male workplaces (Swift and Gilley 1985, 1989; Davis 1991). The small place occupied by half the Irish population in the records (Censuses apart) or in analyses is never questioned. Yet the titles of all these books claim universality in approaching their subject. The lens through which their view is refracted is summed up by the closing words of a keynote contribution by David Fitzpatrick to Swift and Gilley's 1989 collection. His chapter was entitled 'A curious middle place: the Irish in Britain, 1871–1921' but the conclusion makes clear that this was an entirely male location: 'for T. P. O'Connor . . . partial integration into that "British environment" had made the Irish *man* in Britain "broader in *his* outlook" than *his* fellows at home. *He* now occupied "a curious middle place" in British life' (Fitzpatrick 1989: 46; emphasis added).

Only two books take Irish women in Britain as their focus, each presenting a collection of personal biographies and thus providing qualitative material about experiences in the twentieth century. The first, path-breaking, volume was *Across the Water: Irish Women's Lives in Britain* by Mary Lennon, Marie McAdam and Joanne O'Brien (1988). The authors saw this as 'a beginning', a book as much for, as about, diasporic Irish women:

> Rather than a statistical survey of Irish women, we wanted to convey Irish women's experiences of immigration as perceived from the inside – in their own words without commentary from us. Through the photographs, we wanted to contribute a permanent visual record of women's lives in Britain. So few images of ourselves are reflected back to us, and generally the perspective is not ours. We decided finally on a book consisting of edited interviews and photographs.
> (Lennon, McAdam and O'Brien 1988: 11)

A second book, *Leading Lives* by Rita Wall (1991) had a different aim, seeking to celebrate the success of nine individual, named Irish women.

> In this book I wanted to challenge the persistent stereotyping of Irish women. The women interviewed are all visible in Britain, each in her own field – outstanding writers, campaigners, entrepreneurs, professionals. Each one of the women interviewed

has stepped out onto new ground with courage and conviction in her own ability. I have deliberately chosen to allow the women to speak for themselves. Too often, women's talk is not heard or appreciated.

(Wall 1991: 11)

The focus on 'visible' women contrasts with that of the authors of *Across the Water* who selected 'primarily, working class women whose experiences are rarely published' (Lennon, McAdam and O'Brien 1988: 11). Both these volumes intentionally leave readers to make their own judgements about the material presented. They counterpose their method of direct reporting with the distanced historical analyses of the historians of the nineteenth century, and explain that they edited the interviews in collaboration with the women whose stories the books tell.

Original qualitative material is slowly appearing, therefore, and is being followed at a growing rate by interpretative analyses in chapters and journal articles (Walter 1989b, 1991, 1995, 1997, 1999; Rossiter 1992, 1996; Daniels 1993; Kells 1995a, b; Gray 1996a, b, c, 1997, 1999; King and O'Connor 1996; Buckley 1997). There are also a small number of theses which take Irish women in Britain as their focus (O'Connor 1993; Letford 1997; Kanya-Forstner 1997; Roche 1997). Many of these sources have been brought together in an annotated bibliography (Barrington 1997).

Women are also marginalised in the far more extensive bibliography of Irish-American emigration and settlement. In Kerby Miller's (1985) monumental (684 pages) and apparently comprehensive text, *Emigrants and Exiles*, for example, only twenty references to women are given in the index. However in a 1996 collection edited by Ronald Bayor and Timothy Meagher, an even more substantial volume (744 pages), women are much more prominent in a number of chapters, indicating that recent scholarship is less skewed in its coverage. In contrast to Britain, one text specifically analyses Irish women's experience in the nineteenth century, Hasia Diner's (1983) *Erin's Daughters in America*. It provides a wealth of material about the conditions in which Irish women lived and the changes over the course of the century. A small volume recording twentieth century Irish migrant women's oral histories in the United States has also been published, Ide O'Carroll's (1990) *Models for Movers*. As in the British collections, direct experiences are prioritised over analysis:

Although the possible reasons and explanations for this emigration of Irish women are discussed, the major focus of the book is on what women emigrants themselves have to say. Interviews with some women emigrants I spoke to are given in their entirety because, in truth, theirs is the only real picture. Our interpretation of their words is merely one path to an understanding of their life's experiences.

(O'Carroll 1990: 15)

However a breakthrough was marked by the publication of an edited volume entitled *Irish Women and Irish Migration* (O'Sullivan 1995) in Patrick O'Sullivan's series *The Irish World Wide*, which contains a number of case studies of historical and contemporary aspects of Irish women's migration experiences. The editor's aim was 'to draw attention to the paucity of research into the experiences of women. Make the gap visible'. The moves towards closing the gap which have been gathering pace in Britain reflect the larger consolidation of feminist scholarship in the 1990s, a small but steady increasing number of women undertaking research in this area and more open recognition of Irish identities in Britain especially amongst the second generation (Walter 1997).

What is still missing is a critical synthesis of ideas about Irish women in the diaspora. This is the distinctive contribution of my book. My aim is to complement the approaches outlined above by providing a framework which to contextualises these firsthand experiences and detailed case studies within the diasporic spaces of Britain and the United States of America. It is not intended to be a comprehensive survey of diasporic Irish women, but offers ways of thinking about broader processes of mobility and settlement from a comparative perspective. In particular it seeks to locate the specificity of diasporic Irish women's situations within the societies of which they are part. In this way it strengthens the challenge to the invisibility of Irish women outside Ireland already begun and highlights areas for future research.

By raising the issue of Irish women's invisibility outside Ireland I want to question the oversimplified white/black binary construction of 'race' which is so pervasive in Britain and the United States. This universalisation of the centre through shared whiteness marks only certain oppressed groups as different (Carter *et al.* 1993). Such an illusion of coherence is a product of modernist and colonialist discourse, which focuses on the 'other' and categorises itself as a neutral 'same'. In reality, hybridity is a characteristic of all cultures, resulting from 'a long history of confrontation between unequal cultures and forces, in which the stronger culture struggles to control, remake or eliminate the subordinate partner' (Lavie and Swedenburg 1996: 9).

Far from having a fixed, unchanging relationship between culture and terrain, therefore, the white West has long been a 'diaspora space' (Brah 1996). Whiteness certainly carries privileges, but they are not always guaranteed. In order to give back meaning to the apparent emptiness of the 'white' category it is necessary to explore the specificity of white minority experiences.

This book responds to the argument that diaspora discourses must be 'rout[ed] . . . in specific maps/histories' (Clifford 1994: 319). Such a demand is echoed in calls for conjuncturalism, a politics of location in which different axes of domination and the articulations between them can be identified. 'A conjunctural theory of power is not claiming . . . that all such relations of power are equal, equally determining, or equally livable; these are questions that depend on the specific, concrete conjuncture' (Grossberg 1989: 138). The specific map and history of my narrative is that of the outflow of women from Ireland over the last two centuries.

At the time of writing, the Irish Republic is being transformed by the economic success of the 'Celtic Tiger', which has sharply slowed down rates of emigration and led to a net inflow of population, especially after 1996. This contrasts with the situation in the late 1980s when exceptionally high population losses were being recorded, equalling and even exceeding the peak years of emigration in the 1950s. The transformation at home is paralleled by a world-wide commodification of Irishness manifested in theme bars and keg-beer brands. Despite an apparently positive remoulding of Irish images, however, this 'greening' retains a strongly masculine flavour. Moreover it continues to run alongside a deeply-ingrained negative stereotyping of Irish people, especially in Britain.

Chapter I

Diaspora

Key concepts and contexts

In this chapter I examine key theoretical and empirical material which will help the reader to interpret the arguments developed in the book. First, I examine the value of diaspora as a framework for Irish women's emigration and settlement. I show how place is crucially bound up with the concept of diaspora, bringing together spatial and social understandings which constitute and inform each other. Second, I ground these notions in the specific case of Ireland by tracing the empirical background to the exceptionally large-scale movement of women out of Ireland over the last two centuries. Third, I show how representations of women in Ireland have reflected and confirmed the unequal access to power which underlay high rates of emigration. These representations 'at home' also followed women into the diaspora in various forms. In the fourth section, I examine processes of racialisation of women outside Ireland which underpin their social positionings and experiences in the diaspora. Finally I place myself in the analysis by interrogating my own relationship to the Irish diaspora in Britain.

A diaspora framework: spatial and social concepts

> Diasporas . . . take place in the context of both social and geographical uneven development . . . what is always in play is the specific form of the spatiality of power.
>
> (Massey and Jess 1995: 235)

The theme of the spatiality of power runs through this narrative of Irish women and diaspora. Power is often overlooked in the celebration of diaspora and hybridity in contemporary cultural criticism. This leads to 'theories and politics which neglect the everyday, grounded practices and economic relations in which social identities and narratives of race and nation unfold' (Mitchell 1997: 533). I shall use the framework of diaspora to explore the location of Irish migrant women outside and inside the societies in which they settle, grounding these theoretical concepts firmly in the materiality of women's lives.

As Clifford (1994: 302) points out, diasporas are 'always entangled in powerful global histories'. Diasporas must be seen as a product and constituent of international capitalism, which has been the process underlying the large-scale demand for Irish women and men as labour migrants in North America and Britain for two centuries. The Irish diaspora must be also be positioned within British imperialism, re-attaching it to the colonial enterprise from which it is often separated by the black/white binary. Whiteness is thus a key issue in the analysis. Both these global positionings underpin representations of Irish people which exclude women. On the one hand, British colonialism has constructed masculine Irish others. On the other, capital seeks to 'disembody the labor from the migrant worker' (Kearney 1991, cited in Lavie and Swedenburg 1996). Thus while the economic contribution of Irish women migrants underpins profits and growth, their social presence has often been devalued and marginalised. In processes of marginalisation some bodies become highly marked, but others are rendered invisible.

In order to highlight different spatialities of power I have chosen to use a comparative framework in which the United States is contrasted with Britain so as to make the familiar strange. Why aren't Irish identities in Britain as desirable as they are in the United States? Why do Irish women have a strong positive image in the United States and an almost non-existent one in Britain? I examine these questions over the long timespan of the nineteenth and twentieth centuries, to allow both continuity and change to be explored within and between these locations.

Diaspora is a central notion in this book. This is a spatial concept in a multitude of ways. In descriptive terms, it refers to the long-term settlement which follows people's scattering or dispersal from their 'original' homeland (Hall 1995). But contemporary cultural understandings parallel this 'closed' definition with a more 'open' symbolic spatiality, which combines the separate locations of origin, travel and settlement into a 'third space'.

> Diaspora discourse articulates or bends together both roots and routes to construct what Gilroy describes as alternate public spheres, forms of community consciousness and solidarity that maintain identification outside the national time/space in order to live inside, with a difference.
>
> (Clifford 1994: 308)

Instead of a linear journey of migration from 'outside' to permanent settlement 'inside', accompanied by assimilation from identities of origin to those of destination, this notion of diaspora expects the two forms of consciousness to be held at the same time. The concept thus explicitly dislodges many kinds of binary notion: of migrant/settler, insider/outsider, home/away. In place of either/or relationships conventionally associated with the resettlement process, migrants and their descendents are connected by both/and ties to their countries of origin and settlement. Hence one meaning of the title of this book, which appears paradoxical – surely outsiders by definition cannot be inside? – expresses the simultaneous, connected identities of Irish women as both coming from/identifying with an outside and settled/belonging inside.

However the specificity of the relationship between the Irish diaspora and British imperialism problematises this notion of both/and. Using the example of Black-British, Lavie and Swedenborg argue that the hyphen in hyphenated identities becomes the third time-space: 'A space is charted in the interstices between the displacement of the "histories that constitute it"' (Lavie and Swedenborg 1996: 16). This brings out clearly the contrasting situation of Irish people in the United States and Britain. Irish-American is an accepted identity, indicating the possibility of hybridity, whatever the actual content may be. But there is no term for the Irish in Britain equivalent either to Irish-American or Black-British. A hyphenated Irish-British identity does not exist because there is no acknowledged third space for the hyphen to represent. The identities remain oppositional and unlinked.

Place is a notion closely bound up with the concept of diaspora. In fact two very different definitions of place are involved. The common understanding of place is bound up with settledness, enclosure, coherence and boundedness (Massey 1994). This meaning is implicit in the language of 'displacement' in discussions of diaspora. For example Clifford (1994: 306) refers to 'shared, ongoing history of displacement, suffering, adaptation or resistance' amongst diasporic peoples who do not necessarily identify with a specific origin. The significance of a concept of 'home', both as yearning for a place of origin or in the feeling of 'at-homeness' in the place of destination, also refers to a stable, secure place.

However an alternative definition is also congruent with the concept of diaspora. Doreen Massey strongly critiques the dominant version outlined above. She argues for an understanding of place, 'as a meeting-place, the location of intersections of particular bundles of activity space, of connections and interrelations, of influences and movements' (Massey 1995: 59). Places which are 'open, porous and the products of other places' chime with Avtar Brah's (1996: 181) proposal of 'diaspora space' as '"inhabited" not only by diasporic subjects but equally by those who are constructed and represented as "indigenous"'. As such, the concept of diaspora space foregrounds the 'entanglement of genealogies of dispersion with those of "staying put"'.

In other words, those whose identity is defined by migration are necessarily placed relationally with those who define themselves as having 'stayed put'. The 'difference' of diasporic people is constructed through this juxtaposition. Thus the adoption of the concept of diaspora space shifts the focus dramatically by foregrounding shared locations, which are nevertheless contested. Instead of simple binary polarities which underlie conventional thinking about migration and its consequences, Brah suggests that diaspora can be envisaged as 'a cartography of the politics of intersectionality'. Both 'diasporic' peoples and 'indigenous' peoples equally inhabit diaspora space, which therefore becomes a description of the centre rather than the margins.

Contradictions between these views of place in diaspora discourse will be explored in this book. They resonate strongly with gender. The fixed and bounded understanding of place, with its connections to a romantic view of place as 'home', a haven of rest and retreat, is a masculine characterisation. On the other hand the greater emphasis on 'placement' as well as mobility, which distinguishes the concept of diaspora from that of emigration, gives a recognition to everyday issues of importance in women's lives, often overlooked in more exotic tales of travel. However the contradictions need not necessarily be seen as a duality with a positive and negative pole. Lavie and Swedenborg (1996) argue that the third time-space of diaspora could be seen as a borderzone between identity-as-essence and identity-as-conjuncture, which resists privileging the latter.

Representation of the scattering of population from Ireland as diaspora has had a profound effect on the ways in which it is, and can be, understood. It competes with ongoing traditional discourses of emigration, which carry the very different meanings of a one-way outward flow. 'Emigration' has particular political connotations. It reflects the types of explanation offered for such permanent population losses, expressed in the contrasting labels of 'exile' and 'opportunity'. Conceptualising the outflow as exile explicitly connects it with coercive British policy, and its after-effects, and thus fits with a nationalist interpretation, whilst the notion of opportunity offers a 'revisionist' perspective.

Diaspora has been used sporadically as a descriptive term, usually as a shorthand for Irish settlement in the United States (for example, McCaffrey 1976). However the much more recent use of the concept in academic and political discourse is related to the sharp increase in the globalisation of labour supply and the political project of recentring minority populations within hegemonic majorities (Tololyan 1991). It entered the vocabulary of Irish population movement most clearly through the specific intervention of President Mary Robinson, when in her inaugural speech in 1990 she introduced the keynote theme later elaborated as 'cherishing the diaspora'.

The strategy had a number of significant effects. One was to strengthen more inclusive definitions of Irishness. The stress on the large numbers involved – over seventy millions claiming some form of Irish identity worldwide – inevitably grouped together a diverse population over many generations. A large number of the seventy million were Protestants, for example, the numerous descendents of pre-Famine 'Scotch-Irish' emigrants. This could signal inclusion to Northern Irish Protestants, decentring the traditional association between Catholics and 'exile'. The size of this extended Irish population also positioned Ireland to claim a global identity, no longer the subordinate 'British Isle' or even simply a peripheral European state. Such a reorientation was sealed by the appointment of Mary Robinson as the United Nations Commissioner for Human Rights immediately her term of office was completed.

This embodiment of global identity in the President could be seen as part of a wider process of 'feminising the diaspora', evident in the ways in which the diaspora concept was presented. Under Mary Robinson's presidency the theme was couched in feminised language and symbolism, which took an active rather than a passive form. For example, the choice of the word 'cherish' emphasised a positive notion of nurture rather than the self-sacrificing duty of 'caring' associated with a Catholic version of 'Mother Ireland'. An emphasis on the everyday lives of the global Irish population was reinforced by the President's activities. She made a series of unprecedented visits to welfare agencies in Britain and the United States, acknowledging officially for the first time issues such as homelessness and poor mental health amongst migrants, which successive Irish governments had concealed with a rhetoric of 'opportunity'. Many of these welfare issues had particular resonances for women.

Feminisation was also signalled by the domestic symbols adopted to represent diaspora. In her inaugural speech Mary Robinson announced that she would host annual reunions at the presidential 'home' for representatives of diasporic communities, strongly echoing the importance of family and the high profile of the figure of the mother in Irish culture. However the most striking symbol was that of the lighted candle in the window of Aras an Uachtarain, the official presidential 'home', also occupied as a domestic 'home' by the President and her own family. The flickering candle was intended as a permanent reminder to those who had 'stayed put' in Ireland of the absent members of their 'imagined community'. In her address to both Houses of the Oireachtas in 1992 she said

> I had in mind all our exiles, all our emigrants – past and present
> – when I put the light in the window of Aras an Uachtarain. I
> was not prepared for the power and meaning which a modest
> emblem would have. But we have reason to know in Ireland
> how powerful symbols are: that they carry the force of what they
> symbolise . . . that light reminds us – that the community of
> Irish interest and talent and memory extends far beyond our
> boundaries, far beyond Europe's boundaries . . .
>
> (*Irish Times* 9 July 1992: 8)

The candle is a symbol redolent with gendered significations. Candles are domestic objects which resonate strongly with women's lives in the past, though within the memory of many. To men candles may signify a romantic view of the cosiness of home as a haven, overseen by mothers and wives who 'keep the home fires burning'. Again the symbol was personally linked with Mary Robinson herself: she ceremonially 'blew it out' when she left office, strangely ending the 'eternal tie'. It could be argued therefore that

the President used her role to promote more inclusive understandings, of political tradition, religion and gender, through her
adoption of the diaspora motif. Her own personal part in the construction of these meanings gives yet another twist to the
multifaceted symbolic figure of 'Mother Ireland'.

However the application of a diaspora discourse to Ireland
also has its critics. David Lloyd (1994) rejects this representation of Irish settlement in America. He argues that the discourse
of diaspora depoliticises emigration and disguises its economic
causes, which are linked to the earlier history of colonial
dependence. In his view it provides a cultural gloss to the
economic reality of continuing failure by the governments of
independent Ireland to provide employment at home for Irish
citizens. He also sees it as a strategy by which Irish-Americans
can jump on the 'ethnic bandwagon' and claim special privileges to which they are not entitled as fully-fledged members of
the privileged mainstream.

While it raises important political issues, this critique prioritises
two elements of the diaspora, male migrants and a United States
destination. In the first place, it omits consideration of positive
benefits of this conceptualisation to other constituent parts. For
example, whereas men's migration from Ireland might be classed
as primarily economic and therefore directly affected by state
economic policies in Ireland, women's movement is also the
product of much wider cultural and social processes. Kate Kelly
and Triona Nic Giolla Choille, education and information and
information officers with Emigrant Advice Agency in Dublin,
describe the reasons given by women using their services in the
1980s. For many

> Their main reason for leaving was the repressive moral and
> social climate in Ireland. They describe how narrow social atti-
> tudes and restrictive laws which had an impact on almost every
> aspect of their lives contributed to their decision to leave.
>
> (Kelly and Nic Giolla Choille 1990: 21)

Second, Irish communities in Britain cannot be placed with
such confidence within the white mainstream majority as may be
possible in the United States. And even this confident placing may
reflect a viewpoint from a particular part of the United States, the
West coast from where Lloyd writes.

Breda Gray (1997) also critiques the conceptualisation of Irish emigration as diaspora, arguing that it homogenises both gender and class. The apparent inclusivity blurs the boundaries between a variety of different statuses and in reality continues to privilege mobile masculinity, reinscribing a feminised position of stasis and passivity for all those who remain in Ireland. It implicitly references transnational professional classes and especially excludes working-class female migrants. These are compelling arguments which underline the power relationships which continue to underpin emigration. However I would argue that, although the discourse of diaspora may have been appropriated in these ways within Irish society, this does not negate the opportunities it provides for more progressive understandings of identities which are multiple and constantly in process of change.

Issues of identity permeate the concept of diaspora. Identity is drawn from our location, both specifically geographical (which particular place do we feel we belong to?) and positional (what is our place relative to other group identities?). We all have multiple identities, but their salience changes with time and place. Globalisation brings particular outcomes for identity, producing plural and contested identities within 'diaspora space'. These issues become explicit for the first time when Irish women enter the 'zone of contact' with dominant and other subordinate groups.

Identities are thus placed both geographically and relationally in the context of diaspora. Stuart Hall (1995: 176) illustrates the juxtaposition and inseparability of social and spatial location when he writes: 'Having a position within a set of shared meanings gives us a sense of "who we are", "where we belong" – a sense of our own identity'. Geographical and social positionings are clearly conflated in the identities of 'outsider' and 'insider'. The clash between immigration and diaspora discourses is most evident in contests about who 'belongs' inside. The notion of a fixed relationship between a particular culture and a stable terrain continues to hold sway and to be particularly powerful in nationalist thinking. In 'diaspora space' by contrast, there are no pure essences, only hybridities on the part of apparent 'insiders' as well as those designated as 'outsiders'. Moreover the nation is only one of many inside locations. Irish women in the United States and Britain may be perceived as outsiders in their cultural affiliation as 'Irish', and to patriarchal societies as women, but considered insiders as 'white' people.

Irish women's migration: empirical subjects

One of the most striking aspects of Irish women's migration is the large numbers of people involved. The population of the island as a whole fell from its highest point of 8.5 million in 1841 to a low of 3.5 million in 1961. Jim Mac Laughlin (1994) argues that this reflects Ireland's peripheral status in the global economy which has made it a major supplier of skilled, unskilled and professional workers to international labour markets. Although the loss of over a million migrants in the Famine years of the 1840s is well-known, the huge population decline from a lower base in the 1950s is less talked about outside Ireland; yet of women living in the Irish Republic in 1946, one in three had left the country by 1971 (Kelly and Nic Giolla Choille 1990). A further outpouring occurred in the late 1980s with net losses of over 30,000 people per year.

The gendering of this outpouring has been extremely unusual amongst European migration patterns, where women have been markedly in a minority, especially in the nineteenth century. Irish women have left in greater numbers than men in most decades since 1871 when reliable statistics were first recorded. The only periods in which more men emigrated were those of major wars involving Britain, when many Irish men joined the British army (Kennedy 1973). In the post-1945 era, times of extreme economic depression in Ireland were also associated with a higher ratio of emigrant men, notably in the 1950s, when employment in agriculture declined sharply, and again in the 1980s when foreign investment collapsed. As an underlying trend, however, the ratio of women to men in emigration streams increased steadily from 1,010 women per 1,000 men in 1871–81 to a high point of 1,365 in 1946–51.

Why did so many women leave Ireland? In the second half of the nineteenth century women left sometimes for reasons that were similar to those of men, but also for different causes. Following the Famine of 1845-8 the impartible land inheritance system was widely adopted, whereby a single son inherited the entire property instead of subdivision between all the children. Daughters and remaining sons were thus excluded from the family farm land when they reached adulthood (Arensberg and Kimball 1968). This is a classic example of the stem-family system, in which a single genealogical line continues to keep the 'name on the land' while the sibling branches are removed by emigration. One daughter might remain in the locality by marrying a neighbour's inheriting son, but unless other daughters were able to find some means of acquiring a dowry, they could not be supported as single adults. Joanna Bourke (1993) argues that women in some parts of Ireland did make a positive choice to remain as housekeepers to their brothers, preferring the level of independence they could achieve by being mistress of the household to the loss of status and control which would result from domestic work in strangers' households overseas. Nevertheless large numbers did not, or could not, take this course. A few emigrated to earn dowries to bring home, but the majority left permanently.

What is certain is that the substitution of extensive grazing land for labour-intensive arable systems specifically removed areas of women's agricultural work, and in those which remained women were progressively replaced by men (Lee 1978). As Mac Laughlin (1997) points out, this agricultural restructuring was a product both of 'core' British economic needs and core-formation by rural capital within Ireland. By the end of the nineteenth century, remaining areas of women's farm work had been removed. Control of milk production was seized by the creameries and poultry raising shifted away from the farmstead and out into the male territory of the fields (Bourke 1987, 1990). The peak decade for female emigration, after Census records were first available in 1871, was 1881-91 when there was a net decline in the thirty-two counties of 30,400 women (compared with 29,200 men) (Kennedy 1973).

Educational differences too helped to explain greater emigration amongst daughters than among sons. Girls were educated to higher levels than boys, in part to compensate them for the lack of a tangible inheritance of land, and in part to provide them with skills that would make them better providers of remittances from abroad (Fitzpatrick 1986; Nolan 1989). Women were in this way encouraged to emigrate because they were seen as likely to secure regular employment where they could save money, and also because they were less likely to squander their earnings and thus provide support for their families in Ireland.

The establishment of Irish independence increased the limitations on women's lives, ironically in a state whose proclamation of independence made unusual reference to Irishmen *and* Irishwomen. In 1923, very soon after the establishment of the Free State, a 'marriage bar' was introduced prohibiting married women from remaining in paid employment after marriage in certain occupations. This bar was not lifted until 1973, when Ireland was required to repeal it to conform to EEC labour regulations. The 1937 Constitution defined women's roles even more restrictively by placing the family at the heart of the national project:

> Article 41.1.1. The State recognises the Family as the natural primary and fundamental unit group of Society, and as a moral institution possessing inalienable and imprescriptable rights, antecedent and superior to all positive law.
> 2. The State, therefore, guarantees to protect the Family in its constitution and authority, as the necessary basis of social order and as indispensible to the welfare of the Nation and the State.
>
> (Bunreacht na hEireann 1980: 136)

The economic and social options open to women were thus progressively reduced by the two major sources of power in Ireland: landownership and the Catholic church. Many rejected these restrictions, and chose instead to leave the country (Derry Film and Video 1989; Kelly and Nic Ghiolla Choille 1990; Walter 1991). Although the rate of emigration slowed between 1926 and 1936 in the new twenty-six county state, there was still a net loss of 9,400 women (compared with 7,200 men).

Partition in 1921 produced a very different state in the North of Ireland, with distinctive consequences for women. Because of the industrial economy of North East Ireland, especially Belfast, more paid employment has been available for women and their need to emigrate has been proportionately lower than in the Republic. Although the Catholic Church has not occupied an institutionalised state role as it has in the Republic, it has still played a dominant part in the lives of Catholic women. Similarly the Protestant churches are run by male leaders who exert a strong form of control over the beliefs and activities of Protestant women (Sales 1997). Outflows of women and men have been approximately equal (Compton 1992), and the absolute rates have been high. Since 1969 an additional reason for emigration, especially marked in the early 1970s, has been the renewal of open political conflict.

In both parts of Ireland the family occupies a central role in political ideologies (Prendiville 1988; Smyth 1993). Debates over the abortion and divorce referenda in the Republic during the 1980s, and the failure of feminist and other progressive movements to bring about substantial change in these areas, illustrate the continuing power of the Catholic church to control women's lives. Fundamentalist Northern Protestantism equally places women firmly in the home and opposes the right to choose abortion (Meaney 1993).

Representations of women in Ireland

In this section I want to explore some key issues which are central to arguments in the following chapters. They involve ways in which ideas relevant to Irish women and their mobility have been constructed and conceptualised. In later chapters I will examine some of the practical effects of these constructions in Irish women's lives outside Ireland. Issues of representation thread through the book, including both those of women *in* Ireland, which connect with high levels of mobility and are also both reproduced, transformed and contested in diasporic locations, and those of Irish women *outside* Ireland, which play a significant part in constructions of whiteness.

The observation that 'what is socially peripheral is often symbolically central' (Babcock 1978) is strikingly apposite in the case of Irish women. This is reflected in the contrast between high visibility in symbolic representations of Ireland and a marginalised social position in Irish society. Despite the fact that meanings are never fixed but constantly being negotiated and inflected to meet new situations, there are remarkable continuities in the images of, and discourses about, Irish women.

The Catholic church took on a powerful leadership role in the national struggle and imposed a particular version of gender differentiation. After the Famine the Virgin Mary was promoted as a role model for women. Her assigned qualities, which were promoted as ideals for all Irish women, included duty to family, self-sacrifice, submerged sexuality and the elevation of a caring function above all others. Thus restrictive and limited roles for women became Catholic religious ideals and the Church portrayed married motherhood as the only acceptable status, apart from entering into a religious vocation as a nun (Beale 1986). This discourse of 'proper' womanhood has retained a powerful grip on Irish women's identities, enforced by education and social sanctions, and it continues to coexist with alternative feminist discourses.

A major influence has been the contested colonial relationship with Britain, which has placed Ireland in a position of feminised dependence. The fixing of women in the central, but disempowered role of Mary, was mirrored in images of the Irish nation. Britain represented Ireland as Erin, a young, beautiful but weak woman who needed 'marriage' to her strong masculinised neighbour for control and protection. The feminine position of dependence was popularised in the second half of the nineteenth century by Matthew Arnold, who published theories about Irish 'Celticism'. Celts were constructed as a feminised 'race', characterised as artistic and charming, but impractical and unreliable (Cairns and Richards 1988). This clearly illustrates Ashis Nandy's (1983) observation of the 'homology between sexual and political dominance': 'The homology, drawing support from the denial of psychological bisexuality in men in large areas of Western culture, beautifully legitimized Europe's post-medieval models of dominance, exploitation and cruelty as natural and valid' (Nandy 1983: 3).

Feminised representations of Ireland were particularly resisted by Irish men, who responded with hypermasculine self-representations. Thus the increasingly organised and well-supported challenge to British rule was accompanied by aggressively masculine 'Gaelicisation' in Ireland involving an emphasis on athletic male physical prowess (Nash 1996). It could be seen as evidence of repudiation of dependency but also of identification with the aggressor in the colonial culture (Nandy 1983). The post-independence era in Ireland was thus even more exclusive of women in the public sphere, as the 1937 Constitution confirmed, in ways that continued to resonate with the colonial past.

The icon of the family, apparently representing interdependence and unity, has remained dominant in Irish society. All nations represent themselves as families, interconnected and united, but the trope is particularly resonant in Ireland. Ironically it is headed by the figure of 'Mother Ireland', although power clearly resides with father-farmers. Ciaran McCullough (1991) shows how the myth of the strong united family emerged in the late nineteenth and early twentieth centuries to deny and displace conflicts created by the stem-family system of land inheritance. Even the inheriting son remained captive by the forfeiture of an education, until the father died or chose to relinquish control (Limerick Rural Survey, 1965). Material conditions reinforced the reduction in women's status. The change from arable to pastoral farming can also be linked to the increasing demand of Britain for higher-value dairy and meat foodstuffs, although the emerging role of Irish capitalist farmers was also critical. Widespread loss of women's agricultural jobs led to the replacement of cooperative family economic activities with a classically patriarchal structure.

In Irish nationalist constructions, women were given a prominent position at the centre of the nation, but in ways which reinforced their subordinate status. After the establishment of the Irish Free State in 1922, an icon which was widely adopted to signal the parameters of the newly-independent state was that of the family farm (Nash 1993). This image of the 'home' appeared to place women as key figures in the new state. But in reality it reinforced the centrally masculine themes underlying the struggle for Irish national independence, those of territorial ownership, small-scale economic self-sufficiency, a rural as opposed to British urban way of life, and the Irish man's mastery of his own domain and its occupants. Mac Laughlin's (1994) description of Ireland as an 'emigrant nursery' unconsciously echoes the imagery which elides home and nation, placing women in the central but exploited position of raising children for export to labour-poor industrial economies.

The increasingly marginalised position of women in Ireland is mirrored in Irish landscape painting, as Catherine Nash (1993) shows. In the early twentieth century the West of Ireland, which had been chosen to symbolise the essence of the Irish nation and its distance and difference from colonising Britain, was depicted as a landscape with figures of young, untamed Irish women. This theme challenged the association between docile femininity and the Irish nation which British representations of Celticism employed. However in the new nation these images became dangerously unstable, allowing readings of uncontrolled sexuality and the possibility of free choice which might lead to emigration. They were replaced by images in the landscape of old women, who represented the fulfillment of a successful life both in Ireland and in the home. The old had remained in Ireland, where they conformed to the Catholic church's idealised view of women and raised a new generation of children for the state. In yet a further representational shift in the 1920s, paintings omitted all direct images of women. Instead the cottage in the landscape became a symbol of women, who were absent from the frame yet understood to be present within the walls, essential both to the operation of the enterprise and to the continuation of the nation, fixed yet dispossessed. Finally, by the 1930s the

West had become a hypermasculine space, represented by the rugged 'Man of Aran' of Robert Flaherty's classic film.

The progressive exclusion of women from media representation, intended to 'keep them in their place', in fact had the opposite effect of 'displacing' them altogether. As outlined earlier, the 1920s and 1930s were decades of increasingly restrictive social practices, including the introduction of a 'marriage bar' preventing married women from participating in most forms of paid work, punitive sanctions on unmarried motherhood, the banning of contraception, and low pay and status for single women. Large numbers of women were forced, or chose, to emigrate.

Many of these distinctive images are included in the overarching figure of 'Mother Ireland', which has been a powerful point of identification. The image is a contradictory one, both disempowering and empowering. On the one hand it illustrates the restriction of women to the passive symbolic sphere, rather than the active social realm. It limits acknowledgement to women who are mothers, that is those who choose, and are able, to conform to the strong pressures of the Catholic church towards marriage. It also elevates the qualities associated with motherhood, protection of children and the selfless devotion of caring for them. Yet as Belinda Loftus (1990) points out, public representation by a female figure is at the same time transgressive and highly destabilising; outside the home, women belong to the street. Its meaning for contemporary women is therefore ambiguous, at once liberatory and oppressive, vividly illustrated by interviews in the film *Mother Ireland* directed by Anne Crilly (Derry Film and Video 1988). Some women welcomed the strength of the image which recognised the contribution of women, but others saw it as a limiting representation, confining them to maternal roles within the home.

'Irishness' in Ireland is thus deeply gendered, while appearing to encompass all members of the nation in a common image. These 'roots' shaped migrant women's early experiences in Ireland and were recreated in a variety of ways in Irish communities in the diaspora. They continued to be reinforced by the Catholic church in places of settlement outside Ireland and reproduced in Irish families. Moreover very different relationships to Ireland are constructed for and by women and men who have left. Common features of Irishness are shared by Irish women and men but their Irish identities are experienced differently.

Racialisation: otherness and sameness

Outside Ireland, a key aspect of constructions of Irishness is the paradox by which the Irish are represented by dominant Western groups simultaneously as 'other', that is racialised as essentially different in stereotypical ways, and also the 'same' because 'white' people share a similar timeless essence. This process has taken different forms at certain times and in particular places, and must be examined in its specificities. Although one of the features of this essentialising is its unifying function of focusing on 'the Irish' as a homogenous group, all of whom share these characteristics regardless of gender, class, religion or age, in reality these constructions depend on an unstated gendering for their effects.

Construction as 'other'

Racialisation of the Irish as inherently inferior depends on the process of stereotyping. Stuart Hall (1997) argues that stereotyping has three main features. One is the reduction of a person's characteristics to a few, simple, easily recognised traits which are regarded as unchanging, fixed by Nature. The second is its function in the maintenance of symbolic order. It works to set up a symbolic frontier between the normal and the deviant, excluding those who are defined as not belonging. 'Stereotyping . . . facilitates the "binding" or bonding together of all of Us who are "normal" into one "imagined community"; and it sends into symbolic exile all of Them – "the Others" – who are in some way different – "beyond the pale"' (Hall 1997: 258).

Tellingly, in elaborating this part of the definition, Hall draws on a description of the Irish ('beyond the pale') which has become so integrated into the English language that its origins have largely been forgotten. In fact the phrase derives directly from the name given to the area around Dublin, which was fortified by the English crown in the statute of 1488 to protect its toehold in Ireland (Simms 1989). Thus the name came to symbolise the 'civilised' population under English control, those within the Pale, in contrast to the 'uncivilised' Irish in the rest of Ireland. It is now applied unconsciously to any excluded social group.

An important extension of this rejection of 'abnormal' others is their association with pollution, dirt and impurity. In psychoanalytic terms they represent the split-off parts of the dominant group which cannot be acknowledged. One element of this disavowed part of dominant selves, which resonated particularly strongly in the English national identity, and by extension to masculinities in colonial formations with English origins such as the USA, is that of dependence. Englishness is unusual as it is constructed around a middle-class core, in contrast to nationalisms which have a revolutionary origin in which 'the people' have been mobilised. Independence became a key characteristic of the dominant group in England, fostered in the 'public school' system which removed boys as young as seven from their homes for education to become 'manly' in homosocial school environments (Dodd 1986). Women, the working classes and colonized peoples represented the dependence which this class of English men had to deny in themselves, and therefore must subordinate and control in others.

In the nineteenth century, 'dirty Irish' was a common stereotype, used colloquially as a term of abuse but also incorporated into official reports on living conditions in industrial cities. Irish settlement was seen as a cause of decay and ill-health, rather than a symptom of the failure of the economic system to provide adequate housing for the labour force. In the 1830s James Kay Shuttleworth blamed the Irish for 'fatal contagion' of the English nation (Hall 1998: 27). Writing in 1845 Engels linked the Irish with 'dirt' in explicitly racial terms:

> One may depend upon seeing many Celtic faces, if ever one penetrates into a district which is particularly noted for its filth and decay. These faces are quite different from those of the Anglo-Saxon population and are easily recognisable.
>
> (Engels 1971: 105)

The epithet was implied in social scientists' descriptions of Irish 'slums' in British cities in the 1950s (Spinley 1953; Kerr 1958) and is openly used in verbal abuse of Irish people in the 1990s (Hickman and Walter 1997).

Third, stereotyping involves violent power relationships. It is not associated simply with difference, but with 'gross inequalities of power'. Hall (1997) goes on to point out that this is a symbolic power exercised through control of representational practices. These practices have a wide range of effects, including social positioning and economic exploitation, as well as physical coercion.

However there is not a simple, one-way relationship between the dominant and dominated groups. The line between them is less sharply drawn than the stereotype suggests. On the one hand the dominant group has ambivalent feelings, mirroring the splitting process, and thus also exhibits envy and desire (Pajaczkowska and Young 1992). On the other hand the dominated group becomes part of the hegemony; as Ashis Nandy (1983: 2) points out, colonialism 'includes codes which both the rulers and ruled can share'.

Construction as 'same'

Most, but not all, Irish people are now regarded as white. However this construction is far from being an uncontested biological given. As Ruth Frankenberg points out:

> whiteness changes over time and space, and is in no way a trans-historical essence. Rather . . . it is a complexly constructed product of local, regional, national, and global relations, past and present. Thus the range of possible ways of living whiteness . . . is delimited by the relations of racism at that moment and in that place.
>
> (Frankenberg 1993: 236)

The boundaries of the white have been drawn to include the Irish for strategic reasons at particular historic moments. They are continually renegotiated as new conditions arise. Because conditions are different in different societies, the meanings of whiteness vary between places at the same time. How Irish whiteness has been constructed in the United States, and what it now means there, is not the same as in Britain, although discourses flow between the two societies and inform each other. Naming and understandings of the categories 'white' and 'black' differs between the two locations but will be standardised in this comparative account. Attention should always be drawn to their constructedness, but quotes will be used sparingly to ease the flow of the argument.

Irish women occupy a complex position in relation to whiteness. At one level they unquestionably benefit from the universal recognition of whiteness as a signifier of dominance in the late twentieth century. This affords a level of protection from types of racism, including widespread physical violence, perpetrated on black people in Western societies. At another level the shrinking of the discourse of 'race' into the oversimplified black/white binary leads to the forcible inclusion of Irish people in the 'white' category. Other types of racialisation are excluded from common-sense understanding in the United States and Britain, including those which resonate much more strongly in other European countries, such as those of the Jews and Gypsies. Thus in Britain, different processes of racialisation simultaneously construct Irish women as privileged and subordinate:

> As white Europeans, Irish women are constructed as a dominant group *vis-à-vis* black women in and through the discourses of anti-black racism, even when they themselves are in turn subordinated within anti-Irish racism.
>
> (Brah 1996: 90)

One consequence of the inclusion of the Irish as white, and the equation of whiteness with dominance, is that racialisation along other axes of difference is overlooked. Prior inclusion of the Irish within a 'white' category, means that there is a strong tendency to ignore the 'racial' aspects of hostility and discrimination faced by Irish people in Britain on the grounds of inherited negative characteristics. This process of exclusion was epitomised by the operation of the 'ethnic question' in the 1991 British Census. In reality the only options for self-identification were White/non-White (of various kinds). Although it was possible to 'write in' a different ethnicity at the end of the list, this was ignored by counting mechanisms employed by the Office of National Statistics if the respondent had already ticked 'White' (Walter 1998).

The different trajectory of relations between hegemonic and subordinate groups in the United States of America means that the relationship between whiteness and Irishness has been played out very differently. The Irish-American population has largely become part of the privileged white mainstream, placing new immigrants in a very different situation from those entering Britain.

> newcomers from Ireland rapidly learn what whiteness means in America and capitalise upon these different meanings. This, in turn, means that they become part of the forces that shape the complex racial hierarchy of America, rather than

being victimised by its system of race thinking and racial categorisation.

(Luibheid 1997: 257)

The two diasporic locations are not isolated from each other. Meanings cross the Atlantic and reverberate in the very different social settings. In the eighteenth and nineteenth centuries anti-Irish British attitudes were transferred to the United States with the 'Anglo-Saxon' charter group and reproduced in identical cartoons of simianised bodies. In the twentieth century, the theories of Robert Park of the Chicago School of Sociology in the 1920s, which propounded an assimilationist view of Irish ethnicity, were adopted uncritically by British social scientists in the 1960s (Peach 1968, 1975) and are still drawn on (Hornsby-Smith and Dale 1988). Moreover migrants themselves have also experienced both racist marginalisation in London and acceptance into the white hegemony in America when they have moved from London to New York. As Luibheid (1997: 256) argues, Irish immigrants today, many of whom may have experienced racial discrimination in Great Britain, find that the meanings attached to whiteness in the United States, are not at all similar to those prevailing in either continental Europe, or indeed Ireland itself.

The role of gender in the construction of Irish women as white needs to be explored. It has been argued that white Western men have projected their inner fears onto black women as the most extreme other (Gilman 1992). How does this gendering of others play out for Irish women? Does whiteness override gender differences? Are Irish women represented as sexless because of associations with Virgin Mary? How has the whiteness of Irish women been constructed in relation to other subordinate minority women, when they have often occupied similar economic positions? How has the privilege of whiteness operated in representations of Irish women?

These identities are necessarily defined by difference, which is integral to all representation. However the hierarchical character of these binaries need to be challenged. As Iris Marion Young (1990) argues, this involves deconstruction of the homogeneity of the most powerful categories, a process which has hardly begun. In particular the hybridity of 'white' British culture through its colonial encounters at home with its Irish 'others' has yet to be fully explored.

Shared diaspora space

One of the most imaginative and fruitful ways in which this hybridity can be explored is through Brah's (1996) notion of 'diaspora space'. She argues this describes a shared location, only *represented* as inhabited by the binary of central and marginal groups. Thus 'the diaspora space is the site where *the native is as much a diasporian as the diasporian is the native*' (Brah 1996: 209, author's emphasis). This replaces binary constructions with multiple ones, whilst still recognising relational realities within multi-axial fields of power relations.

Rethinking England as a diaspora space is a massive task requiring detailed study of ways in which 'Englishness is continually reconstituted via a multitude of border crossings in and through other diasporic formations' (ibid.: 209). I can make a small beginning by reviewing the narrative of my own family history. Because of strong pressures in British society to incorporate Irish people and render their cultural specificity invisible, particularly after a single generation, the personal ramifications of Irish connections in Britain are rarely traced or acknowledged. I want to use my own biography and family history to identify some of the intersections between particular class, gender and geographical locations in the shared diaspora space of England. By doing so I will highlight key themes which are explored in more depth later in the book. I am a white 'English' woman from a family located as southern and middle-class in my parents' generation. Thus my own biography places me 'outside' the collectivity which is the focus of this book, but 'inside' the shared 'diaspora space' of the place which is central to the analysis, Britain.

Most accounts of Irish women in the diaspora begin, or could begin, by placing the author as part of a family history of migration from Ireland (see for example, Conway 1992, Nolan 1989, Roche 1997). My own family background appears to have no Irish connection, but I am closely related to the story I tell. My 'Englishness' is mutually constituted with 'Irishness', but in ways which are so deeply embedded they have to be teased out of very mundane situations. The interrelationship is vividly presented in Avtar Brah's (1996) concept of 'diaspora space', in which migrants and those represented as indigenous are brought together.

> In the diaspora space called 'England', for example, African-Caribbean, Irish, Asian, Jewish and other diasporas intersect

among themselves as well as with the entity constructed as 'Englishness', thoroughly re-inscribing it in the process. Englishness has been formed in the crucible of internal colonial encounters with Ireland, Scotland and Wales; imperial rivalries with other European countries; and imperial conquests abroad.

(Brah 1996: 209)

My own 'English' identity is not only constructed within a particular set of power relations, including those of class and gender, but is itself hybrid. My father's mother was a Welsh-speaker from mid-Wales and even my 'English' grandparents came from Cumberland, Hampshire and Dorset, regions with differing relationships to the 'Deep England' of the 'Home Counties'. A crucial facet of the concept of diaspora space is its deconstruction of the monolithic 'sameness' of the 'centre', by revealing the hybridities which already constitute it.

At first sight it is particularly difficult to see any connections. I was born and lived – until I left home to go to university in 1966 – in Poole, then a town of 80,000 people on the south coast of England. Although Irish-born people are widely scattered throughout England, this was far from the major centres of settlement in London, Lancashire and the West Midlands. Nevertheless, according to the 1951 Census 1 per cent of the population of Poole was Irish-born, including 525 women. As far as I can recall I knew only one of them, who had been a neighbour in my parents' early married life and remained a friend. She was a nurse who had met and married a sea captain in Ecuador. I remember that my mother laughed affectionately at her 'quaint' forms of speech. The other Irish woman I remember from my childhood was a 'housekeeper' for my mother's brother's family in the West Midlands. I have since learned that my uncle employed six of her male cousins in the large engineering firm in Birmingham where he was managing director. Irish women were hardly present at all in my enclosed life in a middle-class neighbourhood in Dorset. Yet the small contact I had was archetypical, including a middle-class Irish woman, who had been a nurse before marriage, and a domestic servant. Their voices marked each of them as not fitting the category of 'Standard English' which was important in the 1950s when elocution lessons were on my schools' curriculum.

Perhaps more tellingly I remember that Catholicism was regarded with distaste and even fear in my childhood. My mother said I must never marry a Catholic. A Catholic family moved into our Protestant suburban estate of detached houses when I was about six. They came from Manchester which may have contributed to the genteel cold-shouldering. I listened with horrified fascination as the mother threatened her children with black spots on their souls if they misbehaved. At my selective girls' high school in Bournemouth a handful of Catholics had to shuffle late into assembly with the two Jewish sisters, after 'prayers'. They sat selfconsciously on the floor as we stared at them.

It might seem that Irish women were missing from my family social interactions because of our location far from industrial centres or the Irish Sea coast. But recently I was thumbing through listings of 1851 and 1891 Census returns in the village of Hampreston, not far from Poole, where I knew earlier generations of my family had lived. Sure enough their names appeared, described as agricultural workers. As I looked down the birthplaces in the village I was astonished to see about forty women born in Ireland listed at each date. No occupations appeared beside their names; they must have been part of a religious order. Throughout the second half of the nineteenth century, then, there had been a large presence of Irish women in the same village as my ancestors in rural Dorset. Even where there appeared to be absences, therefore, a small amount of digging reveals interactions with the 'outside' which disrupt any notion of a homogenous, local population. Although the nuns may not have reproduced themselves biologically, a stream of women had travelled to Hampreston from different parts of Ireland over at least a forty-year period.

How did I come to choose to write a D.Phil. dissertation on Irish migration to Britain and spend the next twenty years researching and writing on this topic? The narrative I have pieced together to explain this to myself incorporates two strands which resonate with the themes of this book. One is the importance of specific places where 'insides' and 'outsides' are brought together in particular configurations. The other is the hybridity of identities and the ongoing resonances of past dislocations, perhaps over many generations.

The specificity of place relates to Oxford where I studied for my Geography degree in the late 1960s. The course was an unusual one for that time in having options in social and colonial geography, which reflected Oxford's global entanglement with empire. Lecturers used the archives at Rhodes House and Queen Elizabeth House for their research and we could also attend seminars there.

By far the most interesting tutorials offered to human geography students were those about migration and plural societies. Indeed they encouraged a whole raft of students of my generation to undertake research (see Clarke, Ley and Peach 1984). Undoubtedly the exoticism of the 'other' excited our desires as well as chiming with the radical politics of the time.

While I was an undergraduate, one of my lecturers, Ceri Peach, published the monograph *West Indian Migration to Britain* in 1968. He used meticulous academic analysis to expose the myth that Caribbean people were being enabled to escape from overpopulation by the generosity of the 'mother country'. Instead he showed that numbers migrating correlated precisely with demand for labour in Britain. I was attracted by the possibilities the book suggested for linking my left-leaning political sympathies and academic interests. However I also noted that Peach used the Irish as a counterpoint to West Indian population in Britain, in order to demonstrate immutable black/white differences in migrant experience. But evidence to support conclusions drawn from Census statistics on the Irish was missing.

Where had my political sympathies come from? Although this was 1968, I doubt whether more than one or two of my Bournemouth classmates would have shared them. I can vividly remember my horror at discovering that I was the only child at my private junior school who could not be certain that her parents voted Conservative in the 1954 election. I can still see myself standing in the playground debating whether to pretend that they did. However by 1964, the year of the first Labour victory for thirteen years, there was a mock election at my secondary school and I had become more confident about difference. I wanted to be the Welsh Nationalist candidate but ended up as the Liberal agent. No member of the sixth form could be found to stand for Labour; eventually a very junior girl was allowed to take it on, gaining eighteen votes. The Liberal team campaigned very vigorously and converted eighty people. But the Conservative majority was huge and I remember my shock and disillusionment at seeing the staff on the platform erupt to a woman in joy when the result was announced.

Much later I traced the source of my anti-Establishment views to my father's Welsh roots. In my household there was a strange mix of the radical and the conventional middle class. We took the *New Statesman and Nation* as well as the *Daily Telegraph*. Welshness was a daily presence; we had Welsh names, could count to ten in Welsh, and my father still used Welsh phrases he had learned as a child. The mix of religious non-conformity and oppositional politics must have translated into his own Labour voting. My mother's deeply-held Protestant Christianity made her, too, uncomfortable with the triumphalist Conservativism of our neighbourhood, although I now know she voted with them.

So when I came to choose a research topic, after returning from a postgraduate year in the United States, I briefly considered studying Welsh migration to Britain. I had recently married and realised that it would have to be something 'close to home'. But the difficulties of disentangling Welsh threads from the whole seemed too great, and I turned instead to the question of Irish immigration, which seemed to have parallels and whose academic neglect had been puzzling.

My D.Phil. thesis, entitled 'The Geography of Irish Migration to Britain since 1939, with special reference to Luton and Bolton' was completed in 1979 and received enthusiastically by the examiners. Within a few years I realised it was deeply flawed. Feminist geography was bursting into life and drew attention to the discursive trap of 'migrants and their wives'. When I read Linda McDowell and Doreen Massey's pathbreaking essay 'A Woman's Place' in 1984, many things fell into new places. I recognised in the strong, independent women in Lancashire cotton towns they described, the Irish women whom I had portrayed as adjuncts of their centre-stage labouring husbands in Bolton. In fact women were not peripheral but could be seen as central to the story of Irish settlement in Bolton, their work in the mills giving them a key position in the labour migration process and in the economic support of households, as well as a public voice in trades unions.

At about the same time, the Greater London Council was extending its Ethnic Minorities Working Group to include an Irish dimension, and in 1984 it published a *Report on Consultation with the Irish Community*. This marked a breakthrough in the recognition of Irish cultural specificity and welfare needs in Britain and provided a policy-related dimension to my own research. The 1984 Report noted a lack of data on the specific needs of Irish women and I was invited to produce *Irish Women in London* (1988). The research which grew out of that report and flowed in new directions forms the content of this book.

This biography positions me in the narrative which follows, since 'we all write and speak from a place and time, from a history and a culture which is specific. What we say is always "in context", positioned' (Hall 1997: 51). It also highlights key features of Irish women's diasporic relationships with England. First, it points to the geographical specificity of settlement. Very few Irish-born women made their way to Poole during the 1950s (there were still only 547 in 1961), but at this time there was a huge growth in number of Irish-born women in towns and cities in the South East and West Midlands. In Birmingham, for example, where my uncle worked, numbers grew from 16,316 in 1951 to 26,294 in 1961, a 62 per cent increase; in London they rose from 61,739 to 88,752, an increase of 44 per cent. Even though I met few Irish people, a subtext of Irish presence in Britain was still very evident to me in the form of suspicion and distancing of Catholics. Second, it indicates the absence of academic interest in the Irish in Britain. The large inflow of labour from Ireland during the 1950s attracted almost no attention. In the 1960s assumptions about ease of assimilation were made on the basis of uncritical borrowings from the United States of theorisations about ghetto-formation and 'white flight'. The largest absence was that of Irish women, for whom frameworks of inclusion became available only in the last two decades.

The notion of Britain as a diaspora space runs richly through my biography, which seemed at first sight so uncomplicatedly 'English'. My third-generation Welshness continues to be part of my identity. Few Irish women were present, but they were not missing altogether. Finally my encounter with higher education in Oxford was still suffused with colonial links in the 1960s, which provided a context in which plural societies could be part of the Geography curriculum and led to my curiosity about the absent Irish. This interrogation of white sameness in England provides a small case study in the much larger project, which has hardly begun, of acknowledging the hybridity of white British identities and the myriad of ways in which outsides and insides have always constituted each other.

I now explore the tensions between insideness and outsideness on a larger canvas. The specificity of Irish women's movement to and settlement in the United States, which has received more scholarly attention than in Britain, provides an initial comparative point of reference. In Britain, by contrast, silence about Irishness in general and Irish women in particular has been resounding. Moreover, thinking about Britain as a diaspora space has only just begun.

Chapter 2

Outside the Pale

Irish women in the United States of America

This chapter explores the historical specificity of the experiences of women born in Ireland who settled in the United States, and of their female descendants who continued to define themselves, or to be constructed, as 'Irish'. The analysis is begun 'outside the Pale' for two reasons. First, by far the largest number of women leaving Ireland in the nineteenth century settled in the United States, so that their descendants constitute over half of those now claiming an Irish identity. The historical span of five or sixth generations provides a relatively long and well-documented period over which to study changing socio-economic positionings and socio-cultural constructions, and thus to provide a framework for considering the diaspora as a whole. Second, establishing the contours of Irish women's experiences in the United States provides a point of contrast with Britain, both for analytical purposes and as an integral part of Irish women's own understandings of their circumstances.

Using a diaspora framework to re-integrate migration flows from one 'homeland' to different destinations allows comparisons to be made between constituent parts of this larger displaced population, so that the positionings of different strands can be identified. Thus the availability of a more positive trajectory offers possibilities of 'third space' resistance for Irish women in Britain, who can draw on the experiences of their aunts and sisters in the United States to interpret their own situation in opposition to essentialist constructions of the Irish in British culture.

My aim in this chapter is to offer a critical synthesis of existing studies of the Irish in the United States in order to emphasise Irish women's distinctive material and representational roles in the processes of travel, and to draw attention to the significance of 'dwelling'.

Displacement: women's routes

In this analysis, displacement refers to diasporic links outside the area of settlement. The concept of diaspora includes multiple meanings of 'displacement', both empirical and representational. In an abstract sense it is of course the fundamental element in identities constructed by and for diasporic peoples. The very name 'Irish' evokes another 'place' as central to personal and group identities. However displacement is also the product of economic processes and is experienced both personally and collectively in specific ways. Here I examine both grounded practices through which displacement has been and continues to be lived by Irish women, and collective representations of gendered Irishness in the United States.

Empirical subjects: dispersal from Ireland

North America was the major destination of Irish emigrants in the nineteenth century. Data collected from emigrant counts in Ireland and census enumerations at destinations suggest that over 80 per cent of those leaving Ireland eventually crossed the Atlantic. However there was considerable underenumeration of those travelling to Britain, as O'Grada (1973) has demonstrated. This 'missing million' Irish-born people in Britain would reduce the overwhelming dominance of North America in the flow, though by no means remove it.

The peak decade for Irish entry to the United States was 1851–60, the immediate aftermath of the Famine, when 914,119 Irish-born people were recorded as entering directly, 35 per cent of the total immigration volume. Another peak was in the period 1881-90 with a total of 665,482, though by then the proportion of Irish-born had fallen to 13 per cent. In the following decade the total halved to 338,416 and by 1911-20 it was only 146,181, a mere 2.5 per cent of all immigrants.

During the nineteenth century more than four million women emigrated from Ireland to the United States. The vast majority settled permanently, and their descendents are now part of the forty millions who claim Irish ancestry. Fewer than 10 per cent of Irish people returned to Ireland, in contrast to half of all Italian migrants who went back and an even higher proportion in smaller groups, for example Bulgarians where it was over 80 per cent.

Women comprised more than half of the total flow from Ireland, unlike the Italian (and German) migrant populations, for example, where only 20 per cent were women. The greater freedom of Irish women to travel and settle as single people, attached to family networks but outside nuclear families, meant that there was strong demand for their labour in traditional female occupations and helps to explain their unusually large representation.

Gender ratios in Irish emigration changed over time. Before the Famine men were more numerous amongst emigrants but by 1871, when records are first available, more women were leaving in each decade and the proportion rose over time. United States censuses also first disaggregated birthplace data by sex in 1860. One index of the cumulative numerical dominance of women by the early twentieth century is figures of employment in six eastern states with large Irish populations, which show that 22,162 Irish women were employed in the major occupation groups in 1920, compared with 12,612 Irish men (Kennedy 1973).

During the twentieth century, numbers emigrating from Ireland to the United States dropped dramatically, especially after the 1920s. Quotas were introduced in 1921 and 1924 and the inflow fell very sharply to 13,197 in the 1930s. There is some debate about the reasons for the sudden decline. Undoubtedly it was related to the introduction of quotas and to the slump in demand for labour during the Depression. Kennedy (1973) suggests that the establishment of the Irish Free State in 1922 also changed perceptions of Britain as an alternative destination, removing at least some of the negative feelings towards the imperial core.

Stringent immigration regulations, including the 1952 McCarran-Walter Act, which drastically reduced numbers permitted to enter, continued to restrict numbers after the Second World War. Thus only 57,332 of the massive outflow of more then half a million people from the Republic of Ireland in the 1950s travelled to the United States. The Immigration Act of 1965 still further restricted categories of entry to those with close family ties or with skills needed in the United States. By then far fewer Irish people could claim close ties, despite the very large number with connections from earlier generations.

Much more recently a sharp upturn in emigration to the United States took place when the 1980s generation of young adults left Ireland in large numbers (Corcoran 1993). Many chose to become 'illegals' in the United States. A slightly greater number of men left Ireland, reflecting the switch since the 1970s towards more employment opportunities in Ireland for women. Estimates vary about the size of the Irish-born component in 1990; in addition to the Census total of 170,000 Irish-born people officially recorded, the Irish Bishops' Commission on Emigration gave the figure of 136,000 'illegals' in 1987, although the United States Catholic Conference reckoned the number to be as low as 44,000. Overall therefore the Irish population in the United States is heavily weighted towards earlier generations. In 1970 only 250,000 Irish-born people were recorded in the Census compared with forty million claiming Irish descent.

Empirical subjects: personal linkages

For most women the move to the United States has been a one-way, permanent relocation. In the nineteenth century a small number of women saved money for a dowry and returned to marry in Ireland. Fewer women than men returned, including some who had saved their own dowry and others who had married Irish men and returned as part of a nuclear family unit. One example is Frank McCourt's family whose return from New York to Limerick in the 1930s is vividly recalled in his autobiographical novel *Angela's Ashes* (1996). Men who returned to rural areas were often summoned to 'keep the name on the land' when all other family members had left (Brody 1973). Returners were often resented, and referred to disparagingly as 'Yanks', suggesting that the expected norm was a one-way movement towards success and upward mobility for the nation as a whole.

However strong ties with relatives were retained, both in Ireland and with siblings and cousins who migrated to Britain. These took a wide variety of forms. On a material level, remittances were sent to family members at home, tickets for travel and guarantees of jobs were offered, and finally board and lodging provided for those who followed. Fitzpatrick (1986) argues that women were seen as more reliable sources of remittances, because their work in domestic service was assured and they were thought less likely to spend their earnings on drink. They were also more able to offer accommodation to succeeding family and friends. Women's paid work as domestic servants and unpaid work as household heads gave them more permanent addresses than men who needed to travel in search of work. Others, often widows, earned an income as lodging-house keepers. The short distance of moves between domestic jobs also made them easier to locate. A detailed collection of 'Missing Persons' advertised for in the *Boston Pilot* between 1831 and 1857 shows that less than a quarter of these contacts were made by women, suggesting that they kept better contact with their friends and families and were less likely to become 'lost' (Harris and O'Keefe 1993).

Large amounts of information flowed back across the Atlantic, stimulating a desire to leave and providing concrete measures of comparison between lives in Ireland, Britain and North America. Much has been written about the impact of glamorous American lifestyles on impressionable young girls, often by anxious priests. From the haphazard survival of these records it is not possible to compare numbers of letters written by women and men, but the greater reliance on remittances from women, their gendered family obligations and their higher literacy levels suggests that they probably wrote more frequently.

The Irish diaspora has thus been continuously mobilised by links between its various parts. At a personal level, these links have been strongest between adjacent generations, but they also stretch forward and back through time. Children are told about more distant relatives who emigrated or remained, particularly by their mothers and aunts who have been prime keepers of family histories. Richard White (1998) opens his exploration of links between memory and history in *Remembering Ahanagran* with a list of the locations of his mother's stories:

> Sara Walsh, who married and became Sara White, is my mother, and she has told me stories about her life since I was a child. She sets these stories in County Kerry, Ireland, where she was a girl. She sets them on South Mozart Street in Chicago, where she was a young woman. She sets them in New Orleans, where she met my father. She sets them in and around Boston, where she visited briefly when my father returned from overseas after World War I.
>
> (White 1998: 3)

However the links also at times broke down, and attempts to retrieve them had varying degrees of success. The importance of these ties is attested by the urgency with which they were traced and the lengths to which relatives went to try to make contact. The tracing of ancestors is a more recent version of attempts to re-establish links for the purposes of exploring personal senses of identity. Many resources now exist to assist people of Irish descent in genealogical searches, including manuals, websites and a computerised database funded by the Irish Government since 1988, known as the Irish Genealogical Project (Nash 1999). By far the largest national group using these methods are Irish-Americans.

Many of these longstanding links, both active and half-remembered, were revived in the 1980s when young people unable to find work in Ireland became 'illegals' in the United States. Difficulties in finding satisfying jobs, however, together with weakened ties with the United States during the twentieth century, as well as greater possibilities for frequent return to Ireland, meant that far fewer young Irish people decided to settle permanently. Corcoran (1996) describes their extreme ambivalence about emigration and a much greater reluctance to commit themselves to living outside Ireland. In part this indecision was made possible by the very ease of travel between Ireland and other parts of the world, as well as by their ability to maintain close relationships by telephone and electronic mail. These transnational connections epitomise contemporary meanings of diaspora as ongoing displacement.

Representations: refracted images outside the United States

A crucial aspect of the concept of diaspora is the notion of multiple linkages between different strands of the dispersed group, as well as between the 'homeland' and places of settlement. As Clifford (1994: 321) argues: 'The empowering paradox of diaspora is that dwelling here assumes a solidarity or connection there. But there is not necessarily a single place or an exclusivist nation'. Thus connections between the United States and Britain also reverberate.

The film industry has portrayed Irish-Americans in ways which have been influential in Britain as well as Ireland. Especially in the early Hollywood days these confirmed the prominence of men who played active and heroic roles, many played by Irish-American actors, such as Jimmy Cagney, Tyrone Power and Bing Crosby.

Indeed people with other ethnicities adopted Irish names in their search for Hollywood fame.

The overwhelming message refracted back to Ireland and Britain from North America has been one of success. A potent symbol is the widespread display of portraits of John Fitzgerald Kennedy in Irish households, representing shared group achievement at the highest level in the political sphere, which had been appropriated by the Irish since the late nineteenth century. But this was a male route to success. Rose Kennedy was acknowledged in a supporting role, but the arrivals being celebrated were those of Irish men. Knowledge of this upward mobility in the United States is widely diffused in Britain. In a survey which asked an Irish-born sample in London and Birmingham to give an opinion on how Irish people were viewed in the United States and Britain, only 1 per cent felt that they were viewed negatively in the United States compared with 22 per cent who said this about Britain (Hickman and Walter 1997).

Collective myths/memories

Definitions of diaspora generally include reference to its origins in histories of violence, displacement and loss. Myths and memories about such violent episodes continue to reverberate long afterwards, so that the constructed boundaries of the nation are breached by reminders of its constitutive outsides. The Irish Famine of 1847–50 was such a catastrophic event. Although Irish settlement in the United States had been on a significant scale since the early eighteenth century, the Famine marked a sharp break in the process. Richard Williams argues that this was a forced movement in a way which could be compared with the transportation of enslaved people from Africa.

> In both cases the mass movement of people out of their societies was involuntary, one by military force, the other by economic force. The two reflect the different methods by which surplus was extracted within the societies from which the migrants came.
>
> (Williams 1990: 134)

Collective memories of violent origins can wax and wane in importance in different periods but are not necessarily erased by the passage of time. They may continue to have real effects on contemporary communities. Ways in which collective memories are expressed can be permanent, such as museums and monuments, or temporary, in the case of exhibitions or demonstrations. In 1996 the 150 years' anniversary of the Irish Famine took both forms in commemorations in Boston, Massachusetts, revealing and creating a variety of meanings for people identifying themselves as Irish. The geographical specificity of Boston has an important bearing on the form taken by the commemorations and the ways in which they mobilised community feelings. In east coast American cities, Irish experiences differed according to their relationship with the dominant group who defined themselves as 'Anglo-Saxon', as well as other ethnic groups (Clark 1986). Anti-Irish attitudes were particularly strong in Boston, where the intellectual elite had close ties with England and there was a less diversified economic and social structure. The Irish largely remained a disadvantaged minority, the apparent success of the Kennedys having little to do with Boston except as a political affiliation. The city has retained a strongly working-class Irish population, in contrast to New York and Philadelphia where group upward mobility has been much greater.

Two events which took place in the autumn of 1996 illustrate the place of Famine memories, that is memories of displacement, in the present-day 'diasporic space' of Boston. One was the construction of a small Famine Exhibition at the Museum of National Heritage, in Lexington, a suburb of Boston, compiled by historians from the United States and Ireland. The Irish contribution was made by the curator of the Strokestown Famine Museum in County Roscommon, a museum which takes an overtly political stance highlighting the 'view from below' (Johnson 1996). The Exhibition was experiential as well as visual; visitors could enter a reconstructed hovel, see photographs and read selected quotations. At the exit a book was provided for visitors' comments. It contained a wealth of reflections by Irish-Americans who freely registered their feelings and personal connections with what they had seen, whilst also leaving no doubt about their secure identity as Americans.

> My parents were born in County Sligo and County Claire [sic].
> Emigrated to United States, to New Jersey, around 1899 and

1903. Raised a family of 4 children. We are all thankful to be Americans. Very sad about the potato famine.

Very informative and interesting. Will bring my children so they won't forget their heritage.

Thank you for this wonderful exhibit. People should never forget.

I live in America because my great-grandmother had the courage to make the trip. Exhibit was very meaningful to me. My grandmother was Mary Nagle. She grew up, after leaving Boston, to live in Fitzwilliam, N.H. She married a vet, Richard Comerford III, whose grandfather, Peter, came from Ireland. They had three children. Their son, Richard Comerford IV became a judge in Leominster, Mass. Yes, the Irish have contributed much to our country.

Proud to be Irish. It is sad what some races have to go through.

The Irish have proven themselves in all phases of life and government – did they deserve the ridicule and disrespect shown them back in the 1800s? Shame.

The last comment was probably triggered by a quotation from Ralph Waldo Emerson which was displayed in the exhibition. It included an extract from his journal describing the Irish as 'shovel-handed and fit only to be cowcatchers and road graders', and his wish that 'populations of paddies' should disappear. Several visitors expressed their shock, hurt and anger that a central figure in the American literary establishment should have expressed these views.

I am upset over Ralph Waldo Emerson's opinion of the Irish. I will burn all his books that I own as soon as I get home. What a jerk and a bigot.

Clifford (1994: 310) argues that the language of diaspora is 'invoked by displaced peoples who feel (maintain, revive, invent) a connection with a prior home. This sense of connection must be strong enough to resist erasure through the normalizing processes of forgetting, assimilating and distancing'. Such a connection was clearly being revived, or invented, for some visitors to the exhibition, and was strongly present in their own lives, if often submerged. The expression of these feelings suggests the relevance of the concept of diaspora to Irish experience in the United States, despite Lloyd's (1994) concern that it is inappropriate since the Irish are by now 'a fully integrated element of white and mainstream American society'. He claimed that the idea of return is a 'mostly sentimental and fetishising desire to establish their genealogy in the homeland' in an attempt to jump on the multicultural bandwagon and reap the benefits of cultural distinctiveness. Reactions to the Famine Exhibition in Boston, however, suggest that Irish diasporic identities coexist with social incorporation. The important question is how these continuing connections resonate both for themselves and for other parts of the diaspora, particularly Britain.

British imperialism in Ireland has resulted in a complexly-textured diaspora which shares common features with other major displacements of population, but is also profoundly different. Comparisons and contrasts can fruitfully be drawn with other diasporic groupings. Whilst cautioning against simplistic connections between traditions which are disparately derived and internally heterogenous, Paul Gilroy (1993a) nevertheless points to parallels in the experiences of people of African origin and Jewish populations. The common themes of catastrophe, brutal dispossession, loss, exile and journeying he identifies are also central to Famine memories of the emigrant Irish, although there are also significant contrasts between Irish experiences and those of Jews and people of African origin. The incorporation of the Irish middle classes in the United States into an Anglo-Saxon hegemony is a significant breakpoint. This transformation means that Irish people in the United States need not share 'this experience of fear in all its radicality, which cuts across class and gender to the point of touching the bourgeois in the very isolation of his town houses or sumptuous apartments '(Jameson 1988, cited in Gilroy 1993a: 206).

Middle-class Irish-Americans need have no anxiety about the possibility of a retreat from their secure position at the centre of the national narrative of the United States. They fit into the model described by Toni Morrison: 'We live in a land where the past is always erased and America is the innocent future in which immigrants can come and start over, where the slate is clean' (Gilroy 1993b: 179).

However this central place continues to retain traces of earlier marginality which can be drawn on to form alliances with other groups as well as share in their exclusion. A second event during the Famine commemoration activities in 1996 produced a remarkable repositioning of the Irish community in Boston with respect both to 'Yankee' hegemony and a new wave of racialised immigrants. This was the proposal to build a Famine memorial on Cambridge Common, Massachusetts for which permission had to be given by the City Council. The plan was widely understood as an audacious claim by the Irish to be included on equal terms with the 'charter group' of 'white Anglo-Saxon Protestants', by symbolically occupying land alongside monuments celebrating the founders of the nation. Most people expected the challenge to be rebuffed, but the reality was very different.

An article in *The Boston Globe*, on 4 October 1996, under the headline 'Beyond class and clan', captured the dramatic shift which took place during the Council meeting to consider the proposal. The article is reproduced almost in its entirety because of the richness of the story it tells about the place of the Irish in Boston.

> It was supposed to be class warfare. Elite Cantabrigians against working-class townies. Harvard Square against Inman Square. The Yankees against the Irish. The snooty Cambridge Historical Commission against everybody else.
>
> A group of Irish-born and Irish-American residents had asked permission to build a memorial to the 19th century Irish Famine on historic Cambridge Common, where George Washington took command of American forces in 1775. The Historical Commission had replied that it was sworn to defend the Common as a place to commemorate the Revolutionary War.
>
> Yesterday, the townies marched to a public hearing with flags unfurled, chip-on-the-shoulder at the ready. Commission members sat at a large rectangular table, two of them wearing bowties, all of them wearing skeptical faces. But after two hours of passionate yet respectful argument, an extraordinary rapprochement took place. Members of the Historical Commission, criticized by some as stodgy and impervious to

reason, were deeply moved by what they heard and voted unanimously to approve, in principle, the idea of building the famine memorial on the common. The two sides agreed to work together to decide on the final design and location.

It was a decision that neither side expected before the hearing convened shortly after 4pm.

'I guess we made an impression, huh?' asked John Flaherty, the Irish-born co-owner of the Druid pub in Inman Square and the originator of the idea to commemorate the famine that killed one million Irish . . .

Backers of the memorial put together a multiracial group that reflected the diverse population of Cambridge. They were short on Irish sentimentality, but long on the universal lessons taught by the Irish famine – official indifference to suffering – and long on how the Irish experience validated other immigrant groups.

Tiara Dias, a Cape Verdean, said the memorial would provide a positive message about how newcomers as immigrants are being demonized in a country built by immigrants.

Former Mayor Ken Reeves said that while Cambridge Common has been reserved for tombstone-style memorials to those who fought in the Revolutionary War and the Civil War, it was time to reflect the broader experience of Cambridge. 'We should use our common to teach people about history, all history', Reeves said.

The backers had the entire City Council and Mayor Sheila Russell in their corner. The ability of the backers to put together a coalition of the politically influential and the ordinary citizen impressed the commission.

(Cullen 1996)

The incident and its reporting convey complex messages about the positioning of the Irish in relation to both the hegemonic group and other subaltern groups in Boston in the 1990s. In the first place, it is significant that several generations of the Irish diaspora came together to make this claim. At the outset they were labelled by place, their neighbourhood in the city, Inman Square, and described as 'townies' in distinction to the Historical Commission, who belong to Harvard Square but not apparently to the 'town' itself. This illustrates the complex construction of insideness and outsideness in play. The Irish were accepted as local, but excluded from the upper-class 'white Anglo-Saxon Protestant' group which guarded the national identity. Yet during the meeting the Irish outsiders were admitted to a sacred place of the elite over which the Historical Commission had guardianship, through the agreement to allow a Famine monument to be built there. Part of their success lay in the political manoeuvrings their leaders had engaged in prior to the meeting, a classic Irish-American activity on which the urban success of the collectivity had been built in important ways since the mid-nineteenth century.

Of particular interest here is the repositioning of the Irish as a representative immigrant group whose past experiences gave them the authority to speak for others. The memory of the Famine resonated with present-day experiences of other immigrant groups in ways which were recognised both by the newer groups and by key representatives of the 'white Anglo-Saxon Protestant' elite. Yet the power of the elite to control access to the symbolic heart of the American nation was still in place, and the right to be admitted had to be requested and granted. Diasporic myths and memories are thus by no means erased by the establishment by the Irish of a place in the white race, or even in its patrician centre, and continue to be reasserted in new and hybridised forms. The violence of the Famine continues to interrupt from outside the linear progressive narratives of the American nation state and its apparent assimilation of white ethnic differences.

The gendering of these events can also be examined through visual imagery. The instigator of the Famine memorial campaign was an Irish-born man, following in the tradition of Irish male appropriation of political space in the United States. However the newspaper pictures of the supporting march show women taking a prominent part in carrying banners and national flags. They were led by the Mayor, an Irish-American woman. By contrast the Famine monument itself, unveiled the following year by President Mary Robinson depicts much more traditional gender roles (Plate 2.1). It comprises a rectangular block of stone on which is sculpted a small family group of a woman, an adolescent boy and a young child. The boy is standing up, the child in one arm, with the other held out towards the seated woman. He is represented as the mobile, active migrant, leading the way to the new life in America and providing leadership and support for both mother

Plate 2.1 Irish Famine Memorial on Cambridge Common, Boston, Massachusetts, opened by President Mary Robinson, 1997. The common symbolises key events in mainstream United States history. It was first preserved as an open space to commemorate its use as a rallying place for troops in the War of Independence in 1775. To the right of the picture, behind iron railings, is the Soldier's Monument, a memorial erected in 1867 to Cambridge men who died fighting for the Union in the Civil War. In the background are the buildings of Harvard University, which surround the Common.

and child. The woman remains seated, passive, fixed to the rock and dependant on her son's hand for support. She is either reluctant, or too weak, to leave unaided and appears as an integral part of the land, echoing the theme of Mother Ireland (Nash 1993).

This choice of figures illustrates the use of the family to represent the nation, an apparently 'natural' grouping bound by emotional loyalties which conceal the hierarchy of male adult male power. In this case, however, the husband/father is puzzlingly missing, having either emigrated ahead of his family or already perished in Ireland, prefiguring the absent Irish father in Irish-American households.

Women have been distinctively involved in the processes of both displacement and placement of the Irish collectivity. Although Irish women have been unusually well-represented in the migration flow itself, as well as in the forging and maintaining of connections between different locations, they are frequently excluded from accounts. Emphasis on organised political activities, and lack of attention to small-scale domestic routines through which the Irish have become settled in the United States, have largely hidden them from view after arrival. I now explore ways in which Irish women have played distinctive roles in the construction of 'Irish' as a distinctive United States identity.

Placement

Paradoxically, although journeyings are highlighted by the invocation of the term 'diaspora', 'diasporic journeys are essentially about settling down, about putting "roots" elsewhere' (Brah 1996: 182). Diasporic moves are generally assumed to be permanent even though ties elsewhere are retained, so that placement – the development of local and social attachments – is a long-term process of fundamental importance. However the process of settling down lacks the glamour of travel and has received far less attention. The emphasis on travel and displacement is a reason why diaspora has been talked of in unmarked ways which normalise male experience.

A discourse of diaspora gives a very different viewpoint on placement from that of traditional migration analyses which assume a process of adaptation towards the norms of the receiving society. From a diaspora perspective, establishment of 'roots' does not involve the loss of identities but the forging of new ones, so that placement is not simply a process of adaptation; it also involves ongoing political struggles to define distinctive local communities in new ways. These relationships change over time, both in the lifespan of individuals and over generations.

Placement locates Irish women both spatially and socially. The specificity of the locations in which 'roots' are put down has important implications for the social positions women may occupy. In turn these social positions locate them relative to dominant and subordinate collectivities. In this section I will explore first, the material conditions within which Irish women have settled in the United States and second, representations of their placement. By far the greatest weight of evidence available from secondary sources refers to the nineteenth century when immigration from Ireland was at its height, so my analysis is skewed towards this period.

Empirical subjects: spatial contexts

Irish women have settled within the United States in a nested hierarchy of spatial contexts. At the largest geographical scale, their regional distribution has had markedly different consequences according to economic opportunities and social attitudes. At the urban level, women have been clustered or dispersed within neighbourhoods and workplaces. At the most local scale their day-to-day lives, like those of most women, have been based in households.

Data sources at these different scales vary greatly. Regional comparisons depend on case studies of Irish settlement in various locations. Most detailed study has been made of large east coast Irish communities such as Boston (Handlin 1941; Thernstrom 1973; O'Connor 1995, 1996); Philadelphia (Clark 1973, 1986) and New York (Bayor and Meagher 1996). Smaller cities in Massachusetts, such as Lowell (Mitchell 1986; Marston 1986) and Worcester (Meagher 1986) have also been examined. Case studies of mid-west locations have been made, principally Chicago (Skerrett 1986, McCaffrey, Skerrett, Funchion and Fanning 1987), though also St. Louis (Towey 1986) and Butte, Montana (Emmons 1992), with a small number focusing on the Irish community on the west coast in San Francisco (Burchell 1979; Sarbaugh 1986). However it is rare for women to feature more than peripherally in these accounts which tend to emphasise the public face of Irish community life, notably political organisation. Interestingly, Irish women are much more central to studies which select specific workplaces, showing that their economic presence was highly significant though not specifically acknowledged. Thomas Dublin's (1979) clear and detailed account of working women in Lowell, Massachusetts *Women at Work,* is very largely a study of Irish women, who made up 60 per cent of Lowell's female workforce in 1860. Similarly Faye Dudden's (1983) study of *Serving Women* necessarily focuses to a considerable extent on the conditions of Irish household servants.

By far the largest proportion of Irish women settled in eastern cities. Here their relationship with the dominant 'Anglo-Saxon' as well as other ethnic groups varied markedly according to patterns established in the nineteenth century (Clark 1986). Thus as the study of the Famine memorial in Boston in 1996 suggested, anti-Irish attitudes were particularly strong in Boston, where the Irish working classes generally remained a larger and more disadvantaged minority far longer than elsewhere. In Philadelphia, by contrast, a more socially-differentiated but cohesive Irish population developed, with a middle class remaining attached to the community. This followed a serious anti-Irish riot in 1844, after which a parallel set of institutions were constructed which set the Irish population as a whole apart. Thus whereas Irish Catholic mayors were elected in Boston in the nineteenth century, this did not happen in Philadelphia until 1963. A very different picture can be painted of New York where a mix of newcomers was the prime feature and the Irish epitomised this characteristic, becoming distributed according to their socio-economic positions. Wealthy Irish people distanced themselves residentially and socially, though the majority of the Irish remained confined to the poorest areas throughout the nineteenth century.

Far fewer travelled west, though the minority who did so encountered very different conditions. Like all women, those from Ireland or of Irish descent were in a minority among the 'pioneers', who were dominated by young, single men. Nevertheless they were an integral part of the 'homesteading' process. Irish women who travelled as far as the West Coast were in strong demand as servants and wives and wages were far higher than in the east because of gender imbalances (Diner 1983). Earnings were $4–7 per month in New York in the 1850s, but $50–70 in San Francisco. In 1852 only 30 per cent of the Irish-born population of San Francisco was female, though by 1860 this had reached 47 per cent and after 1870 women were in the majority. Bob Burchell (1979) argues that anti-Irish attitudes were less in evidence in San Francisco for a number of reasons, including the dilution of 'Anglo-Saxon', the fact that this was a second stage of settlement for Irish people, and the generally buoyant economy in the mid and later nineteenth century.

Types of work available to Irish women varied widely according to their location. Factory work was distinctly clustered in particular New England towns such as Lowell and Worcester in Massachusetts, as well as in Philadelphia. But for the majority of women domestic service was the principal source of paid employment. As late as 1920 the occupational distribution of Irish-born women in six states (Massachusetts, New York, Pennsylvania, Michigan, Minnesota, Wisconsin) included 81 per cent working in domestic service and 10 per cent as semi-skilled operatives in textile factories (Kennedy 1973: 77). Experiences in these two types of workplace are examined in more detail in the following section. Here I simply want to note that the consequences for women were very different. In mills they were working with other Irish people, some women later becoming prominent in union leadership, whereas as servants they were isolated, often in Protestant employers' homes. Thus the smallest spatial scale, that of the household, has archetypally defined and contained Irish women in the United States. Two types of household were equally important and strongly intertwined with each other. On the one hand were the households in which they were employed as domestic servants, often the first place of settlement after the journey from Ireland; on the other were households established by Irish women for their own families. These different locations were connected in many ways, and large numbers of Irish women spent substantial periods of their life in each. Yet they were geographically separate. In employers' households many Irish girls were isolated within Protestant middle-class enclaves, whereas their own homes were located in Irish Catholic neighbourhoods.

At the local level much material relating to Irish women was collected by various agencies concerned with the problems they were thought to pose. Diner used these extensively and believes that many sources remain to be tapped: 'The major problem . . . I encountered in putting together this study of immigrant Irish women was that the mountains of material from government, charity and church sources, particularly at the local level, seemed almost insurmountable' (Diner 1983: 115). This abundance contrasts strikingly with the absence of similar material in Britain, where there appear to be very few recorded mentions of Irish servants, and certainly no qualitative analysis has been done.

The view from within, on the other hand, produced by Irish women themselves, remains scanty. From the nineteenth century the major source is letters which have been preserved in an *ad hoc* manner. As yet no systematic analysis of what they reveal about Irish women's view of their worlds has been made. Diaries do not appear to have survived and memoirs were not recorded. Thomas O'Connor (1995) contrasts these absences with other diasporic groups in the United States who kept written records. He suggests that the Catholic system of confessions was associated with oral tradition so that family histories relied on 'the encyclopedic memory of some elderly grandmother or maiden aunt who kept it all in her head' (1995: xvii). A more recent attempt to capture Irish women's own accounts of their lives was made by Ide O'Carroll (1990) who interviewed women who had emigrated as early as the 1920s and arrivals in each decade up to the 1980s.

Empirical subjects: Irish women's workplaces

Women who left Ireland in and after the mid-nineteenth century were part of a massive transfer of labour between a peripheral area of the European world capitalist system and a land-rich/labour-poor United States. Richard Williams (1990) argues that the surplus labour force generated in Ireland needed quick access to the means of survival, which was available in the form of wage labour in the United States. Their need for wages coincided with a transformation in the United States economy involving three areas of internal change: the shift from a dependence on merchant capital to industrial capital, transformation from home to factory production and a move away from the primacy of independent skilled craftsmen to the requirement for cheap, unskilled wage labour. Since there was not a large enough home labour market in the United States to supply these needs, migrants were desperately needed.

Williams' discussion of the recruitment of poor, landless Irish peasants as the first United States urban proletariat omits all reference to their gender, usually a sign that it is implicitly taken to be male. In fact the slots into which the Irish labour force was inserted were distinctively gendered, which in turn affected the ethnic and racial constructions of 'the Irish' as a social group. Two large areas of work depended largely on female workforces: textile mill work and domestic service. While mill work is discussed by Williams as a prime source of demand for migrant labour, albeit without reference to its female composition, he does not consider domestic labour and its place in a structural economic discussion of the development of United States society must therefore be added here.

Women workers in textile mills

The major area of employment for Irish women in the public sphere was mill work. Dublin (1979) describes how Irish women became the principal group working in the cotton mills in Lowell, Massachusetts, in the mid-nineteenth century. This development took place after 1836, when only 3.7 per cent of workers at the Hamilton Company Works were foreign-born. By 1850 the proportion was 38.6 per cent and by 1860, it had reached 61.4 per cent, of whom three-quarters were Irish. The reasons for this dramatic shift hinged on the decline in numbers of available 'Yankee' girls, both because of depletion of rural migration sources and because better employment opportunities were opening up for them. These changes coincided with the arrival of large numbers of post-Famine immigrants from Ireland who were willing to work in increasingly demanding technical conditions for low wages. Irish men were also recruited to do the 'women's work' in mills at the same low wages, linking practices of subordination by gender and ethnicity.

It was largely through mill work that women entered the public sphere of political organisation. Although Irish men were the prime union organisers, Irish women provided much of the female trade union leadership in the second half of the century. Diner (1983: 100) argues that 'the real enthusiasm and involvement of [Irish] women deviated sharply from that of most employed women'. In 1878, for example, Irish women workers shut down the carpet mills in Philadelphia for six months in a strike against a 10 per cent wage-cut. The strike failed, but the experience strengthened women's membership of the Knights of Labour (Clark 1986: 82). After the First World War, campaigns organised by Mary O'Reilly against child labour in the Philadelphia textile mills led to the industry leaving the city and moving to the non-unionised South where black workers could more easily exploited. 'Mother Jones' and Elizabeth Gurley Flynn, well-known socialist political activists, both moved on from trades union bases. Elizabeth Gurley Flynn, daughter of an Irish-born mother and second-generation Irish father, worked actively for the International Workers of the World and was finally elected National Chairman of the Communist Party in 1961. She attributed her activism to a determination to avoid the limitations of her mother's domestic world:

A domestic life and possibly a large family had no attractions for me. My mother's aversion to both had undoubtedly affected me profoundly. She was strong for her girls 'being somebody' and 'having a life of their own'. I wanted to speak and write, to travel, to meet people, to see places, to organise for the IWW.

(Flynn 1955: 113)

She also described her ancestors as 'immigrants and revolutionaries', linking her passion for political justice with her father's stories of family and national histories.

There had been an uprising in each generation in Ireland and forefathers of mine were reputed to be in every one of them. The awareness of being Irish came to us as small children, through plaintive song and heroic story. The Irish people fought to wrest their native soil from foreign landlords, to speak their native Gaelic tongue, to worship in the church of their choice, to have their own schools, to be independent and self-governing. As children, we drew in a burning hatred of British rule with our mother's milk. Until my father died, at over eighty, he never said 'England' without adding, 'God damn her!'.

(Flynn 1955: 23)

Diner (1983) suggests that the unusual political involvement of Irish women in the workplace reflects their specific relationship to the economy. They had arrived as labour migrants and, as single women, depended on their own wages. As wives Irish women were valued in the United States, as in Ireland, for the money they could bring to the partnership.

Domestic service

Although Williams' otherwise elegant and persuasive analysis of the construction of an urban proletariat appears to centre around the direct labour needs of industry, a major component of the unskilled labour force required in the United States after the mid-nineteenth century was that of domestic servants. He does not explore the rise of the 'cult of domesticity' which accompanied industrialisation, and which again demanded a large new unskilled immigrant workforce. This omission is surprising given the excess of women in the Irish migration flow.

The new urban middle classes found it increasingly difficult to find servants through personal networks and were obliged to employ strangers. As with factory workers, there were no entry requirements; indeed as Faye Dudden (1983: 48) points out, the ability to do housework was viewed as 'practically a secondary sex characteristic'. If so, this was an ironic misreading of women's lives in Ireland in the groups from which migrants were drawn, where there was no experience of the kind of housework required in middle-class American households. The 'cult of domesticity' defined masculinity as the ability to create economic wealth while femininity was associated with unpaid domestic work and studied leisure. These lifestyles demanded symbolic cleaning rituals, such as polishing silver and furniture, and cooking luxury items such as meat, all of which were far removed from peasant life in Ireland. Thus, paradoxically, servants were required to free middle-class women and their daughters to develop the privacy and intimacy of the private hearthstone, but the only labour available for the task was that of outsiders. Moreover the cash nexus, and low pay, meant that domestic workers were constantly on the lookout for higher remuneration creating the 'servant problem' of 'unfaithfulness'.

The demand for Irish women's labour as domestic servants was created by an extreme shortage of American-born women willing to take on such menial duties. It is this which provided a major reason for the large numbers of Irish women workers and the unusual Irish gender ratio in the United States. In the 1850s, 80 per cent of women in paid household labour in New York were Irish. Community studies in smaller North American towns reveal the extent of dependence of Irish women's domestic labour. In Kingston, New York, for example, 240 out of 254 servants in 1860 were Irish (Dudden 1983: 61). African-American women were much more likely to be self-employed, notably as washerwomen; nearly half of all African-American adult women in Philadelphia in 1849 were in this trade. Since African-American men had far fewer alternatives as unskilled workers than Irish men, African-American women became chief earners in households, much closer to the margins of survival than Irish women who were similarly placed.

Young Irish women were far more available than those in other

European birthplace groups because of their unusual level of independence from nuclear family ties. Girls and young women travelled from Ireland within networks of siblings and parents' siblings, as result of the stem-family system in which their parents remained fixed to the family farm in Ireland. In other national groupings, such as the Italians, men usually emigrated alone to North America and were later joined by wives travelling in family groups. Even after arrival relatively few women in these groups were permitted to work or live outside the family home. Where women from other European regions did enter service, the different conditions in which they worked meant that they occupied more marginal positions in public perception. German women tended to work only for German employers and to remain within the ethnic ghetto, whilst Swedish women were fewer in number and geographically concentrated (Dudden 1983: 62).

In turn, it is argued, domestic service was an attractive occupation to Irish migrant women, providing board, lodging and clothing for new arrivals, and the opportunity to save money both for sending back to Ireland as remittances and to fund their own later marriage. In 1845 alone £1.7 million was sent to Ireland. According to Diner (1983) single women were responsible for a large proportion of this. Household work was healthier than that in factories and also relatively independent of downturns in the economy, which caused high levels of unemployment for Irish men, for example in the depression years of 1873 and 1893. Demand for Irish women as servants increased over time because of their continued willingness to take jobs as live-in servants. Wages rose so that in 1906 the only women to earn more were schoolteachers. In 1920, in six states with large Irish-born populations, 81 per cent of Irish-born women were in domestic service, compared with 32 per cent of British-born women and 8 per cent of those from Italy (Kennedy 1973).

However the view that domestic service was embraced by Irish migrant women for its positive advantages may be overstated and may over-rationalise the placing of Irish women in this low-paying sector. Dudden (1993: 63) argues that the life was extremely harsh and only desperation persuaded Irish women to put up with it. She quotes the writer Harriet Beecher Stowe who observed 'were it not for the supply of poverty-stricken foreigners there would not be a domestic for each family who demands one'. Some measure of the demand is given by the placing of women in paid work by the New York reception centre in 1869. Of 12,111 placed, 11,673 were in domestic positions. The reliance on Irish women continued during the 'heavy waves' of 'New Immigrants' from southern and eastern Europe who arrived during the 1880s.

> The New Immigrants immediately entered into economic competition with the Irish by displacing the Irish from many unskilled occupations. One exception was the area of domestic jobs, where many of the newly arrived Irish women worked but members of most other ethnic groups avoided.
>
> (McKivigan and Robertson 1996: 311)

Irish women in the United States could save their earnings from live-in domestic work to provide their daughters with an education, enabling them to avoid domestic service (Perlmann 1988). In 1913 E. A. Ross calculated that 54 per cent of first generation Irish women were servants or waitresses but only 16 per cent of the second generation (cited in Diner 1983: 94). Conversely fewer than 5 per cent of all Irish-born women in the United States in paid employment in 1900 were 'white blouse' workers, whereas more than 14 per cent of the second-generation were teachers, bookkeepers, accountants or typists. In 1908 20.7 per cent of all New York public school teachers had Irish-born parents (Weisz, cited in McCaffrey 1996: 230) and by the 1930s jobs as schoolteachers were cited as the most sought-after career for second-generation Irish women (McKivigan and Robertson 1996). The jump in upward mobility was far higher than that registered for other groups (Nolan 1989) or for Irish men (Diner 1983). One reason for the large-scale movement of second-generation Irish women into school-teaching was the control over local public appointments by Irish-run political administrations. In this occupation too, second-generation Irish women became union activists, as for example did Margaret Haley in Chicago, appointed vice-president of the Chicago Teachers' Federation in 1901 (Nolan 1995).

The proportion of Irish women in domestic service declined after the turn of the twentieth century and a number of commentators argue that in New York the Irish reached 'class-structure parity' with the 'WASP' hegemony by the early twentieth century (McKivigan and Robertson 1996: 312). But live-in service and waitressing continued to be cited as key areas of work for Irish women during the 1920s and 1930s (Casey 1996), though by the 1990s women of Irish-American descent were unlikely to be in these jobs in New York (Reimers 1996). By contrast, however, new arrivals continued to depend on paid domestic work, especially in the 1980s, in a direct echo of nineteenth century patterns. A survey of the 'new Irish' in New York in 1987–8 showed that the majority of young women 'illegals' were working as nannies or companions in private homes (Corcoran 1993).

Irish women's households

Irish women in the United States spent longer periods in full-time paid employment than other immigrant groups. They married later than average, and more remained single. In Cohoes, New York, for example only 8 per cent of Irish-born women aged twenty to twenty-nine were married in the late nineteenth century compared with 13 per cent of the English-born. Among those aged thirty to thirty-nine the difference was even greater: 44 per cent were married compared with 84 per cent (Diner 1983). This difference reflects high rates of celibacy in Ireland. In 1891 only 42 per cent of women aged twenty-five to thirty-four were married compared with 67 per cent in England and Wales (Kennedy 1973). However, many Irish women did marry at some time, and the great majority of these became mothers, often of large numbers of children. Once married, Irish women rarely combined paid work outside the home with family care. The household could be a source of paid labour through taking in boarders and lodgers and Irish women provided accommodation for new arrivals from Ireland, both kin and strangers. This was one way in which family care and a small cash income could be combined.

In contrast to rural Ireland, where women were subordinate partners in farm households (Kennedy 1973), in the United States Irish women were often controllers as well as managers of households. Not only did they bring their saved earnings to the partnership, but they were disproportionately affected by the loss or absence of husbands. Irish men worked in dangerous occupations, and indeed were considered more expendable by employers than enslaved people who had to be bought and maintained (Ignatiev 1995). The rate of deaths from industrial accidents was high, leaving widows to support families. One estimate placed

Irish men's survival in the United States at an average of six years from arrival. Many men travelled widely in search of work or undertook contracts which involved lengthy absences. Some even returned to Ireland without their wives and children.

Empirical subjects: women in neighbourhoods

Too little is known about Irish women's participation in worlds outside the home and workplace. Most accounts of Irish life focus on Irish men's political involvement. This appears to exclude women from an active role outside the home, yet this absence was more apparent than real. Within Irish neighbourhoods the work of women underpinned both formal and informal community institutions, but their invisibility in named positions of leadership, except in trade unions, has helped to hide this involvement. They also took part in street fights although there are only glimpses of this kind of activity in the surviving records.

More recognised areas of neighbourhood involvement included Catholic church membership and the informal structures which supported immigrant life, such as bars and boarding houses. Although Irish women were historically denied access to formal Catholic church structures, they were indispensible to the more informal realms of religious practice. Not only have women been the most assiduous attenders, they have continued to assume responsibility for maintaining the faith of the next generation. In the nineteenth century, for example, commentators in the United States remarked approvingly on the religiosity of Irish women (Diner 1983). Indeed some parishes consisted largely of Irish women domestic servants. Colleen McDannell quotes a Paulist priest who claimed that Holy Innocents parish was 'decidedly a woman's parish: that is, it is situated in a hotel and brownstone, district, and, having in it but few tenement houses, the church going population is chiefly composed of domestics' (McDannell 1996: 248).

The Catholic parish was also the hub of social events in Irish neighbourhoods. McDannell (1996) argues that parish fairs, which flourished between 1870 and 1900, were sites of a role reversal between Irish women and men. Whereas men dominated the public space of St Patrick's day parades, women took charge of organising fairs, which involved directing male activities. The indoor, semi-domestic environment of fairs made them feminine spaces, and their fundraising aims chimed with the economic importance of women's work in the paid employment sphere. This was an area where middle-class Irish women could also play a role outside the management of their own households, although all social classes were involved. In contrast to male-organised parades, which celebrated Irish difference, fairs brought Irish women into contact with people of other ethnicities in the parish and reinforced religious rather than ethnic loyalties.

During the nineteenth century there were groupings of Irish populations in distinct neighbourhoods. Ethnic clustering was encouraged both by Irish male political bosses requiring blocs of Democratic Party support and the Catholic church which could keep better control over adherents within ethnic parishes (Miller 1990). One of the most famous was the 'Bloody Old Sixth' Ward in south east Manhattan, New York, but other large towns and cities had similar Irish residential clusterings. The Sixth Ward continued to house the poorest immigrants and their descendents but by the end of the century the large majority of Irish people had moved out, though often to suburban Irish neighbourhoods. In the case of New York a large proportion of the population was Irish. In 1890 there were 200, 000 Irish-born residents and 400,000 second-generation, together comprising over a third of the total. By 1910 this had fallen to 20 per cent and by 1945 it was 10 per cent, though Snyder (1996: 444) gives the higher figure of 20 per cent in 1950 after the post-War 'baby boom'. By the 1960s, however, the Jewish influence had become predominant and although the Irish had become an important constituent of the remaining ethnic mix, they were no longer the major one (McNickle 1996).

Irish women were at the forefront of decision-making about where families should live; after their children were born they searched for a 'comfortable and respectable' way of life. Marion Casey (1996) argues that movement to the suburbs of New York in the 1920s and 1930s represented 'horizontal mobility' for families. Women rearranged the household's existing finances to find accommodation with cheaper rents at a greater distance, or supplemented the higher costs by taking in boarders, accepted jobs as janitors in the apartment complex, or even sublet for the summer whilst moving to even cheaper seaside locations. In other large cities also, Irish-American neighbourhoods persisted until the 1960s but gradually fell away with further upward mobility on the

part of the Irish and in-movement of African-American populations and later other groups such as Latinos (Snyder 1996).
Boston is very unusual in retaining distinctively Irish urban neighbourhoods, in a 'frozen historical experience' (McCaffrey 1980).

Representations of Irish women

Working lives: gendered constructions of the Irish as an ethnic group

The social 'placement' of Irish people in the United States derives
from their construction as an 'ethnic' group. Indeed the name
'Irish' has a very specific origin in the mass migration of poor,
landless Catholic peasants during and after the Famine of the
1840s. It thus refers to a limited specific sub-section of the population originating in the island of Ireland, whose perceived
characteristics became generalised as 'Irish'. In response to this
negative stereotyping, earlier arrivals renamed themselves
'Scotch-Irish', emphasising their Protestant religious affiliation.
Williams (1990) argues that the notion of ethnicity developed as a
way of categorising the massive influx of unskilled wage labourers
in the 1840s and 50s, who filled a newly-created lowest stratum
within the free market economy. Its equivalent categorisation in
the lowest stratum of the unfree, or slave, economy was 'race'.

Unpacking the historical specificities of diasporas makes it
easier to identify the constructed nature of social groupings originating in labour migration. Williams (1990) shows how their
transformation into apparently 'natural' categories has hampered
their theorisation. The establishment of the black/white binary of
race was logically and socially prior to the construction of ethnicity, since ethnicity was a means of further subdividing one half of
the 'race' binary. But the two concepts share their origins in the
existence and creation of stratified social systems. In both cases
they result from the assignment of sectors of older stratified
systems to lower structural positions in the newly-created social
system of the United States. Thus black people were drawn from
the lower stratum of West African society and the Irish were similarly in the lowest position on the periphery of Europe.

Williams (1990) also argues that skin pigmentation became the
marker of 'race' because of the particular bodily characteristics of
the group who were available when large quantities of unfree

labour were needed to exploit the newly-colonised North American continent. A second period of massive labour shortage occurred in the middle of the nineteenth century, when the change from an agricultural/merchant-based economy to an industrial manufacturing one was taking place. At this time the available labour supply was from Ireland, and it was distinguished from the earlier European populations by the assignment of cultural as well as skin pigmentation (white) attributes, which then became understood as 'ethnic'. Thus ethnicity became the mark of vertical classification in the free labour system, signalling the split between the skilled and unskilled labour forces. Ethnic identity thus has a very specific meaning, referring to the labelling of a group of individuals with a particular social value, as reflected in stereotypes.

This detailed analysis of the construction of the ethnic group labelled 'Irish' is particularly important in locating the specificity of experiences in different diasporic locations. It underlines the need to avoid essentialist definitions of groups according to shared origins. Being Irish in the United States has not been and is not the same as being Irish in Britain. Williams (1990: 87) contrasts the placement of Irish people in relation to Britain and the United States by highlighting the movement of the Irish from being 'the lower race (Irish and Catholic as opposed to English and Protestant) into the lower slot of the upper race (Irish and White as opposed to African and Black)'. Thus in Britain the Irish have been racialised as different, while in the United States they have been racialised as the same, but ethnicised as different.

The categorisation of groups as constituted by race and ethnicity depends on the process of stereotyping whereby individual variation is overlooked and a limited number of traits are attributed to total populations. Gender plays a key role in stereotyping, introducing a further dimension of power differentials in the placing of subordinate groups. What is striking about the gendering of representations of 'the Irish' in the United States in the nineteenth century is the equal, if not greater, prominence given to women. The stereotype which had crossed the Atlantic from Britain with earlier settlers had been that of 'Paddy', the violent, unreliable, rebellious male 'other' to English masculine authority (Knobel 1986) . But after the mid-nineteenth century, 'Bridget' began to appear beside or even in place of 'Paddy' or 'Pat'. This is brought out in the word order in which H. Giles, in the *Christian*

Examiner in 1848, presented his definition: 'Irish means to us a class of human beings, whose women do our housework, and whose men dig our railroads' (cited in Luibheid 1997: 257). The wider variety of personal names also used to refer collectively to Irish women also reflects the high visibility of the stereotype. 'Mary', 'Norah' and 'Maureen' were all understood to indicate the Irish population as a whole. This was in stark contrast to Britain where no such naming of Irish women took place, despite their similar location in domestic service.

In 1856, *Harper's Monthly*, later known for the viciously simi-

MR. DONE BROWN'S VALENTINE.
" What does Snip mean, I'd like to know ?"

MR. LIONEL LAVENDER'S VALENTINE.
" Oh yes, Dinah!   But—"

BRIDGET MALONY'S VALENTINE.
" Sure, Patrick is a jewel ov a boy."

CÆSAR WASHINGTON'S VALENTINE.
" Dat is a fac, an' no mistake !"

Plate 2.2 Four of a set of sixteen cartoon representations of American stereotypes in 1856. The Irish are represented by a female servant, Bridget Maloney, whereas the central African-American figure is male, Caesar Washington. By contrast Dinah, a washerwoman, is a secondary character, whose occupation illustrates the displacement of African-American women into domestic service outside the homes of white Americans.

anised images drawn by its cartoonist, Nast, printed a lighthearted set of cartoons for Valentine's Day (Plate 2.2). They depicted a variety of people stereotyped by class and ethnic group, opening their Valentine cards and giving appropriate reactions. Physical appearances, surroundings and speech patterns give readers immediate clues as to the group identities of each character. The Irish are represented by Bridget Maloney, a cheerful, simple woman opening her Valentine from Pat in her employer's kitchen. 'Pat' hides his true uncouth character, probably racialised as simian, by appealing to Bridget's good nature, causing her to exclaim 'Sure Patrick is a jewel ov a boy'.

This representation brings out a range of gendered responses towards the Irish in the mainstream white society of *Harpers' Monthly* readers. Irish women, epitomised by 'Bridget', were firmly placed within a working-class framework, their peasant background and naivety still clearly evident. Many complaints about their clumsiness and poor cooking skills were made. Yet they were also shown as 'cheerful' and, as Diner (1983) suggests, 'lovable'. Clark (1991: 39), for example, discusses Nast's cartoons in the 1870s, which 'showed Brigid, the clownish Irish maid, enacting follies or having tantrums in domestic situations' whereas 'the [male] Irish' were depicted as 'ape-like, corrupt, violent and religiously depraved'. Although the overall picture of Irish women is a negative one in contrast to the sophistication of white 'Anglo-Saxon' middle classes, there was ambivalence about their status. This is illustrated by their association with Catholicism, which was thought to contribute to their reliability and honesty as servants, even though it confirmed their Catholic 'otherness'. Irish men on the other hand were portrayed with much greater hostility and condemnation.

In the cartoon, 'Bridge' is positioned inside a white American home, whereas in another cameo, 'Dinah', the African-American washerwoman is outside the door delivering a parcel of clothes to 'Mr Lionel Lavender'. She is clearly in need of money, conveyed in the picture by her presentation of a washing bill, instead of the Valentine he had been expecting through the post. Unlike Bridget, Dinah is a peripheral character within the frame of the cartoon, not the recipient of the Valentine; this more central role of representing the black population was reserved for a man 'Caesar Washington'.

Strong negative stereotypes of servants in general, however, became particularly associated with Irish women, whose ubiquity and financial need made them conspicuous. One widespread complaint was that they were 'faithless'. Dudden (1983: 59) cites the example of Caroline White of Brookline, Boston, who complained that 'the Irish were the source of all the servant problems' and repeatedly pronounced herself 'heartily sick of the Irish' and 'sick of all the race'. Dudden argues that blaming the Irish avoided the perplexities of free market explanations and absolved employers from any responsibilities. But what was labelled the 'servant problem' by employers could also be interpreted as evidence of Irish women's resistance to the identities and social positions constructed for them.

Stereotypes of Irish women in their own households

Assimilation has been a central tenet of the national ideology of the United States and informs the language of diversity, with terms such as 'minority' and 'immigrant' which locate groups relative to the mainstream rather than as part of a globally scattered population. Whilst servants were negatively stereotyped, Irish mothers were represented much more positively. Thus the enhanced visibility of Irish women in the United States also reflects mainstream society's approval of their behaviour as mothers. According to Diner (1983) they were regarded as agents of 'Americanization', as 'civilizers' of their families. They were cast as pillars of family strength, applauded for keeping their families together and credited with advancing the collective status of Irish-Americans. The image of the 'Irish-American matriarch' was thus strongly related to the distinctiveness of an Irish ethnic identity, including the retention of Catholic religious affiliation and a strong sense of family loyalty. But this approval was at the cost of negative representations of Irish men. They were seen, by contrast, as a source of family disorganisation because their primary allegiances appeared to be to male groupings, in political organisations or among drinking companions, and because they frequently left home to seek work.

The move 'from shanty town to lace curtain', which was a widely recognised metaphor for Irish mobility from urban proletariat to lower middle class, was thus seen largely as women's achievement. This very telling phrase signals a shift from the masculinity of the construction workers' life in roughly built 'shanty' housing to the femininity of the 'lace curtain', simultaneously representing a spatial move from the working class 'ghetto' to the edge of middle-class respectability. According to this narrative Irish women would have observed – and washed – the lace curtains in their employers' houses, and aspired to replicate them when funds allowed. Upward mobility was thus firmly linked to the home and women's immersion in the tastes and property of mainstream society. But the phrase is also edged with scorn for the pretensions of higher status, and suggests a continuing exclusion from a secure place in the hegemonic 'Anglo-Saxon' group.

Academic commentators reinforce the interpretation that domestic service produced aspirations to emulate the white middle-class American households. Thus, using evidence from Irish women's letters to family and friends in Ireland, Kerby Miller (1995: 55) argues that domestic service 'certainly increased and refined, if they did not create, bourgeois aspirations both material and socio-cultural'. Describing women's aspirations, Colleen McDannell (1986: 73) similarly argues that 'with the open approval of the Catholic hierarchy, they aspired to create the "right" kind of home . . . which then would make them the "right" kind of people'.

However Williams (1990: 144) questions the view that the upward mobility of the Irish was linked to the assimilation of 'Anglo-Saxon' values. He argues that upward mobility was accompanied by changes in attitudes towards the Irish by dominant groups, rather than by Irish choice to conform. Negative stereotyping of the Irish did diminish as they were able to occupy better paid occupational slots in the hierarchy, but it was transferred to new immigrant groups, such as the Italians, who filled the unskilled wage labouring stratum. This interpretation chimes much more closely with the conceptual framework of diaspora, which allows for the retention of difference rather than the assumption that those 'dwelling-in-displacement' automatically move towards 'assimilation'.

Irish women and constructions of whiteness

A central aspect of Irish people's movement into the centre of the American nation from an initial location on its margins was their 'whiteness'. As the group most closely positioned to enslaved and free black workers by timing of arrival and economic position, the Irish occupied a pivotal role in the construction of whiteness as a social category in America. This relationship has only very recently begun to be analysed in depth, and it remains largely ungendered (Williams 1990; Roediger 1991; Allen 1994; Ignatiev 1995). Yet as bearers and reproducers of the 'races' and as economic competitors in domestic service, women played a major part in this construction. Irish women have been praised as 'civilizers' of American families, an acknowledgement, in part at least, of their success in securing a place for their children in the hegemonic white supremacy. But their place in the construction of whiteness has been ignored.

When they first arrived in large numbers early in the nineteenth century, Irish people shared the same occupational niches and neighbourhoods as free African-Americans in eastern cities of the United States. Their social standing was therefore place-based, linked with conditions of poverty. According to Noel Ignatiev (1995) the 'colour line' was by no means fixed and often ignored. He uses the complete absence of reference to segregation by 'race' in Philadelphia prisons in the 1820s to argue that such distinctions were later social constructions to meet particular needs among sections of the 'white' population. He goes on to describe a variety of ways in which the Irish and 'black' populations initially intermingled and were linked together by the 'Anglo-Saxon' mainstream. Some saw the two populations as almost interchangeable, using labels such as 'niggers turned inside out' for the Irish and 'smoked Irish' for the free blacks. Others identified some difference, but also tended to consign the Irish to an intermediate 'race' category.

In some situations it appears that African-Americans were valued more highly than Irish people. Thomas Sowell (1978: 21) amasses examples including advertisements in the mid-nineteenth century which stipulated 'Any color or country except Irish' and 'A colored man preferred. No Irish need apply'. In New York hotels African-American waiters were paid higher wages than Irish ones and in Boston in 1860 the occupational status of free African-Americans was slightly higher than that of the Irish. Perhaps the most striking comparison is that made by slave owners in the South, who hired Irish men to do the most dangerous jobs, while using enslaved people for work that was simply dirty or degrading. One owner commented: 'The niggers are worth too much to be risked here; if the Paddies are knocked overboard, or get their backs broke, nobody loses anything' (Sowell 1978: 28).

The gendering of these various constructions has not been fully considered. There is evidence that mothers played a particularly significant role in this early ambivalence about the place of the Irish in relation to whiteness. Children of Irish mothers and African-American fathers were quite common in New York and Boston in the 1860s and it was often speculated that 'racial amalgamation' would take place, spearheaded by Irish/black unions (Ignatiev 1995, Hodges 1996). Irish women were involved in this process to a much greater extent than men. Ignatiev (1995) comments on the irony that Huckleberry Finn, an icon of American identity, was probably of mixed Irish/black background. The Irish were by no means automatically included as 'white'. According to Ignatiev, the change took place during the period of industrial expansion in the 1840s and 1850s when new industries gave organised white labour the opportunity to exclude African-American workers on the grounds of 'race'. The textile industries were at the forefront of this process, as result of the expanding home population's demand for cloth. Ignatiev fails to note that the New England textile mills were in fact dominated by a female Irish workforce.

The rise of the textile industry was a critical development in securing a place for the Irish within the white race. Because Irish workers were employed in the lowest skilled areas, designated women's work, while the more skilled jobs were taken by British and German male immigrants, women were at the forefront of this construction of whiteness. Ignatiev (1995) argues that employers initially favoured European immigrant labour in the textile mills, partly because of the new arrivals' experience of industrial life and partly for their willingness to accept low wages. Once established, however, these white groups protected their position by setting up trade unions which designated the jobs they were doing as 'white men's work'. For work to be defined in this way, it had to be in areas without black workers, and this could only be ensured in new industries where there was no legacy of black involvement. By the mid-century, trades unions had effectively been taken over by the Irish, who were thus heavily implicated in the definitions of whiteness they constructed.

David Roediger (1991) offers a broader explanation for the emergence of whiteness as a significant social category. He relates

this to the context of class formation rather than simply competition for jobs, and develops DuBois' notion that the white working
classes in America were persuaded to accept low monetary wages
because of the compensatory 'wage' of public and psychological
deference associated with being 'white'. They agreed to accept
their inferior class position because they were 'not slaves' and 'not
blacks'. Beyond this, whiteness was 'a way in which white workers
responded to a fear of dependency on wage labour and to the
necessities of capitalist work discipline' (Roediger 1991: 13). It
therefore chimed with the heritage of the American revolution in
which independence was a 'powerfully masculine personal ideal'.
Enslaved black workers were hated and feared because of their
dependency. Indeed as pawns of the rich and powerful owners,
they were seen as 'anticitizens', the opposite of free men. It should
be remembered that rejection of dependency had particularly
strong resonances for the Irish in their own attempts to end the
colonial relationship with Britain.

However the strongly masculine underpinning to these explanations is at odds with the apparent centrality of Irish women in
the workplace. It again suggests that women had a looser connection with whiteness than Irish men. The easier conflation of Irish
women with the servility associated with blackness was illustrated
in the names used to describe them as workers. Although the fear
of dependency and servility had resulted in the avoidance of the
word 'servant' for white domestic maids in the early decades of the
nineteenth century– it was replaced by 'hand' or 'help' – it was
returned to use as Irish women came to dominate these jobs by
the 1830s. In 1845 Lowell female textile workers chose to describe
themselves as 'slaves' in their demands for improved conditions.
In the 1850s Irish women, who constituted the largest group of
prostitutes in New York City were described as 'white slaves' or
'Irish niggers'.

Yet at the same time that Irish women shared a position with
African-American women, they displaced them from unskilled
jobs on racial grounds. An important issue is the extent to which
the whiteness of Irish women enabled them to displace free black
people in domestic service. If this is the case then women were in
the vanguard of creating 'the wages of whiteness' whereby they
accepted lower wages in return for preference over black people
in a competitive labour market. Acceptance as white constituted
part of the reward. This could be interpreted as a market decision

in which individual Irish women were willing to undercut African-American women's wages because of their own need. For example, by the period 1826–30 the New York Society for the Encouragement of Faithful Domestics was already reporting applications from 8,346 'Irish' people, compared with 2,574 'Negroes', 3601 'Americans', 642 'English' and 377 other foreigners from other countries, indicating the strength of demand for work by the Irish. By 1849 only 156 out of 4,249 servants living with white families were black, all women.

Although Ignatiev (1995) argues that this initial phase of competition was not in itself a 'race' issue, a term which could not be applied until systematic exclusion by unions used whiteness as a condition of employment in certain industries, Dudden (1983: 64–5) provides strong evidence that African-American women were being excluded on grounds of skin colour. She cites reports from European travellers in 1830s about the difficulties experienced by those who employed both white and black servants in the same establishment, arguing that this led to the simpler expedient of hiring all-white staff. If this is the case it predates the process identified by Ignatiev in which unions in new industries marked the turning point in defining workers as 'white'. Perhaps the most interesting point is that in both areas of work Irish women were the key group being constructed as white and against whom blackness was judged to be inferior. Dudden lists other examples including that of a Philadelphia employer who chose to employ an all-black staff and was punished by neighbours who destroyed the garden and sent a threatening note demanding the dismissal of the black servants. The author Louisa May Alcott observed that she had managed to find a white woman to work with her black cook, but that it had proved 'an insurmountable problem to all the Irish ladies who had applied'. However by the 1920s the proportion of domestic servants who were Irish had declined sharply and their place had been taken by African-American women moving into northern cities, who rapidly comprised over 70 per cent of the total. Perhaps this suggests a much more tenuous relationship between whiteness and domestic service which could easily be reversed.

The hegemony which had originally been centred on the 'Anglo-Saxon race' alone was not finally widened to include other white Europeans until there was a need to reconsolidate the racial order after the tremendous disruption to it threatened by the

abolition of slavery (Omi and Winant 1986). After the American
Civil War Irish immigrants actively reinforced 'racial' hierarchies,
engaging in notorious mob violence against the black population
(Luibheid 1997). Women were deeply involved in these
exclusions, prominent in moves to all-white neighbourhoods and
in leading trade unions which reserved workplaces for white
women (Snyder 1996).

Again, however, place-specific evidence must be used. Recent
research in New York suggests a much more nuanced picture (Bayor
and Meagher 1996). Thus Graham Hodges (1996) entitles his study
of the Sixth Ward between 1830 and 1870 'Desirable companions
and lovers'. He argues that shared hardship in this extremely poor
neighbourhood surmounted 'racial' differences, citing many
examples of mixed work and household patterns between Irish and
African-American inhabitants. Irish women's partnerships with
Chinese men were also caricatured in *Harper's Weekly*. John Kuo Wei
Tchen (1996) traces the shift of Irish men into the 'white' category
through their presentation of themselves as stage performers, in
which they increasingly aligned themselves with mainstream
Protestant audiences, caricaturing Chinese and African-Americans
in yellowface and blackface masquerades. He argues that Irish men
chose this route and demanded that Irish women conform: they
'were essentially told to make a choice, or else'. This suggests a much
slower, more variable and differently-gendered pace in the construction of whiteness in the United States.

The place of the Irish within the white hegemony remains
complex. Although the case study of the 1996 Famine memorial
issue in Boston appeared to position them in a continuing subordinate position to 'Anglo-Saxon' hegemony and in solidarity with
new black immigrants, this may have have been the atypical
product of a specific geographical placement within America.
Moreover the solidarity being expressed and accepted was
between migrants, white and black, rather than between long-
settled Irish and African-American people. When 'Harvard
Square' recognised the Irish as archetypical migrants, it did not
include descendents of enslaved people. Eithne Luibheid (1997)
paints a very different picture of the contemporary manipulation
of their whiteness by 1980s migrants to achieve their ends. Her
interview with Cora Flood, Anti-racism and Immigrant Outreach
Co-ordinator of the Irish Immigration Center in Boston, starkly
expresses this different relationship:

Our people are one of the groups that caused pain to Black people. They're one of the groups, they're not the only group. I've spoken with African Americans who left Boston because of the Irish. I've spoken with African Americans who were denied jobs because of the Irish.

(Luibheid 1997: 270)

Luibheid argues that Irish-Americans have been deeply implicated in the 'white ethnic revival', which opposes moves towards racial equality through policies such as affirmative action in order to preserve the prevailing racial hierarchy. New Irish immigrants have been drawn into this movement, although they occupy a very different relationship to it through the problems they share with subordinate groups, particularly those with illegal status and poor socio-economic circumstances. The struggle to secure 'diversity immigrant visas' brought together earlier generation Irish-Americans and new arrivals from Ireland to secure advantages in the Immigration Acts, which compensated national groups adversely affected by the introduction of quotas in 1965. This powerfully illustrates the 'white dividend' on which Irish-Americans could draw. As a result Irish people benefited disproportionately from Donnelly visas in 1988 and Morrison lottery visas in 1990 and 1995. They were able to achieve this by presenting themselves as desirable white migrants, implicitly playing on the racial anxieties of the hegemonic group.

Among the 1980s immigrants from Ireland, however, elements of the nineteenth-century experience have been replayed. The most common jobs for women 'illegals' have been in low-paid domestic work, including care of children and the elderly, and restaurant and bar work. Gender differences are clearcut, both in the nature of manual work done and in the status within the sectors, men being much more likely to move into management positions in bar work, for example (Corcoran 1996). Yet even in these low-paid casual jobs, the whiteness ensures preferential treatment. White nannies are preferred to black ones by middle-class white American families.

Spatial contexts: representational variation

Stereotyped images of Irish women in the United States are based on the perceived characteristics of those settled in the eastern seaboard where the great majority of Irish women were clustered into towns and cities. However despite the prominence of representations of 'Bridget', the lives of Irish women often remain hidden behind those of men who are chosen to represent stereotypical ethnic characteristics in each type of location.

In describing the synonymity between the Irish and the city of New York itself by the 1920s, Dennis Clark chooses almost entirely masculine imagery, which he claims mirrors that used by the collectivity itself:

> The city's Irish, still numbered in the hundreds of thousands were by now as much a standard part of the city as Central Park and the Chrysler Building. Had they not laboured to build the Brooklyn Bridge, the technological symbol of the nineteenth century in the city? Had they not dug its tunnels, policed its streets, sung in its cafes, paraded, danced East side and West side, and commanded its political legions for decades? Of all the groups in the city's melange, the Irish saw themselves as pre-eminent New Yorkers. 'We built it. We won it. We run it!' was their slogan.
>
> (Clark 1986: 64)

The masculine imagery associated with westward migration is also striking. Although no analysis of this aspect of Irish settlement has been made there are clear pointers to its resonances. The Irish epitomised the heroic icon of the 'frontiersman', engaged in feats of physical prowess as builder of canals and railroads, or as miner, assumed to be a single man displaying the positive traits of independence, physical strength and risk-taking. The names of many famous frontiersmen and cowboys attest to the prominence of Irishmen, though this association is often overlooked, probably because of their Protestant origins: Bill Cody, Davy Crockett, Daniel Boone, Billy the Kid. While it is true that husbands left home for months on end to find this work, leaving wives to raise families in the East, some women were also present in shadowy forms on the frontier. The flow to the west included many settlers, where the 'homestead' was a symbol of women's work in the same way that the 'cottage' in the Irish landscape represented the invisible processes of childrearing and daily family renewal. But accounts of the peopling of the North American frontier largely efface women's roles. Clark again prioritises male experience when commenting on the recollections of Charles O'Keeffe, whose father apparently abandoned his wife and eight children. The mother's role in managing the subsequent homesteading process as the lone adult is not mentioned.

> The trek west was an epic of discomfort, and later romantic views of it do the reality a disservice. As a boy, Charles O'Kieffe [sic] left Nebraska with his parents and eight brothers and sisters in 1884. The father later disappeared and the family travelled 500 miles westward to homestead in a sod house in territory still roamed by the Sioux. No boy could ever forget such an experience.
>
> (Clark 1986: 143)

More recognised female roles included boarding house and saloon bar keepers, where women also needed strength and independence. Stories of individual 'frontier' Irish women were celebrated, but the reporting of their activities often hinged around references to their sexual attractiveness to men. Again Clark colludes with and reinforces such romantic stereotypes in his reporting:

> Flame-haired Kate O'Leary, as tough as she was good-looking, ran a saloon and sporting house in Dodge City. In addition to fighting Indians when she was a girl and shooting dead an overly active cowboy on her doorstep, she was not above keeping order in her establishment with a few well-placed shotgun blasts.
>
> (Clark 1986: 145)

Conclusions

This discussion of the discursive and material place of Irish women in the diaspora space of the United States highlights sets of experiences at national, regional and local geographical scales as a result of economic positioning and relationships with other groups. Its purpose is to illustrate the specificity of Irish women's positioning and representation in particular global locations. As Brah points out:

> Diasporas, in the sense of distinctive historic experiences, are

often composite formations made up of many journeys to different parts of the globe, each with its own history, its own particularities. Each such diaspora is an interweaving of multiple travelling; a text of many distinctive and, perhaps, even disparate narratives.

(Brah 1996: 183)

What the evidence presented shows is that Irish women in the United States were highly visible, especially in eastern seaboard cities, partly because of their numbers, but also because of their clustering in paid domestic service which brought them into contact with more powerful groups identifying themselves as 'Anglo-Saxon'. Hegemonic discourse focused around their unreliability and lack of 'faithfulness'. Yet these were also traits which fitted with the capitalist ethic of selling labour to the highest bidder and using all possible means to support and advance individual interests. While Irish women failed to satisfy employers using 'Old World' criteria of servility and deference, they fitted closely with the 'New World' ideology of upward mobility by economic means. Another element in the image is that of the powerful Irish-American matriarch controlling her 'first-generation American' children. These stereotypes of strength and independence came to predominate so that overall Irish women have a strong positive image in the United States at the end of the twentieth century. Bayor and Meagher (1996: 7) give examples from television programmes networked throughout the Western industrialised world, such as *Cagney and Lacey* and *Northern Exposure*, where 'Irish women, long symbols of strong-willed women in American popular culture, continue to play that role as television writers seek images of resolute and independent women in the wake of the feminist revival'.

However despite the centrality of this theme in the national ideology of the United States, the story is not simply one of linear upward progression for Irish women. Renewed immigration from Ireland in the 1980s, in which undocumented women re-entered insecure, low-paid domestic work, and the revival of myths and memories of the Famine in the 1990s, show how displacement continues to resurface in changing forms. Even, and perhaps especially, for those who have embraced their 'placement' in the United States, the 'doubleness' of continuing 'displacement' may be regarded positively. This theme is examined by Charles

Fanning (1996), using the writing of Elizabeth Cullinan whose recent novels chart 'the lives of female protagonists from Irish backgrounds who have landed sanely on their feet in the wider New York world'. In her story 'Commuting' the Irish-American narrator travels between the outer boroughs and Manhattan, in a metaphor for her own upward mobility. Cullinan presents this as enriching and liberating.

> Commuting means literally going back and forth daily between two parts of a life, and is of course central to the experience of many New Yorkers, ethnic and otherwise. Cullinan's story reverses the usual rhythm of urban American commuting in that her narrator travels from a life in the city to a job in the old neighbourhood, and yet the richness of comparative contexts is still the point. Everything that she sees during the commute she sees twice, and thus more clearly – as the Irish girl from the Bronx that she was, and the New Yorker she is now.
>
> (Fanning 1996: 530–1)

The current place of the Irish in the American nation is thus a complex one. On the one hand they are archetypically successful European immigrants, who started in the poorest circumstances and after two or three generations made the 'American Dream' come true. The Kennedy story is a powerful confirmation of this success, although its male hero contrasts with the matriarchal structures through which upward mobility was achieved. More generally Irish ancestry is a popular identity, chosen by preference over their other origins by nearly 20 per cent of Americans, the second most popular ethnic identity after a German one. On the other hand, memories of exclusion have not been completely erased and the surprise registered in Boston by the success of the Famine memorial application is a reminder of these traces. But it is the acknowledgement and celebration of Irish-American identities and experiences which provide such a sharp contrast with the lives of Irish women in Britain. The comparative context of the United States provides a starting point for understanding a different journey to a diaspora space much 'closer to home'.

Chapter 3

Inside the Pale

Constructions of Irish women's place in Britain

The openly acknowledged, if not widely studied, place of Irish women as strong mothers and independent, upwardly mobile daughters in the United States of America contrasts strikingly with that of their sisters, aunts and cousins who settled in Britain. Members of the same family, with similar childhood experiences, levels of education and cultural backgrounds, entered societies where they were represented and positioned very differently. In the following chapters I examine Irish women's place in Britain from a range of discursive and material perspectives which are brought more sharply into focus by juxtaposition with the United States experience.

This more detailed exploration of Britain is necessary for both theoretical and empirical reasons. Britain occupies a key role in analyses of the Irish diaspora because the relationship between Britain and Ireland both underlies the more immediate causes of dispersal and is a central strand in attitudes towards the Irish in different diasporic locations. Discursively, Irish women are much more invisible than Irish men in Britain. There has been no widely recognised stereotype of 'Bridget' to match the public, taken-for-granted representation of 'Paddy'. Indeed Irish women are simply included as 'Paddies' when they are recognised at all. At a practical level much work remains to be done to make visible Irish women's lives in Britain since little data has been collected or analysed. This invisibility mirrors the wider denial of difference to the Irish collectivity in Britain as a whole. Both these issues of exclusion intertwine and will be explored here.

Dissimilarities between the two countries are nowhere more apparent than in recognition of hybridity. 'Irish-American' is proudly proclaimed, but where is the equivalent category in

Britain? While uneasy moves towards hyphenated categories are being made in the case of other diasporic groups, including Black-British, there appears to be no space into which to insert a comparable term for the children of Irish migrants. Ironically 'Anglo-Irish' is occasionally resurrected by British commentators, striving to find an appropriate term for the upsurge of second-generation Irish creativity and popular appeal in Britain in the 1990s, and unaware of its distinctive historical provenance in the colonising class. However local Irish identities in Britain are used more freely in the same way that they are adopted in the United States. 'London Irish' and 'Manchester Irish' are claimed and recognised identities, just as 'New York Irish' and 'Boston Irish' have specific regional nuances. These are quintessentially diasporic labels, simultaneously locating the second generation as 'belonging' in Britain at a local level, while remaining significantly attached elsewhere.

There are parallels between Irish women's lives in the United States and Britain. Similar representations of Irish femininity are recreated within Irish communities on both sides of the Atlantic, reinforced by the Catholic Church with its global, though nationally differentiated, ideology. Above all, paid domestic service has characterised and helped to shape women's working lives in both locations in all periods. Moreover family ties link sisters, aunts, nieces and cousins and lead to permanent and temporary moves between the two countries.

My aim in this chapter is to explore the discursive positionings of Irish women in Britain as a starting point for uncovering their material consequences for women who have settled in this 'diaspora space'. Ironically, Britain has usually been omitted from academic discussions of the notion of the Irish diaspora, which has frequently been assumed to be synonymous with Irish dispersal to the United States of America. One of the earliest uses of the term appeared in 1976 in the title of Laurence McCaffrey's book *The Irish Diaspora in America* where the possibility that this was one strand amongst several was not discussed. Even in the most recent period, when a broader, more theoretical understanding of diaspora has been widely adopted, this assumption continues to be common. For example, in 'a pioneering reference guide', *The Penguin Atlas of Diasporas* (1995), the authors discuss 'the Irish diaspora' only in terms of settlement in the United States as though this was the complete story. Yet their map (confusingly ahistorical and wrongly labelling the two islands 'United Kingdom' and 'Ireland') shows up a smaller, but distinct flow to Britain (Chaliand and Rageau 1995: 158).

These taken-for-granted exclusions of Britain from conventional understandings of diaspora implicitly reinforce a colonial perspective in which Ireland remains attached to Britain so that movement between the two is seen as simply an internal rearrangement of bodies. However ways of rethinking the relationship were signalled by President Mary Robinson's inaugural speech in 1990.

> Beyond our state there is a vast community of Irish emigrants extending *not only across our neighbouring island* – which has provided a home away from home for several Irish generations – but also throughout the continents of North America, Australia and of course Europe itself.
>
> (*Irish Times* 1990: 3, my emphasis)

She repositioned Britain as central to the process of diaspora, openly acknowledging that it was a 'home away from home' rather than part of the 'same' home which its exclusion from conventional diaspora discourses had implied. This phrase recognises a key aspect of diaspora, that of 'dwelling-in-displacement', which fundamentally challenges traditional historical and sociological interpretations based on notions of assimilation. By specifying the possibility of belonging to 'homes' both inside and outside the British nation, it begins to provide a way of unravelling the 'double bind' in which Irish people have been placed discursively through their simultaneous representation as 'the other' and 'the same'.

I shall start by exploring the specific processes underlying ongoing racialisation of the Irish in Britain, and ways in which they are gendered. Like racialisations of other minority ethnic groups these processes are intimately bound up with constructions of the boundaries of the British nation and also the formation of internal hegemonic group identities. However the Irish case is distinctive in a number of ways. The history of 'othering' is very long, pre-dating colonial expansion outside Europe by several centuries. The colony/centre boundary was apparently erased between 1800 and 1922 when Ireland was subsumed into the United Kingdom of Great Britain and Ireland, albeit under different conditions from other parts of the kingdom. Moreover colonial 'business' remains unfinished, with an unresolved national dispute in Northern Ireland.

Despite explicit and widespread simianisation of representations of the Irish in the nineteenth century, which extended as we have seen to the United States, in the post-War period Irish difference has been submerged by the rise in importance of the black/white binary as the dominant model of racialised identities. As a result the Irish have been forcibly included with people of British origin in a common whiteness, which remains largely undifferentiated by ethnicity. The taken-for-granted nature of this boundary is summed up in the apparently inclusive titles of 'race relations' publications of the 1960s and 70s, such as Hiro's (1971) *Black British, White British* and *Black Migrants: White Natives* by Lawrence (1974). In these titles white migrants and their descendents are either subsumed into the British population, or forgotten altogether. By contrast, the same misunderstanding of racism as a black/white phenomenon is unthinkable in continental Europe, where references to 'race' would instantly bring to mind Jewish experience (Miles 1993: 20). Far from being a widely applicable analytical concept, therefore, the idea of 'race' is an ideological construct which is highly specific both in time and location.

The assumption that the Irish in Britain assimilate rapidly also follows from beliefs about whiteness representing 'the same'. In the 1960s, when geographers began to publish analyses of post-war migrant settlement in Britain, the connection between inevitable 'progress' towards assimilation and whiteness was taken to be self-evident. To some extent this was a mistaken transfer to Britain of constructions of 'race' in the United States. In the 1960s British academics seized the theoretical ideas of the Chicago School of Human Ecology in order to explain and predict the residential patterns of immigrant groups, but in doing so the historical specificity of relationships between dominant and subordinate groups was often lost. Even where evidence of similarities in the experiences of white and black migrants was reported, British analysts drew very different conclusions about the two populations.

A geographical analysis of patterns of immigrant settlement in 1961 found that 'The distribution of West Indians in both London and Birmingham was similar to that of the Irish' (Peach 1968: 87).

However the wider dispersion of Irish settlement throughout the city was used as evidence that in reality there was a 'fundamental distinction' between the two groups although it was acknowledged that this could be explained by the very much longer history of settlement and much greater numbers of Irish people involved.

In another comparative study of immigrant residential distribution in Birmingham it was stated that: 'the assimilation of the Irish immigrant is merely a matter of time, and the segregation which exists now, and may well persist, is one of socio-economic status' (Jones 1967: 44). Yet no evidence was provided to support this assertion, which was challenged by the contemporaneous findings of a study of Sparkbrook, Birmingham, where survey material revealed that hostility against the Irish was as least as great as that against 'coloured people' and sometimes higher: 'Mr C saw the Irish as the main problem-group among newcomers. Riddled with North–South animosities, they got "boozed up to the eyeballs", became fighting mad, and punched and kicked one another in the street' (Rex and Moore 1967: 70). There were no favourable mentions for the Irish in Sparkbrook, although all other groups except the Pakistanis had some. However the total number of unfavourable mentions was slightly greater for 'coloured' than for the Irish and 'tinkers' combined (ibid.: 82–3).

During the postwar period, therefore, the Irish have become invisible in the discourse of 'race' in Britain, despite ongoing evidence of undisguised anti-Irish hostility. The construction of this invisibility is gendered according to the representational and material places occupied by Irish people. The apparent homogeneity of the 'white' population contrasts strongly with increasingly recognition of the diversity amongst 'non-white' groups (Modood et al. 1997). Meanwhile denial of difference to the Irish in the late twentieth century coexists with strongly negative attitudes, which continue to draw on centuries-old negative stereotypes. Although the need to problematise whiteness rather than allow it to remain 'the absent centre' has now been acknowledged, it remains a homogenised category, which allows anti-Irish racism to be ignored. The dualism of 'other' and 'the same' is thus constantly undermined by contradictions, but always present in representations of the Irish in Britain.

Gendered constructions of the Irish in Britain as 'other'

Defining the Irish as 'other' has played an important part in constructing the identities of, and according positive attributes to, hegemonic groups in Britain. These boundaries have been drawn both externally to the British nation, defining the line between national belonging and exclusion, and internally, dividing the powerful from the disempowered within the nation. Because the Irish can be constructed simultaneously as outsiders and insiders, they have played key roles in both processes which in turn interlock with, and reinforce, each other.

Ways in which the Irish are constructed as an 'other' to British identities at a national level have been explored in detail (Hickman 1995), but their roles in the construction of class and gender formations in Britain have been less fully recognised. In particular the gendering of these processes needs to be made more explicit. I shall offer some ways forward in conceptualising the place of Irish women through examining their discursive positions at both the margins and the heart of the British nation. Images of Irishness are not gender-neutral. Their representations are inscribed on bodies whose gender is integral to processes of construction of national identities.

External boundaries: gendering of the margins

Racism is a key part of the process of constructing British national identity, although it is usually decentred onto racialised groups and represented as a reaction by the indigenous majority to the unsettling presence of particular groups of diasporic peoples (Donald and Rattansi 1992). Thus 'race' appears to be an attribute of those racialised as inferior, rather than those at the centre. However the use of 'Anglo-Saxon' as a synonym for 'English', a term which was widely adopted by those of white English ancestral origin in the United States of America, indicates the importance of a racialised representation of the powerful as well as the marginalised, and the interchangeability of 'race' and 'nation' in the construction of the hegemonic group. As Miles argues: 'The ideologies of racism and nationalism can be interdependent and overlapping, the idea of race serving as a criterion of simultaneous inclusion and exclusion so that the boundary of the imagined "nation" is equally a boundary of "race" '(Miles 1993: 79).

Constructions of British national identities have included the racialisation of the Irish as part of a repertoire of different exclusions, as Cohen and Bains (1988) highlight in the title of their book *Multi-racist Britain*. The Irish have been represented as racially inferior since at least the twelfth century, with a remarkably consistent range of negative stereotypes. Thus the racialisation of the Irish is so ingrained in British culture as to be barely recognisable for what it is. Moreover there is now deep resistance amongst white British people to acknowledging it. One reason for the failure to recognise anti-Irish attitudes as racist is the preoccupation with skin colour in many late-twentieth-century Western societies. But this is only one of many signifiers of inherited inferiority. As Phil Cohen points out:

> in pursuit of natural symbolisms of inferiority, racist discourses have never confined themselves just to body images. Names and modes of address, states of mind and living conditions, clothes and customs, every kind of social behaviour and cultural practice have been pressed into service to signify this or that racial essence. In selecting these materials, racist codes behave opportunistically according to an economy of means; they choose those signs which do the most ideological work in linking – and naturalising – difference and domination within a certain set of historical conditions of representation. To make the issues of in/visibility depend on physical appearance is to bracket out precisely these historical realities.
>
> (Cohen 1988: 14)

Naturalising Irish difference as innate and inherited has included both body images and culture (Hickman 1995). The notion that the Irish are simply 'white' and therefore not racialised by body image overlooks a whole range of ways in which bodies can be labelled 'other' in addition to pigmentation. The body has a particularly strong resonance in othering because of its place in the body/reason binary which took its strong hold in the Enlightenment. Thus the physical appearance of Irish people has played an important part in their construction as different. It has also given different roles in the construction of difference to Irish women and men.

Persistent stereotypes of Irishness are related to the external political threat offered by a disaffected colony and unreliable neighbour, but have had a much wider currency as a reminder of what Britishness is not. Although they have been presented more starkly and virulently in times of political crisis, these images have persisted even in times of relative peace. I will examine some of the overtly political media images of the Irish in Ireland and then consider more generalised representations of the Irish in Britain which predate, draw on, and extend beyond, them.

Political threat: colonial resistance

The contemporary coupling of 'race' and blackness in the context of diasporas associated with colonies in the Caribbean, Africa and Asia has blocked out memories of nineteenth-century scientific racism which included the Irish as a related low branch on the 'Tree of Man'. Indeed in the second half of the nineteenth century, explicit links between body shape and pigmentation were made to establish equivalences between black African and Irish physical characteristics. Measurements of 'nigrescence' and the 'facial angle index' proved the 'white negro' status of the Irish, and provided a scientific basis for assuming similar cultural characteristics of 'violence, poverty, improvidence, political volatility and drunkenness' (Curtis 1971). These echo descriptions of the interchangeability between Irish people and African-Americans in the United States in the early years of the nineteenth century. They demonstrate the provisionality of the 'white' category into which the majority of Irish people are now placed.

The images, which were popularised in *Punch* cartoons aimed at middle- and upper-class English readers, later crossed the Atlantic to be reproduced by Nast in *Harper's Monthly*. Even so Irish independence had different meanings in the United States, even paralleling its own separation from Britain in the eighteenth century and offering no direct threat in the nineteenth and twentieth. In both countries cartoon images were particularly widespread between 1860 and 1880, and were closely related to increasing political unrest in Ireland which threatened to undermine the Union.

By the 1860s no respectable reader of comic weeklies – and most of their readers were respectable – could possibly

mistake the sinuous nose, long upper lip, huge projecting
mouth, and jutting lower jaw as well as sloping forehead for
any other category of undesireable or dangerous human
being than that known as Irish.

(Curtis 1968: 29)

These were strongly gendered representations, ape-like Irish men
being depicted in real-world situations such as political protest,
while women were shown only in allegorical representations.
There are clear parallels here with the construction of national
monuments, which similarly depict real men on war memorials,
but use women's images only allegorically to represent 'peace' or
'freedom' (Johnson 1995). In cartoons, therefore, men carried
the full weight of the negative qualities stereotypically attributed
to the Irish, since women were missing from scenes of active participation in public view. By contrast feminine images of the
allegorical Hibernia represented the opposite extreme of an
Ireland looking to strong, masculine Britain for protection, and
apparently colluding with its controlling intentions. The femininity and dependence of Hibernia illustrates Nandy's (1983)
observations about the 'homology between sexual and political
dominance'. Both masculine and feminine representations justi-
fied continued British rule while bolstering images of the ruling
centre as the antithesis of these negative characteristics.

Visual images which have been widely circulated retain their
power over long periods and can be revived very quickly. Curtis
argues that the *Punch* cartoons had lost their currency by 1914,
and ape-like Irishmen made only a fleeting reappearance during
the bitter guerrilla war in the early 1920s. They were followed by
the generally positive, but still masculine, image, of the 'stage
Irishman'. However the earlier images were reintroduced with
extraordinary ferocity whenever the British press wished to
express outrage and incomprehension at the outbreak of the
'troubles' in Northern Ireland in 1968. John Kirkaldy traces
changes in newspaper images over the period 1968 to 1970 as the
conflict intensified and identifies striking growth in the virulence
of anti-Irish imagery in *Punch* during this period.

Here, in a slightly more sophisticated form, are many of the
crudities of Victorian imagery which could easily have come
from the pages of the same magazine a century or so before.

> The Irish, or particular Irish groups, are seen as mad ('there is always one round the bend'), stupid ('it is their substitute for thinking'), reactionary ('notice their habit of taking ten steps backward for every one step forward') and lethargic ('you must watch closely as movement is almost imperceptible').
>
> (Kirkaldy 1979: 63)

Once again bodily images were used to represent the Irish as inferior. Right-wing newspapers reverted directly to cartoons portraying ape-like figures and animals while even liberal journalists showed their condescension and distaste. Kirkaldy describes Simon Winchester, a well-known *Sunday Times* writer, as 'almost obsessed with the smallness and inferiority of the Irish and the largeness and commonsense of the English'. He lists many instances of male Irish politicians being described as 'little' together with some other unflattering adjective: 'foxy', 'cunning', 'dumpy'.

The focus of the imagery was on men in the formal political sphere or as political sympathisers and potential activists. However some of the strongest ridicule and anti-Irish imagery was called forth in response to one woman who became prominent as a newly-elected Member of Parliament in 1969, Bernadette Devlin.

> Almost the entire British Press refused to take her seriously, ignoring her views or representing them as something of a joke. Fleet Street treated her like some kind of clockwork doll, an amusing diversion from the mainstream of parliamentary life: the general coverage of her early days as an MP combined sexism with patronising trivialisation and a refusal to see her in any other terms than 'swinging youth' and the then fashionable mini-skirt.
>
> (Kirkaldy 1979: 56)

Clearly she was 'out of place' in the public, political sphere and representations of her body, through her clothing and appearance, were used to remind readers that she was an aberration. In one cartoon in the *Daily Mail* in 1972, her body was replaced in its more traditional alignment as a metaphor for the land of Ireland, echoing the feminised representations discussed in Chapter 1 (Walter 1999: 83). This image showed Nationalist and Unionist paramilitaries trampling on a prone, high-heeled and mini-skirted figure labelled 'Ulster'. Irish men (labelled 'faceless, senseless, brainless') were again represented as active political figures, while the woman was relegated to a passive, helpless echo of the nine-teenth century 'Hibernia'. Implicit in these images of Irish inferiority, once again, are their opposites: English rationality, patience, toleration and moderation.

Ireland and its inhabitants have thus remained external 'others' with remarkable continuity over many centuries as the history of colonisation has produced resistance, often in a violent form. Inhabiting a country literally on the boundary of Britain, they are both an ongoing social exterior informing Britain of its contrasting virtues, and a dangerous point of defensive weakness. Media images produced at times of political conflict between Ireland and Britain provide the most visible and widely consumed representations of national and racial otherness. These images are directed at British audiences and therefore have a currency for this particular diasporic location.

Political threat: anti-Catholicism

An interlocking strand in the political threat represented by the Irish is anti-Catholicism. From the time of the English Reformation in the sixteenth century, Protestantism has been central to English national identity, counterposed to Catholicism which represented the danger of invasion from Continental Europe and of internal revolt from dissident groups within (Colley 1992). Protestantism has also represented rational indi-vidualism, in contrast to the 'mindless' dependence of Catholics on Papal dictates. Because of the huge inflow of people from Ireland following the Famine in the mid-nineteenth century, Catholicism has been identified as synonymous with Irish origins, masking the existence of a Protestant minority amongst Irish migrants.

Most Irish people are thus excluded fundamentally from core Britishness by their religion. Membership of the Protestant estab-lished church, tied to the monarchy – chief symbol of Britishness – continues to define full participation in the collectivity (Nairn 1988). Anti-Catholicism unites the separate nationalisms of England, Scotland and Wales (Colley 1992), rupturing the shared Celticism which denies Irish racialisation. Different forms of politicised Protestantism are deeply intertwined with these national identities. The Kirk came to occupy a central role in Scottish politics after the emasculation of the state under the Act of Union (Harvie 1977).

State attempts to incorporate the Irish by interdenominational education failed in the mid-nineteenth century because of English fears of contamination, expressed at the municipal level, rather than separatist Catholic demands (Hickman 1995). The resulting dual education system, still firmly in place, has reinforced religious differentiation, while the common secular curriculum renders invisible the national context of Irish identity. Religion has thus been a prime means of controlling threatening Irishness in Britain.

Catholic identities are strongly gendered in ways which parallel the patriarchal family. The leadership at all levels remains exclusively male, while women take on responsibility for children's religious observance and school attendance (London Irish Women's Centre 1984). Thus women play an active role in reproducing a central aspect of Irish ethnicity and are placed in most visible opposition to dominant cultural norms. At the same time a social life which revolves around the Catholic church removes Irish women from interaction with the majority population and may hide their existence, especially in the more Protestant South of England (Walter 1984).

Anti-Catholicism remains deeply embedded in British nationalisms. Although frequently denied and presented as an historical phenomenon with no contemporary relevance, anti-Catholicism in Scotland simmers only just below the surface and erupted into the public arena again in 1999 in the wake of the establishment of the Scottish National Assembly (Bradley 1995, Guardian 1999). In England anti-Catholic attitudes are less systematically expressed, but were still openly voiced in the 1950s and 1960s (Fielding 1993).

British stereotypes of Irish migrants

Both aspects of othering have contributed to the specific forms taken by stereotypes of Irish people in Britain. The familiar strands of stupidity, violence, dirt and drunkenness can all be related to the specific political background of the relations between Ireland and Britain. Moreover they serve to construct the Irish as the antithesis to the unstated qualities of those at the centre.

The bodies which collectively represent Irish people living in the 'diaspora space' of Britain have been predominantly masculine, the most commonly recognised image being that of 'Paddy'. This male, working-class stereotype draws on nineteenth-century images of navvies, whose manual labour characterises them by their bodies. Marella Buckley (1997: 105) draws parallels between the 'highly visible urban physicality' of Irish men in Britain and that of black male populations in Britain and the United States.

These outdoor workplaces also literally associate Irish people with 'dirt' which symbolises their 'abnormality'. 'Dirty Irish' is an epithet which was frequently used in the nineteenth century. Dirt is literally defined as 'matter out of place' and clearly conveys the message of exclusion. There are numerous example of middle-class professionals using this language in reports. For example in 1837 Dr John Black's observations in the cotton town of Bolton in Lancashire were made in the context of more widespread stereotypes:

> Concerning this latter class of strangers, few observations are to be made beyond what are general to the Irish labourers throughout the kingdom. At first, destitute, ill-clothed, and reckless in their habits, they in time, become more orderly, industrious, and cleanly, when they are planted in small numbers among Englishmen; but when they begin to occupy sections and streets in any town, as they are beginning to do in Bolton, their native dissoluteness, dirtiness, and tendency to drunkenness and quarrels, are kept up in all the vigour of the green sod of Ireland.
>
> (Black 1837: 66)

Although Black appears to be describing the unwelcome attributes of male 'labourers', the references to 'dirt' are associated with their homes, implicating women. Almost identical comments were used by James Phillips Kay in 1832 to describe Irish domestic disorder in Manchester (Hall 1998). Dirt was frequently invoked in the nineteenth century as a characteristic consequence of Irish households rather than as a consequence of the conditions in which their low pay confined them. Irish women were despised for lacking domestic skills and being associated with 'dirt'.

The association has continued into the twentieth century. In the Second World War there was reluctance to employ Irish women for the same reason: Penny Summerfield records the responses of welfare managers in Britain who needed to employ additional workers and 'expressed surprise when the negative stereotypes of Irish women ("dirt" and "drunkenness") were not confirmed' (1984: 59). These continue to feature strongly in verbal harassment of Irish people today (Hickman and Walter 1997).

Other associations follow this positioning on the body/reason dualism. Thus Irish men's uncontrolled and uncivilised bodies can be represented as 'naturally' prone to physical violence. Often this is associated with excessive drinking, which reduces reasoning powers and leads to bodily clumsiness. Violent bodies are linked with irrationality, making political protest appear inexplicable and not requiring a considered response. (By contrast the violence of British imperialism is described as necessary military force, a rational response to uncivilised behaviour in 'others').

At the same time the body/reason dualism legitimates beliefs about Irish 'stupidity'. This is most strongly reproduced in the 'Irish joke', a pervasive form of humour in the English media as well as in workplace, neighbourhood and leisure sites. School playgrounds are places where anti-Irish 'jokes' are implanted in succeeding English generations. There is strong resistance amongst English people to defining these 'jokes' as racist. Those who attempt to do so are told that they 'have no sense of humour', a quality which is positively evaluated in the English stereotype of themselves.

Buckley argues that anti-Irish jokes carry a weight of representation missing from other interactions between Irishness and Britishness which remain submerged, perhaps too powerful to be acknowledged.

> The joke is a very significant hinge in Irish–British relations because it is one of the few locations or moments when reference to Irishness rises to the surface of British discourse. Politically, it matters because it simultaneously expresses and obscures racism, facilitating racist interaction while with the same gesture exculpating it as mere fun. When directly addressed to an Irish person, it can constitute an invitation to social bonding which rests on an oblique, mutual awareness of the uneven power-relations which the Irish person is invited to accept. The loaded dynamic typical of Irish jokes in British discourse cannot be carried over so lightly into joking with, or

about, Blacks or Asians, where there is no sharing of a white
skin to disguise and whitewash the power-relations.

(Buckley 1997: 101)

Notions of stupidity are easily reinforced by different use of the
English language (including sentence construction, vocabulary,
accent), elite uses of which are believed to correlate with superior
reasoning powers. As Raymond Williams suggested, the 'Standard
English' of southern English middle-class voices:

> became a badge not simply of power but of knowledge. There
> was a curious convention that to speak in that way was to know
> something, to be more authoritative. I think that is loosening
> now, but it was very successful here.
>
> (quoted in Osmond 1988: 16)

The establishment of a standard dialect of English was itself a by-
product of the 'public' school education system and remains
strongly associated with the upper- and middle-class 'establishment', as its labelling as 'The Queen's English' and 'BBC English'
indicates (Nairn 1988). National and regional variations in pronunciation, syntax and vocabulary are used to signify class
difference, with very little reference to the objective socio-
economic status of speakers. The association with superior
knowledge is a sharp contrast with the dominant representation of
the Irish as 'stupid'. Thus Irish voices are often sufficient to trigger
this stereotype. Women's speech is already branded as less author-
itative, and the added assumptions of an Irish accent serve literally
to silence them (Spender 1980).

Through the homogenising 'Paddy' stereotype therefore, men
have been made to stand for the Irish population as a whole and
have taken the brunt of the racialising discourses. There has been
remarkable continuity in this gendering. Music hall sketches in
Manchester in the late nineteenth century, for example, depicted
Irish men as small and weak figures, heading households where
they were overshadowed by domineering wives. Rather than
acknowledge the dangerous possibility that Irish women might be
the prime household providers, and recognise the precarious
earning power of male migrant workers, English audiences were
invited to ridicule the 'racial' weakness of Irish men in contrast to
the patriarchal strength of Victorian English husbands (Tebbutt

1983). This denial of the economic importance of Irish women contrasts with the celebration of their strength in the United States. Irish women were not being invited to become 'British' in the way that their aunts and sisters were being praised for leading the 'Americanization' of their families.

However Irish women's bodies were implicitly present in stereotyping through their role in the processes of reproduction, especially their 'excessive' fertility. Although the domesticity of Irish women favoured by the Catholic church appears on the surface to be congruent with English ideas about women's place, anti-Catholicism is a subtext for the fears expressed about larger than average family sizes. The rhetoric focuses on families and their threat to the English way of life both biologically and culturally. These include 'swamping' and racial degeneration, the weakening of Protestantism, unfair demand for resources and lack of control over bodies, both their own and those of unruly, dirty and over-numerous children. This was particularly marked in the 1930s when the white British population was declining as result of widespread adoption of contraception.

Anxieties were expressed in a number of official and academic research contexts. In 1938 the Association of Municipal Corporations demanded legislation for 'compulsory repatriation of chargeable persons coming from the Dominions' (Glynn 1981). Clear links were made between excessive fertility and a threat the reproduction of the British 'race': 'the problem of the Irish immigrant is not confined to public assistance and services, but is placing a burden on all social services including housing and the supply of milk to necessitous expectant and nursing mothers'.

The frightening consequences of this fecundity were expressed in 1941 by the social scientist R. S. Walshaw:

> We have already noted that the United Kingdom is faced with a decline in population. Also we have seen that the policy of the United Kingdom Government is to use public money to help English, Scotch and Welsh to emigrate to the Dominions. At the same time Southern Irish enter Great Britain literally by the thousand. Would not these three facts taken together seem to suggest that the United Kingdom has not only decided to become peopled from Eire but is determined to bring about the change as quickly as possible?
>
> (Walshaw 1941: 75)

He advocated an alternative policy of sending Irish people to the 'Dominions' where their excess fertility would be welcomed, arguing that 'in their struggle for British stock, the Dominions should not overlook this important source of population'. His analysis brings out clearly the different levels of belonging accorded to Irish people. While not wanted in Britain, they were seen as quite suitable to boost the 'white' populations of the 'Old' Commonwealth.

Anxiety about excessive fertility linked with 'dirt' and feck-lessness was also the subtext to official discourse about 'slums' in the early post-War period. 'Overcrowding' in British cities was directly linked with Irish settlement in Betty Spinley's (1953) classic study *The Deprived and the Privileged*. With very clear reverberations with Black's description of Bolton in 1837, she wrote of her field study area:

> The district is notorious in London for vice and delinquency; it is a major prostitution area and is considered by the Probation Service the blackest spot in the city for juvenile delinquency. A large proportion of the inhabitants are Irish; social workers say, 'The Irish land here, and while the respectable soon move away, the ignorant and shiftless stay'.
>
> (Spinley 1953: 40)

Spinley specifically commented disapprovingly on the large number of children in the area:

> whether it is a school day or a holiday there always seem to be children playing in the road or going to and fro with shopping baskets and ration books. Women and a few men stand in doorways or sit on the house steps; and everywhere there are dogs.
>
> (Spinley 1953: 39)

An additional reason to distrust and penalise housing applicants was Irish neutrality during the Second World War, a further consequence of the colonial relationship. Spinley's example of a case reported in the local newspaper of one family clearly signals the Irish origins of new arrivals from the Irish Free State:

> A father, mother, and seven children living in one room, with

no kitchen, and carrying water from a tap on the landing; these people have been told that they are low on the borough's priority list because they have not been in the borough long and the father was not in the forces.

(Spinley 1953: 41)

The theme of excessive demands from the Irish migrant population continued to be voiced in the post-War period. In the 1950s, sustained immigration from Ireland, often directed towards towns in South East England which had little previous experience of Irish settlement, meant that new Catholic schools were needed to educate the rapidly-expanding second generation. One such town was Luton (1961 population: 130,000), thirty miles north of London, where numbers of Irish-born people rose from less than 2,000 in 1951 to over 7,000 in 1961. In 1961 there was a lengthy correspondence in the *Luton News* from English people complaining about taxes being used for state contributions to the provision of Catholic schools (Walter 1986). The theme still echoed in the 1990s in the labelling of Irish benefits claimants as 'scroungers', implying that they take resources which rightfully belong to the indigenous population (O'Flynn 1993).

Harassment of Irish families continues to draw attention to their deviance in having more children than the 'English' norm. A front-page article in the *London Evening Standard* was headlined 'Family from hell ruin £180,000 house' and subtitled 'Single mother and 10 children turn home into "human pig sty"'.

The family, which claimed more than £400 a week in state benefits, punched holes in the walls, ripped out electric cables, covered wallpaper with graffiti and defecated on the carpets in the £180,000 house.

However Mrs S– was defiant today. She said: Yes, I am on benefits, but some people only think about money. My family are all that matters to me, not money. The problem with England is they treat dogs better than they treat the Irish. They just don't like big families.'

(*London Evening Standard* 4 March 1998)

Whatever the facts of the case, the stereotype was recognised by the Irish woman concerned and reinforced by the reporting. The headline also revived a nineteenth-century association between Irish people and pigs, originally deriving from migrants who continued their peasant economy in British cities by keeping pigs in their houses, but subsequently applied to Irish people themselves. There was an outcry from the Irish community when John Junor, editor of the *Daily Express*, used the headline 'Wouldn't you rather be a pig than be Irish?' after an IRA bombing in Britain in 1981.

The overall effect of stereotyping is to construct a limited image of the Irish community in Britain whose public face is male and working-class. Lurking in the shadows are the mothers of their over-large families, reminders of the alienness of Catholicism and its threatening material implication of invasion from within.

Variations within Britishness: national, regional and local identities

Representations of the Irish as an inferior 'other' rely on an unspoken concept of a superior 'same'. Britain is therefore a constructed entity whose homogeneity is emphasised. It is a particularly unusual nationalism in deriving its identity from an imperial position, rather than claims about shared internal ethnicity. This imperial basis has contributed to the strongly masculine character of Britishness, which has the qualities attributed to colonial rulers: independent individualism, a sense of justice, the 'stiff upper lip' of suppressed emotions. Within the overarching British identity, however, are multiple ethnicities and more localised senses of belonging. Irish identities are placed in different relationships to this plurality of identities.

Many of the characteristics of Britishness are interchangeable with the core internal identity of Englishness. This is because the identity of Englishness has colonised Britishness, while appearing to leave it as an inclusive term.

Englishness itself is also uncertainly British, a cunning word of apparent political correctness invoked in order to mask the metanymic extension of English dominance over the other kingdoms with which England has constructed illicit acts of union, countries that now survive in the international arena only in the realm of football and rugby. The dutiful use of the term 'British' rather than 'English', as Gargi Bhattacharyya observes, misses the point that in terms of power relations there is no difference between them: 'British' is the name imposed by the English on the non-English.

(Young 1995: 3)

Yet even stereotypical characteristics of Englishness itself are represented by only part of the national space, its 'epicentre' of the south-east corner. John Osmond (1988) argues that the key to the domination of the entire national territory is an even more limited section of this region, the City of London. This relic of imperialism represents continuing divorce between finance and industry which lies at the heart of the displacement of other regions and the working classes.

The 'Home Counties' which literally provide the domestic space for City workers, are symbolised in the British national imagination by a rural arcadia, where English gentlemen are cared for and pursue their leisure lives (Short 1991; Wright 1985). This contrasts strongly with the Irish working-farm rural idyll in the West of Ireland. Images of Irish men are generally absent from this 'deep England', their living and working lives being arranged around manual work in British cities or large scale road construction in the countryside, though they have been involved in agricultural work in the past (Walter 1991). Irish women however are present, though invisible, as domestic workers, and are thus paradoxically located at the very centre of the British heartland. This 'insideness' gives Irish women a distinctive role in constructing masculine British identities and is explored in greater detail later in the chapter.

In other parts of Britain, Irish people may be less clearly identified as outsiders, sharing displacement from the British core. This leads to an ambiguous relationship. Mary J. Hickman (1990) describes the ease with which Irish people in Liverpool transmute their national identity into an English regional one. She contrasts working-class people of Irish descent in Liverpool, who describe themselves as 'Liverpudlian', with those in London where a firmly Irish identity is retained. Similarly Irish respondents in Bolton, near Manchester in Lancashire, in the 1970s reported much closer links with their English neighbours than those in Luton in Bedfordshire, just north of London (Walter 1984). The importance of accent in the acceptance of two Irish doctors in working-class Leeds in the 1930s was noted by Richard Hoggart: 'Their voices did not mark them out and off as 'Them' as the voice of the English doctor did'

(1988: 80). Very similar comments were made to Mary Kells (1995a: 28) in the 1990s by the young, middle-class Irish people she interviewed in London, who saw more in common between themselves and people from northern England. To them, the 'English' were in reality middle-class and from the south.

Differences between the nationalisms of Scotland and Wales and those of Ireland are frequently downplayed by uniting them in the notion of a 'Celtic fringe' to an unmentioned 'English core'. It has been used by British geographers, for example, as a shorthand for migration to England from other parts of the archipelago (see Coombes and Charlton 1992). It was also the basis of a claim for an equal right to additional resources by Scots in Birmingham when the issue of Irish ethnic status was debated (*Guardian* 1986). However crucial contrasts between Ireland and the other two sub-nationalisms cast considerable doubt on such an alignment. The imperial foundation of Britishness was deeply shared by the heartlands of Scotland and Wales, if not their peripheries, but only by the north-east of Ireland (Miles and Dunlop 1987). Tom Nairn points to a crucial difference in economic development: 'Although unusually close geographically to the metropolitan centre, Southern Ireland had in fact been separated from it by a great socio-political divide, by that divide which was to dominate so much of the epoch: the "development gap"' (1977: 11).

Thus Scotland and Wales could be firmly placed amongst developed industrial nations while most of Ireland shared more closely the experiences of Britain's African, Caribbean and South Asian colonies. Moreover anti-Catholicism is a key feature of each of the separate nationalisms of England, Scotland and Wales (Colley 1992) shown by the history of anti-Irish racism in Scotland (Handley 1947; Miles 1982) and Wales (Hickey 1967; O'Leary 1991).

Women and men are, however, positioned differently in the nations and regions of Britain throughout which the Irish-born population is scattered (Walter 1989b). As their stereotypes indicate, the identities of most nations/regions have been strongly masculine. Wales, 'the land of our fathers', is characterised by mining and steel manufacture, male voice choirs, patriarchal religious non-conformity and rugby football (John 1991). Scotland, as suggested by the name of its national newspaper *The Scotsman*, has a strongly masculine basis to the twin traditions of 'Tartanry' (epic military endeavour) and 'Kailyard' (kirk-dominated parochial society) (Nairn 1977; McCrone 1992). Regions within England also have different sets of gender relations, often related to their economic structure. For example patriarchy has been stronger in areas dominated by heavy industry, where full-time paid work has been mainly for men in the past (McDowell and Massey 1984). This is unconsciously confirmed by Osmond in his description of North East England as characterised by a 'network of activities and institutions that gave the community meaning – trades unions, social clubs, football teams, even allotments' (Osmond 1988: 14). Unusually in North West England women shared a more equal status through their access to paid work in textile mills (McDowell and Massey 1984). However the growing feminisation of Englishness in all regions during the 1950s, albeit challenged in popular media, illustrates the continuing renegotiation of gendered national identities (Webster 1998).

Thus while Britishness as an overriding national identity is powerfully masculine, the ways in which this is inflected at more local levels is more complex and need to be taken into account when empirical evidence is considered. Irish women will be placed within specific sets of gender relations in the particular geographic locations they occupy. As Floya Anthias and Nira Yuval-Davis (1992) point out, women in ethnic minorities are subject to two sets of relations around gender: those of the dominant group and those of their own ethnic group.

Internal boundaries: Irish domestic servants and constructions of middle-class male identities

While the overlaps between nation and race have been quite thoroughly analysed in recent literature (Miles 1993; Anthias and Yuval-Davis 1992; Jackson and Penrose 1993), much less attention has been paid to ways in which class and race are mutually constituted discursively within the nation. Deconstruction of the imagery of inferior and alien peoples viewed as originating, and belonging, outside the boundaries of the nation/race is familiar, but this internal othering has remained a much more hidden process. One reason is the taken-for-grantedness of the social class hierarchies which remain submerged within the apparent unity of the 'imagined community' of the British nation. Thus the nation legitimises a variety of hierarchical differences, including centrally that of social class, in the same way that ideologies of the family conceal marked inequalities of power beneath a socially approved and supposedly benign exterior. In the 1990s, for example, the lengthening list of equal opportunities used in advertisements for paid jobs includes gender, race, ethnicity, sexuality, age and disability, but never class, despite evidence of negative attitudes towards certain speech patterns.

However some of the processes whereby the working classes, or certain sections of the working classes, have been constructed historically as 'other' by racialisation, are now beginning to be recognised and have a crucial bearing on the place of Irish women in Britain. I argue that the overall invisibility of Irish women, and their submergence within an overarching masculine 'Paddy' stereotype, can be explained at least in part by their large contribution to domestic service from the mid-nineteenth century. To date not only has remarkably little attention been paid to this occupation, but the contribution of Irish women to the workforce has never been examined or acknowledged.

Internal racialisation

Internal racialisation by social class has been traced to the pre-colonial period by Robert Miles. He argues that the post-war emphasis on the exterior colonial origins of racism has obscured its much deeper roots in the interior of Europe which lie in the 'civilising mission' of ruling classes intent on legitimating their own authority. Class was thus used to distinguish inferior 'breeds' of people, including peasantry or the urban proletariat, as well as those distinguished by ethnic and cultural difference. This ideology was integral to the constitution of nationalised bourgeois formations in Europe, and was subsequently exported to the colonial situation. It is thus 'more deeply threaded through the historical evolution of capitalism' than has been fully acknowledged (Miles 1993: 104). Rather than emerging as a reaction to 'strangeness' in external colonial encounters, racism was available to be applied to new situations because it was already used in constructions of otherness at home.

These representations were given new impetus at the height of imperial expansion when the analogy between the 'slum' and the 'colony' became part of the rhetoric of urban debate in the second half of the nineteenth century. This discourse of degeneration was a response to crises both at home, where experiences of economic depression and poverty were paralleled by the growing resistance from socialism and feminism, and in the colonies where there was imperial rivalry from Germany and the United States. At the same time there was increasing unrest in Ireland over demands for Home Rule, leading to the much stronger simianisation in representations of Irish men in Britain in this period. A racialised discourse was freely used to describe the 'rough' element in British cities as 'a race apart'. Engels, writing in 1845, explicitly adopted this rhetoric in his declaration of the existence of 'two radically dissimilar nations as unlike as differences of race could make them' (Engels 1971). The 'residuum' of the 'undeserving poor' could be constructed as a mirror image of the law-abiding, respectable English worker by attributing its characteristics to 'natural' rather than socio-economic causes.

Jennifer Davis (1996) argues that the racialisation of the 'residuum', that is the unregenerate poor, was dependent on preexisting racialised representations of the Irish. Moreover this internal 'othering' was also explicitly gendered. In parallel to the political violence in which they engaged externally in Ireland, Irish men were portrayed as socially violent within Britain, engaging in riots, communal fights and attacks on the police. Activities were labelled violent when the Irish were involved, but would have been described differently with non-Irish participants. There was a tendency to conflate all such activity without seeking individual causes. Irish women were also featured disproportionately in accounts of street brawls and drunkenness. Davies argues that this laid the ideological antecedents for late-twentieth-century discourses in Britain connecting identification of an 'urban underclass' with the 'black inner city'.

Similar ideas are developed by Anne McClintock (1995) who links conceptually the parallels which were being drawn between the 'slum' and the 'colony' to their joint origins in the 'cult of domesticity'. She argues that overseas colonies were ruled in ways which echoed the control middle-class Victorian men held over their own households. The language used to describe the conquest and annexation of the colonies showed their feminised relationship and the aim was 'civilisation' through 'domestication'. Thus 'as domestic space became racialised, colonial space became domesticated'. Irish women were implicated in both spaces, reinforcing their association with degeneracy.

The cult of domesticity

A central element in the construction of white, middle-class British male identities, both at home and in the colonies, was the cult of domesticity. In Britain its function was to disavow the social and economic value of female manual and domestic work in order to portray the domestic sphere as a realm of natural sub-jugation. Feminine dependence in the private sphere provided the boundary for identities of white men of propertied descent as sovereign individuals. Their defining characteristic as autonomous and independent, economically successful male authors of progress depended on the counterpart of dependent, non wage-earning, anachronistic females. What McClintock does not pursue is the national origins of the servant classes in Britain on whom this structure was built. I suggest that the racialisation of the servant underclass incorporated an understanding of their Irishness, in a similar way to Davies' arguments about the discourse of 'slums'. This means that the construction of white middle-class British masculinity crucially depended on the identity of Irish women as a significant component of the female servant class.

The importance of Irish women's contribution to the servant workforce has been overlooked so far. Although it has been widely acknowledged that domestic service was the principal source of paid work for Irish women, no connections appear to have been drawn between representations of the Irish and the symbolic roles of servants as representing the 'other' to white middle-class men. This may reflect the relative isolation of Irish Studies from mainstream academic history in Britain so that knowledge about the Irish remains 'ghettoized'. Thus although it is widely known that Irish women were mainly employed as servants, their proportion of the servant population as a whole is not commented on. This is an example of the problems arising from a discourse which does not acknowledge Britain as a 'diaspora space' historically, in which the narratives of 'out-siders' and 'insiders' are mutually constitutive.

The neglect of the presence of immigrants in nineteenth century Britain can be illustrated in the work of historians of domestic service. For example, a pathbreaking work about the significance of domestic service in nineteenth century Britain, first published in 1974, *Mastered for life*, leaves the contribution of

Irish women in a strange limbo. In a footnote the author, Leonore Davidoff, adds:

> Note that during this period Britain had neither an indige-
> nous nor imported ethnically or religiously disadvantaged
> population (*with the possible exception of the Irish*). Such groups
> often make up the majority of domestic servants and thus blur
> the effects of the master-servant relationship. Contrast [this]
> with the American experience.
>   (Davidoff 1974: 423, my emphasis)

Again in a later overview she elaborates on the 'particular obsession' in England in the mid-nineteenth century with denoting
distinctions between sections of the population, especially when
confronting a growing waged and urban working class (Davidoff
1995: 5). However, she identifies this obsession as 'paradoxically
partly due to lack of external differentiation', earlier describing
the 'the remarkable homogeneity of the English nation *with the
constant exception of Irish Catholics*' (my emphasis). In this theorisation, class differentiation alone is seen as a sufficient explanation,
leaving the Irish as an anomaly which on the one hand disturbs
the homogeneity of the English nation but, on the other, is not
sufficiently different to be classified as an external group.

Davidoff offers an interpretation of domestic service in the mid-
nineteenth century as both symbolically and materially
representing the 'whole underside of bourgeois culture', observing
that it linked beliefs about gender and class through notions of
disorder, pollution and dirt. The cult of domesticity was a crucial
process in the definition not only of femininity but also masculinity.
Middle-class men needed to mark their separation from men in the
two other major strata of society, that is, the aristocracy and the
working classes. The former were characterised by their lack of
money, since they had continued to depend on the declining asset
of land rather than seizing the opportunities of commodity capitalism. The latter were identified by their lack of property. Control of
both money and property had therefore to be clearly assigned symbolically to middle-class men and the cult of domesticity allowed
boundaries to be drawn which accentuated this.

The key aspect of women's domestic service was that it was paid
labour in a space, the home, which was represented as the antithesis of the market place. Exclusive male rights to the generation of

money could only be asserted by the suppression of knowledge of women's contribution to the economy. The domestic sphere must therefore to be portrayed as 'natural' and outside the cash nexus. Thus the notion of paid women's work in the household was highly threatening and had to be hidden from sight. This led to the invisibility of the work performed both by middle-class and working-class women so that 'the domestic labour of women suffered one of the most successful vanishing acts of modern history' (McClintock 1995: 163).

Middle-class women performed the 'labour of leisure', whereby the appearance of idleness was cultivated by all, but only achievable in reality by the richest. Idleness was not therefore the absence of work but the conspicuous consumption of leisure in order to highlight men's ability to create wealth through work. However the main burden of the work involved in maintaining this outward appearance was thrust onto paid domestic servants. In addition to carrying out household maintenance, servants performed work to underpin the symbolic aspects of middle-class women's leisure, including the provision of elaborate costumes which prohibited any strenuous movement, and the cleaning and polishing of large numbers of emblems of household prestige.

This role gave servants a dangerously powerful position which was crucial to the functioning of the economic system. In the late nineteenth century, domestic servants made up the largest labour category after agricultural workers, yet the importance of their labour was, and remains, unacknowledged in ways that parallel the erasure of slave labour as a foundation of modern industrial power. In order to contain this threatening intrusion of waged work on a massive scale into the domestic sphere, a number of strategies were used to hide servants and their work from view and to represent them as degenerate 'others'.

The invisibility of domestic servants

The erasure of the work of domestic servants in nineteenth-century Britain remains extraordinarily intact. The lack of information, or even debate, about their social and economic place in nineteenth- and twentieth-century Britain or their personal experiences is sharply at odds with their numbers. Overall figures from Censuses show that this was the second largest category of employment after agricultural work. Numbers rose from 750,000 in 1851 to 1.3 million in 1891 and never fell below one million until the late 1930s. Yet in her 1974 article Davidoff described nineteenth-century residential service as an 'exceptionally elusive' area of study (Davidoff 1974: 407). Even when women's history was embraced in the 1970s, little attention was paid to this topic. More than twenty years later, in her overview of research on the topic in 1995, she continues to describe it as 'swept under the carpet' (ibid.: 1). This is despite its intriguingly anomalous position, outside both the private world of the family and the public world of the paid workforce, which should provide particular interest to historians.

Part of the explanation for academic neglect is that residential domestic servants were also remarkably hidden during their own lifetimes, and have therefore left few traces. Contemporary representations are very meagre, again contrasting with the outpouring of commentary in the United States of America. As Davidoff points out 'Considering the numbers involved, both autobiography and fiction were strangely silent' (Davidoff 1995: 3-4). In addition, popular images of working women in the nineteenth century also ignored servants, focusing instead on 'mill girls, or possibly the milliner or seamstress' (ibid.: 21).

These absences are congruent with the physical and symbolic invisibility of servants within British households. In the first place, they were literally hidden from the view of the outside world within the homes of their employers. In fact Davidoff (1974) argues that unlike servants in continental Europe, those in England were unusually segregated: 'The intense privacy of the English middle-class household in individual dwellings often surrounded by gardens in isolated settings or suburbs separated from working-class districts, made English domestic service exceptionally confining' (ibid.: 408–9). This may be another source of contrast with the experiences and representations of Irish servants in the United States. It also underlines the difference between Irish men's working lives in the open air, as construction workers visible to passers by and Irish women servants confinement behind closed doors.

At a smaller scale, servants were further excluded within the household from spaces where the ideology of female idleness was on display, bolstering the illusion of middle-class female leisure. This spatial segregation also removed female servants from direct comparison with their male employers, thus confirming the latter as economic providers. It was achieved by confining servants 'below stairs' or to sleeping quarters in the attics, the boundaries being marked by symbols such as the 'green baize door'. Low rates of pay also hid the massive quantity of effort expended both in substituting for the domestic labour of the middle classes and in concealing the necessary products of manual labour.

Finally, evidence of the manual work of servants was removed in an excessive display of cleanliness through the Victorian dirt fetish. Much of the punishing regime of female domestic work involved symbolic removal of dirt, particularly at the boundaries of the domestic sphere in halls, porches, doorsteps and uniforms. In the process, servants came to be associated with the dirt and disorder they were employed to remove. They 'absorbed dirt and lowliness into their own bodies' (Davidoff 1995: 5). Servants 'stood on the dangerous threshold of normal work, normal money and normal sexuality, and came to be figured increasingly in the iconography of "pollution", "disorder", "plagues", "moral contagion" and "racial degeneration"' (McClintock 1995: 154). This reinforced the existing associations of Irish women with 'dirt' through their occupation of the 'uncivilised' spaces of Ireland and English 'slums'.

The absence of servants from public discourse was not therefore an indication of their lack of importance, but rather a measure of the inadmissability of their power. Not only did they represent the necessity of, and middle-class men's dependence on, women's paid work, but their relationship with middle- and upper-class children placed them in an extraordinarily important position. Servants raised children and played a key role in the early experiences of middle-class men, while mothers were excluded from close contact by the necessity to appear untouched by manual labour. Children also represented disorder and dirt, which meant that they too had to be segregated into particular parts of the house and fed at separate times. Boys spent more time with nurses and domestic servants than with their own mothers, before being sent off to boarding school, ironically being closely influenced by the very class from whom their fathers protected themselves. The Catholic beliefs of Irish servants could have been transmitted much more directly in this way.

Irish women in paid domestic work have been rendered invisible in Britain as part of the wider process of denying the importance of this form of labour. However a fascinating extension of this idea is the possibility that their national/ethnic origins have also contributed to the construction of invisibility of the servant class as a whole through the double association of their externally and internally racialised identities. In other words just as the 'residuum' in inner city 'slums' could more easily be identified as 'a race apart' because of its Irish character, so the Irish origins of servants, and particularly their Catholic beliefs, may have contributed to the fears about recognition of the presence of this group of working-class women.

In order to examine this connection more fully, detailed work needs to be undertaken to assess the nature and extent of Irish women's participation in the residential domestic labour force. This work has not been possible until recently because the published Census tables have not linked occupation with birthplace. Again the effect of this statistical representation has been to emphasise the homogeneity of the population rather than to allow the diasporic importance of migrant labour to be taken into account. All that can be gleaned from existing sources is that over the course of the nineteenth century Irish women became a much more important and sought-after source of domestic labour for a number of reasons which will be discussed further in Chapter 4. They include increasing problems of supply in Britain and improvements in the perceived 'quality' of available Irish women.

However the invisibility of domestic servants in Britain, necessary to the maintenance of the cult of domesticity, helps to explain the absence of Irish women from racialised stereotypes of the Irish. Whereas the waged labour of 'Bridgets' in the United States could be recognised as part of the economic relation of the marketplace, in Britain the economic underpinnings of class position had to be denied. Thus the absence of references to Irish servants in Britain, which contrasts with the outpouring of comments found by Diner (1983) in the United States, is part of a wider pattern of denial of women's household work. But whereas historians have now begun to reclaim British servants' lives, there is still a resounding silence about the experiences and contribution of Irish paid domestic workers in Britain.

Gendered constructions of the Irish as 'the same'

Omission of Irish servants from historical discourse of the nineteenth century is part of a much wider pattern of exclusion and more active denial of difference. Ironically the notion of sameness has taken stronger root in the post-war period, during which the Republic of Ireland became fully separated from Britain and left the British Commonwealth. At the same time that the twenty-six counties were following up their neutrality in the Second World War with a complete severance of political ties with Britain through the declaration of the Irish Republic in 1948, Britain chose to proclaim a continuing 'special relationship'. In 1949 it was asserted that the new Republic was 'not a foreign country' and that its citizens could continue to travel freely to Britain and indeed be entitled to vote immediately on arrival.

An important reason why the 'difference' of the Irish in contemporary Britain can be denied is the omission from mainstream historical accounts of the presence of immigrants before 1945. 'Immigration' has been constructed as synonymous with the post-War movement from the so-called New Commonwealth. This period is represented as one of new diversity in contrast to the 'racial' homogeneity of the immediate past.

> It would be impossible to write a history of the USA without reference to the central issues of slavery and immigration. However in Britain histories of the country constantly appear without reference, for instance, to Irish and Jewish immigration during the nineteenth century . . . The situation in Britain is aggravated not only by a reluctance to accept the role of immigration in the country's history, but also by the national myth, which revolves around the concept of Britain as a tolerant state.
>
> (Panayi 1996: 834–5)

The discursive interchangeability between 'immigration' and 'race' means that even in the post-war period, white migrants have continued to be omitted from public and academic discourse. Wendy Webster (1998) argues that central to constructions of British national identity in the immediate post-war period has been the figure of the indigenous white woman. She is constructed against not only black women but also migrant women. However the conflation of the two removes white migrants from sight and disguises the commonalties between black and white migrants.

Sameness is therefore enforced by the 'myth of homogeneity' in British society before 1945 and the restricted construction of difference in the post-War period. However the failure to acknowledge difference does not mean that 'othering' has disappeared. Indeed there are strong continuities in representations of Irish people in Britain which coexist in reworked forms with denial of difference.

Constructions of belonging

Geography: the 'Island Race'

British national identity depends on the notion of unity. In reality British identities are plural, always including at least one additional national sub-identity. As James Anderson (1989) points out, the very need to proclaim 'unitedness' of the Kingdom hints at its imperfect unity. In face of these divisions, emphasis on the geographical integrity of the islands of the 'North Atlantic Archipelago' helps to naturalise notions of unity, even though it requires an international border to be disregarded.

A refusal to sever ties incorporating the whole island of Ireland into the British state is unthinkingly demonstrated in naming and mapping behaviour. This is most obvious in continued reference to 'the British Isles'. Other phrases in common use include 'mainland Britain' in discussions of Northern Ireland (implying that it is 'offshore Britain'), and 'the Celtic fringe' (of the absent centre, England). The confusion, but also its consequences, is highlighted by the presentation of a report based on 1991 Census data on ethnic minority disadvantage in London (Storkey 1994). A number of tables in the report included the category 'born in Ireland' and indicated significant levels of disadvantage. But the map showing places of origin of the ethnic minority groups under discussion was entitled 'Communities over 10,000 who were born outside the British Isles and now live in London'. Despite the evidence they had themselves presented, therefore, the researchers reverted to a 'commonsense' choice of geographical names and thus excluded the largest ethnic minority by migration from visual representation.

This choice reinforces one of the underlying aspects of this imagery. Miles (1993) argues that the 'myth of British homogeneity' which has been fostered in the post-war period represents black people as unassimilable and inevitably alien. A key element of this homogeneity is 'racial' similarity. In contrast to nineteenth-century representations of superior 'Anglo-Saxon' and inferior 'Celtic' characteristics, therefore, these two groups are made to appear close and complementary. Together they constitute the 'Island Race', a powerful image which was invoked by Margaret Thatcher in 1982 to rekindle British patriotic self-esteem at the time of the Falklands War. Paul Gilroy (1987) argues that the image blurs the distinction between 'race' and nation and relies on this very ambiguity for its effect.

Exclusionary ideas about 'race' lie at the heart of British national identity. Such boundaries can only be sustained if the island of Ireland is included. This helps to explain why immigration from Ireland is generally overlooked when the 'numbers question' of settlers from outside is being considered. The term 'immigrants' has taken on very specific meanings, referring to post-war migrants from the colonies and ex-colonies of the Caribbean, Indian sub-continent and Africa who are also seen as 'black'.

One consequence of this is the absence of a discourse of migrant/indigenous difference, which is subsumed into the black/white binary. White migrants are thus hidden from view and ways in which they are also excluded from national belonging are obscured. Wendy Webster (1998) argues that in the 1950s notions of Englishness came to be constructed around the home, a private and apparently classless definition, in contrast to the 1930s constructions of two nations, rich/poor, employed/unemployed, North/South. This produced strongly gendered as well as raced understandings of national identity, with white indigenous women at the centre and black migrant men as their 'other'. Migrant women, both white and black, were omitted from this construction.

In fact migrant women played a vital role in supporting the existence of the English home, by enabling indigenous women to perform their primary roles as wives and mothers (Webster 1998). Whereas the 'good mother' devoted her life to children and husband, only taking on part-time paid work, migrant women filled the full-time jobs for which female labour was required, particularly in textile mills, domestic service and various branches of the expanding welfare state. White migrant women were permitted to work inside the homes of indigenous English women as nannies and cleaners, but black women were not seen as suitable for this work. Instead they were distanced from the personal lives of white English people and given public domestic work, such as hospital cleaning.

The homes of migrant women themselves were outside this construction of Englishness and belonging. In the first place it was difficult to obtain housing, particularly for women with children. The signs 'No blacks, no Irish' specifically excluded migrants from the rented accommodation they needed. Una Cooper described her experience of searching for rooms in London after her arrival from Dublin in the 1950s to join her husband with two small children. As soon as her Irish accent was heard, she would be told that it was no longer available. Families with children were especially unwelcome (Lennon, McAdam and O'Brien 1988). Difficulties were still being experienced in the 1960s. John Rex and Robert Moore interviewed a large Irish family in Sparkbrook, Birmingham, consisting of an older woman, Mrs C, her eight children and seventeen grandchildren: 'The general consensus of opinion among the Cs was that, although the Irish should expect no special privileges in England, they were, in fact, heavily discriminated against, especially in housing' (Rex and Moore 1967: 88).

The image of home which represented Englishness was therefore a very specific one, and excluded migrants in particular. Webster (1998) describes 'a distinction between a common Englishness of well-kept homes and families in opposition to "blacks next door"'. The well-kept homes, typically on new estates, were being built by a labour force, that included, ironically, a large proportion of migrant Irish men. The migrants themselves, however, were included in a discourse of 'problem families', applied above all to full-time working mothers in poor housing. Irishness was often explicitly associated with this label, as Spinley's (1953) account illustrates. This drew on racialised stereotypes, rather than making connections with conditions of migrant labour: difficulties in obtaining housing, long working hours, low wages, the need to send remittances, and the absence of an extended family to help with childcare.

Focus on the home as the central representation of Englishness produced a more homogenised version of national identity in the 1950s, which Webster describes as classless, private rather than social. Whiteness could appear to be synonymous with this unitary category. The lack of acknowledged diversity thus excluded Irish people from view even though on specific occasions it was also made clear that they were not part of the category.

Whiteness

A central feature of British identity in the late twentieth century is whiteness. Indeed the presentation of Census data in 1991 underlined this categorisation. In what was described as an 'ethnic' question, the dominant group was classified first as an undifferentiated 'White' group, against whom all 'others' were either implicitly or explicitly labelled black and then further fragmented by their geographical origins.

Certainty that the Irish belonged to the 'white race' was much weaker in Britain in the nineteenth century. There are strong similarities to the United States of America where Noel Ignatiev (1995) traces 'How the Irish became white'. But the routes are not identical. In the United States the Irish were seen as interchangeable with 'free blacks' in the first decades of the nineteenth century, but the binary distinction had become more fixed by the 1860s after the Civil War. However in Britain the parallels were drawn with colonised African peoples in the second half of the century. Similar tropes of representation were used for both Irish and African peoples, including feminisation, characterisation as 'children', and relegation to a world outside 'progress' as measured by the industrial work ethic. Explicit links were made between the two groups and the Irish were freely described as 'white negroes' or 'Celtic Calibans'. Both Africans and the Irish were depicted in their 'native' surroundings as idle and untidy, sitting in dirty rural places rather than engaging in useful labour. In both cases, portrayal of unkempt and slovenly houses contrasts with the cleanliness and order of British homes where the cult of domesticity underpinned industrial capitalism. Although women were not necessarily included in the images, domestic scenes directly implicated them in the disorder (McClintock 1995).

Despite these common features, at another level shared whiteness resonated very strongly. It echoes the deep anxieties admitted in the well-known lines by Charles Kingsley, writing home to his wife from Ireland in 1860:

> I am haunted by the human chimpanzees I saw along that hundred miles of horrible country . . . to see white chim-

panzees is dreadful: if they were black, one would not feel it
so much, but their skins, except where tanned by exposure,
are as white as ours.

(Kingsley, quoted in Curtis 1971: 84)

However, moving away from the simple binary of black/white and
echoing the theme of a 'third race' from the early-nineteenth-
century United States, Cohen (1988: 74) argues that the Irish were
made to represent

> a missing evolutionary link between the 'bestiality' of Black
> slaves and that of the English worker as well as dangerous
> currents in European thought, including republicanism. As a
> result they were caricatured as a 'monstrous race' and set
> apart.
>   Once isolated within this magic circle, all sorts of conjur-
> ing tricks could be performed to make the Irish in Britain
> disappear; they could be assimilated through the civilising
> mission of their own Catholic church or converted to the
> British way of life via trade unionism. Most of all the image of
> their political threat could be dissolved into its parody.
>   The paddy joke is the one place where the different
> elements of the code meet up . . . dangerousness is de-fused
> by turning it into mere social incompetence.

(Cohen 1988: 74–5)

Cohen's suggestions about the specificity of the location of the
Irish in Britain moves away from the either/or of whiteness and
focuses instead on processes by which the Irish have been incorporated into British society, through the denationalising
activities of the Catholic church for example (Hickman 1995).
His notion that the Irish have been 'made to disappear' does not
equate with the hegemonic view that they have voluntarily
'assimilated', an interpretation of Irish experience in Britain
which has a very firm hold on academia in the work both of historians and sociologists.

Christianity

There are some indications that shifts towards non-denomina-
tional Christianity in the construction of a national culture have,

more recently, helped to strengthen the process of homogenisation. While anti-Catholicism has closely underpinned anti-Irish hostility in Britain, and indeed remains the predominant form taken in Scotland, there are signs that the growing divide between the Muslim and non-Muslim worlds may reduce the importance of splits within Christianity in future, at least in certain parts of the state. This was underlined by the 1988 Education Reform Act which required all state schools in England to have a daily act of Christian worship, replacing the multi-faith assemblies which many had adopted, giving Christianity therefore 'an affirmed legal status as the ideological cement of national cultures' (Saghal and Yuval-Davis 1992).

Further evidence of a willingness to include Catholicism within the national religious fold in certain circumstances was provided by the outpouring of expressions of respect from non-Catholics on the death of the Catholic Archbishop of Westminster, Cardinal Basil Hume, in 1999. Although newspaper reports made references to his non-Irish origins, which in a veiled but pointed way permitted this sea-change in attitudes, it nevertheless signalled an unprecedented level of acceptance for a religion which British sovereigns are still banned from espousing. But anti-Catholic attitudes, if weakened, have by no means disappeared. The previous year a frisson of disapproval had been registered when the Prime Minister, a practising Protestant, attended Mass with his Catholic wife more frequently than usual. A negatively-phrased headline in *The Guardian* proclaimed: 'Blair denies intention to convert to Catholicism' (5 March 1998).

The renewed significance of religion as a source of identification, coupled with the rise of a broad inclusive 'Christian' category, is illustrated by the introduction of a 'religious question' in the 2001 Census. There are six named boxes: Christian (including Church of England, Catholic, Protestant and all other Christian denominations), Buddhist, Hindu, Muslim, Sikh and Jewish. This apparent sinking of Protestant/Catholic differences chimes with trends towards trans-national Europeanism where Catholicism is now a norm.

Religion remains, therefore, an area of considerable ambivalence. Christianity linked with whiteness appears to emphasise Irish sameness, because of current and emerging constructions of otherness based on both bodily visibility and culture. But beneath the surface differences continue to resonate.

Denial of difference

The overall effect of these homogenising discourses has been to promote a commonsense view that the Irish are very close to the British. A survey on British attitudes towards the Irish published in 1994 revealed that 31 per cent of people identifying themselves as English made no distinction between themselves and the Irish. When the same sample was asked to compare their closeness to the Scots and the Irish, 14 per cent felt closer to the Irish, 23 per cent to the Scots and 57 per cent felt the same towards each. With the pairing Irish:Welsh, the proportions of English attitudes were almost identical, 20 per cent feeling closer to each group and 59 per cent making no distinction. On the other hand both the Scots and Welsh felt significantly closer to the Irish than to the English (*Irish Post* 17 December 1994).

Yet set against this claiming of sameness and acceptance is evidence of ongoing racism and discrimination. Perhaps the clearest indication of the denial of difference is a general refusal to acknowledge that anti-Irish discrimination is racist or indeed needs to be addressed at all. This can be illustrated by reactions to recent activities of the Commission for Racial Equality (CRE) which showed that denial of difference to the Irish is fiercely upheld in public discourse in the media.

Although the Irish clearly fall within the remit of the Race Relations Act of 1976 (which defines discrimination on 'racial grounds' as including 'colour, race, nationality or national or ethnic origin') which the (CRE) was established to support, little progress towards including them in anti-racist policies was made until the 1990s. It was not until 1993 for example that the CRE recognised the need to include an Irish category in ethnic monitoring and made this a recommendation. Although there had been a few earlier complaints of discrimination brought to industrial tribunals before this time, the number slowly increased as awareness of this option grew.

The extent to which this reluctance mirrored wider British attitudes was revealed by media responses to the announcement of these moves. Howls of anger and derision in the press greeted even the small amounts of compensation to two men who had lost their jobs as result of discrimination.

A storm erupted last night over a £6000 compensation to an Irishman tormented by jokes at work,

MPs denounced it as 'political correctness gone mad' over what was little more than shopfloor banter.

They said it could open the floodgates to claims from every conceivable minority, costing employers millions.

Machinist Trevor McAuley, 36, told an industrial tribunal that the daily abuse ruined his work and affected his family life. He did not mind Irish jokes but drew the line at being called a 'typical thick Paddy'.

(*Daily Mail* 8 June 1994: 1)

One of the more depressing aspects of Trevor McAuley's victory against the Irish joke in an industrial tribunal this week was the po-faced triumphalism for the Commission for Racial Equality. After the hearing one of the Commissioners named Aubrey Rose issued a statement to the effect that Mr McAuley's case would send a signal to employees and shop floor workers that abuse against ethnic minorities was unacceptable.

Of course it is, but it must be clear to even the most serious-minded members of the CRE which financed Mr McAuley's complaint, that the telling of Irish jokes is a matter entirely beyond legislation and that nothing will prevent the canteen wit from setting off with the dreary line "did you hear the one about the Irishman . . . "

Irish jokes are part of us . . .

(*Daily Telegraph* 9 June 1994)

Prat's life

Sticks and stones may break your bones, names can make you rich.

The idea of being awarded almost £30,000 damages because a colleague calls you an 'Irish prat' is obscene.

Especially when a murder victim's life is valued at only £7,500.

It is bad enough that college lecturer Alan Bryans – more of a pansy than a prat – should claim that silly jibes at work had ruined his life.

But what's worse is that a politically-correct industrial tribunal should believe him.

The truth is that WE'RE the real prats . . . For letting these people chuck public money down the drain.

(*The Sun* 23 September 1995: 6)

By contrast most broadsheet papers reported the outcome of the case in factual terms and included the statement from the tribunal which was not mentioned in the reports above. This categorised the treatment as 'an appalling case of discrimination upon discrimination'. Ironically both these men were Northern Irish Protestants, a group who have traditionally regarded themselves as 'British' to a much greater extent than the Catholic population of Northern Ireland. Thus the homogenising 'Irish' identity easily subsumes all other forms of difference.

Similar virulent abuse was triggered by the announcement of the first research project on anti-Irish discrimination in Britain, funded by the Commission for Racial Equality in 1994. The project was the result of lengthy lobbying by Irish community and welfare groups since the late 1980s. It received very modest funding, but even this was challenged and derided.

> Funnyman Frank Carson reckons the £50,000 survey into racism against Irish people in Britain is "a load of codswallop". We agree with him.
>
> (*The Sun* 22 January 1994: 9)

The tabloid newspaper *The Sun* dismissed the research with a page of vitriolic anti-Irish jokes to 'give the researchers a flying start'. Almost all the forty one jokes figured Irish men (variously Mick, Paddy and Murphy and including a doctor) demonstrating aspects of their 'stupidity', usually through linguistic misunderstanding. Only one figured an Irish woman, a nameless barmaid, emphasising the strongly male gendering of overt Irish negative stereotyping. This is an important issue and is examined in greater detail in Chapter 5.

When the results of the project were publicly presented in 1997, the reception by the press still included a strong element of ridicule and dismissal. The refusal to accept 'joking' as a racist practice is used to parody the findings.

> Heard the one about the latest ethnic minority?
>
> (*Daily Mail* 26 June 1997: 1)

> Why did it take the Commission for Racial Equality two years to ask the Irish if they are an oppressed minority?
> The answer could be that those interviewed had difficulty

in answering the question. Or at least it might be if this probe
– which cost £50,000 of our money – were in any way funny.

These claims will surprise my Irish acquaintances. Indeed
the typical immigrant from across the water is likely to
conclude that the only 'ethnic' insult they have suffered in
this country is the importuning overtures from the CRE and
its associate pressure groups.

(Birmingham Sunday Mercury 29 June 1997)

It is quite true that the Irish are the butt of jokes depicting a
fey obtuseness, but these are as free of malice as they are of
wit. Scottish stinginess, English snobbery, and Welsh devious-
ness are similar stock-in-trade of feeble British inter-tribal
banter.

(Eastern Daily Press 28 June 1997)

The extraordinary level of hostility and ridicule unleashed by
these announcements suggests that the denial of Irish difference
masks exclusion and rejection, rather than the surprise and
incomprehension claimed. What accounts for this paradox?
Ongoing anti-Irish racism is apparent in both the cases brought
and the press reactions. Yet their message appears to be that the
Irish experience is no different from that of other internal
national and regional groupings.

Conclusions

The Irish in Britain are excluded from full membership of British
society in unconscious and unacknowledged ways. Exclusion itself
is denied, and assimilation of the Irish is asserted by British academics and assumed by official bodies and agencies who refuse to
accord the label of 'ethnic' to the Irish.

However, in a further twist to the contradictions between hostility and denial of difference, a certain kind of Irishness in Britain
experienced an upswing in popularity in the 1990s. Writing about
Manchester, Jack O'Sullivan observed in *The Independent*:

A remarkable surge in cultural self-confidence is taking place.
We are seeing nothing short of the greening of England, as
the Irish in Britain set aside a traditional low profile, moving

out of the ghetto, beyond the enclaves of clubs and into the mainstream . . . Suddenly Irishness is hip. 'Irish culture is seductive. It has become a signifier for hedonism with soul,' says Frank Cottrell-Boyce, a former scriptwriter for Coronation Street. 'There was a decisive moment during the World Cup, when Ireland was there and England wasn't, when people came out as Irish who hadn't been before. Irishness could represent them on the world stage.' And fashion for the *craic* is surviving even the IRA's latest campaign.

(*The Independent* 1 July 1996)

This positive reappraisal, associated with popular music and entertainment, applies to a particular section of the Irish community united by age rather than generation. Well-educated 1980s migrants and the British-born children of those who arrived in the 1950s are at the centre. But it continues to coexist with the racism powerfully exhibited in reactions to the CRE engagement with Irish issues. This illustrates Brah's (1996) argument that racism should not be conceptualised in terms of simple polarities of positive and negative, but 'simultaneously inhabits spaces of deep ambivalence, admiration, envy and desire'.

My analysis has focused on the construction of a gendered Irish 'other' in the process of identifying the boundaries of Britishness, and its consequences for Irish women. I have argued that the content of the category 'Irish' has retained a recognisable core which continues to resonate, while contradictory and ambivalent meanings can co-exist at different times. However this discussion of racialised national identities has necessarily homogenised both 'Irish women' and the 'Britishness' against which they are constructed. Gendered collectivities are also internally diverse (with variations of class, age, generation, religion and sexuality) and situated in relation to other diasporic groups. Moreover hegemonic unity is imposed representationally on diverse national, regional and local conditions which articulate with Irish identities in very different ways. In the following chapters I will explore these differentiations and their material consequences for Irish women.

Chapter 4

Material lives in Britain

Geographical contexts of settlement and work

The majority of Irish women have arrived in Britain as labour migrants, and their lived experience in Britain is crucially influenced by their places of work on a number of geographical scales. These have determined the nature of work, its demands and financial rewards, and the social positioning of Irish women relative to the dominant majority and other subordinated minorities. They are the contexts of diasporic 'placement' in areas where Irish women have established their 'homes away from home'. These placings within local, regional, and subordinate national, contexts offer a more nuanced relationship to the majority British nationalism which excludes Irishness.

The nested scales include the national, (England, Scotland and Wales) where different economies and social relationships to the hegemonic centre prevail, as well as regional subdivisions. Within these broader regions Irish women have settled in urban centres of varying sizes, and are then connected with specific neighbourhoods. At the smallest scale are workplaces, including the households where unpaid domestic labour is performed.

Economic factors are thus central to an understanding of the specificity of Irish women's placement in Britain. They articulate with the discursive positioning outlined in Chapter 3, and begin to ground it in the materiality of everyday life. As Lavie and Swedenburg (1997) point out 'The economic horizon of capitalist internationalism remains crucial to any understanding of how sensibilities of identity are dislocated between cultures and territories' (1996: 6). Katharyne Mitchell argues that many cultural theorists use concepts such as diaspora and hybridity in ways which are 'increasingly disarticulated from history and political economy'. The context of labour migration is thus central to understandings of Irish women's place in Britain. They are integrated into the economic system however their social positions are represented.

Throughout the nineteenth and twentieth centuries emigration from Ireland has been articulated by demand for labour in the English-speaking industrialised world. Women's labour has been in particularly strong demand and Irish women have migrated as independent single workers. They have therefore been available to fill gaps in labour markets abroad which cannot be met by local women. During the nineteenth century, when the substantial majority of Irish women went to the United States, slightly fewer women than men came to Britain, though the totals were quite similar (Figure 4.1). After the introduction of quotas by the United States in the 1920s, Britain became the major economy using Irish labour as a flexible source to meet changing demands, mainly for manual workers. The number of women exceeded that of men in every decade thereafter. The greatest increase in total numbers was in the 1950s when a massive 'haemorrhage' of people from the Republic of Ireland took place, often called the 'second wave' since

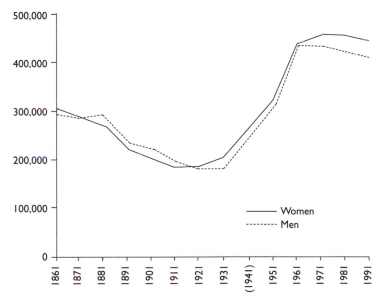

Figure 4.1 Total Numbers of Irish-born women and men in Great Britain, 1861–1991

it marked the renewed upturn after a continuous decline since the earlier post-Famine peak in 1861. Numbers of Irish-born women, from both parts of Ireland, living in Britain rose from 364,663 in 1951 to 478,828 in 1961, an increase of 32 per cent. The rise was much slower in the 1960s, only 4 per cent, and in the following decade (1971–81) the total actually fell by 2 per cent as the Irish Republic registered its first net population growth since before the Famine of the 1840s. However emigration resumed sharply in the 1980s, an upturn referred to as the 'third wave'. Although the overall number of Irish-born women in Britain remained almost static, in some locations there was a dramatic inrease. In London, for example, the number of young Irish-born women aged 15–24 rose 82 per cent in the census period 1981–91. The discourse of 'waves' is critiqued by Clare Roche (1997), who argues that it emphasises male experience of response to economic changes, whereas the social factors underlying women's movements are more continuous.

As we have seen the importance of Irish women's labour in Britain has rarely been acknowledged. Irish migrants are recognised as a source of manual labour, especially in the nineteenth century, but the stereotype is of navvies, outdoor male workers visibly grouped in 'gangs' whose Irish accents signal their difference on building sites and afterwards in 'Irish pubs'. Academic analyses have reinforced the impression that men's work is more significant. For example, John Jackson's (1963) classic work *The Irish in Britain*, still the only comprehensive survey of Irish settlement in the nineteenth and twentieth centuries, contains a chapter entitled 'Nineteenth century toilers: occupations of the Irish immigrant since 1800'. Only half a page at the end of the chapter describes women's occupations, confirming that the earlier, unmarked, discussion of involvement in the 'roughest, heaviest and dirtiest form of unskilled labour' did in fact refer only to the norm of men's work.

Yet there are glimpses of a different ordering of the importance of women's and men's work in reality. According to the 1845 Parliamentary Report into the State of Large Towns and Populous Districts, 'the girls are those who succeed the best' among the Irish , because of the age and sex specificity of textile employment and domestic service. Another telling piece of evidence that unseen Irish women's work was of greater importance is also contained in a memo from the British Minister of Labour in 1932, when repatriation to ease unemployment levels during the Depression was being considered:

> If it were decided to repatriate all persons in this country born in the Irish Free State there might be some temporary dislocation in the case of employers, particularly in Liverpool and Glasgow . . . but there is no doubt that under present conditions the total number of workers born in the Irish Free State *with the possible exception of those engaged in domestic service*, could be replaced rapidly and without much difficulty by workers born in Britain.
>
> (Glynn 1981: 63, my emphasis)

In this chapter I take a long-term perspective, examining Irish women's work over two centuries. This time period includes up to six generations of migrants direct from Ireland, and the same number of generations of descendents from the early nineteenth-century settlers as far as they can still be identified. Although the economic background has changed dramatically over time, the persistent thread of the migration flow provides a unique opportunity to explore continuities and changes in trends in generations of settlement from Ireland. Moreover the 'roots' Irish women have established in specific geographical locations, the solid facts of their placement, make it important to take account of past structures. The existence of networks of family and friends have particular salience for single women migrating to find work, and can persist over generations, outlasting the economic factors which initially attracted their grandmothers and aunts.

The small amount of available data about Irish women migrants and their descendents means that this will be a patchy and incomplete analysis, but the fragments which can be traced have the makings of a framework within which subsequent research can be placed. They also highlight absences which would otherwise remain unremarked. British Censuses did not publish tables of occupation by birthplace on a national scale until 1951 so that only sporadic case studies based on individual researchers' extractions from Census enumerators' returns between 1841 and 1891 are available. The exception was a special tabulation of the 1911 Census of Scotland which provided a comprehensive listing of the Irish-born population's occupations by gender. Only once, in the Sample Census of 1966, was the tabulation provided on a regional scale, and this will

be examined in some depth. In the absence of other data therefore, inferences must be drawn from regional population
distributions, fleshed out by more detailed evidence gleaned from
local case studies.

Geographical patterns of settlement in Britain

A close analysis of the geographical patterning of Irish settlement in
Britain provides clues to gendered demand for migrants' labour, and
raises many questions about the social consequences of such a distinctive mix of clustering and dispersal. Mapping Irish settlement in
Britain produces a very uneven set of Census snapshots, which have
changed sharply over time. During the nineteenth and early twentieth centuries three regions/nations dominated the distribution –
Scotland, North West England and South East England – which
together accounted for about 80 per cent of the total. Very low proportions of Irish people have lived in four regions – the North of
England, Wales, the East Midlands and East Anglia – since the first
Census records became available in 1841 (Figure 4.2).

In certain parts of Scotland (especially Clydeside, Ayrshire and
Dundee) and North West England, therefore, there has been a long
history of entanglement between British and Irish populations on a
large scale. Very substantial sections of the present-day populations
in these areas have some Irish ancestry, and institutions such as the
Catholic church and its associated schools, no longer viewed as
specifically 'Irish', have become embedded into everyday life. At the
other extreme, large swathes of southern England have little firsthand experience of Irish settlement, and are more completely
immersed in background Protestantism. Changes in the distribution
of Irish labour to match regional shifts in the British economy bring
Irish people into contact with these sharply different local backgrounds. For example, new migrants to Luton, just north of London,
found themselves socially isolated in a strongly Methodist Protestant
area in the 1950s, where their Catholicism was treated with suspicion
and resentment (Walter 1986).

This experience is part of a more general trend after the Second
World War, which has seen South East England become increasingly important in the pattern of Irish settlement. By 1991 nearly
half of all Irish-born people in Britain lived in this region, reflecting both new migration destinations and a redistribution of the

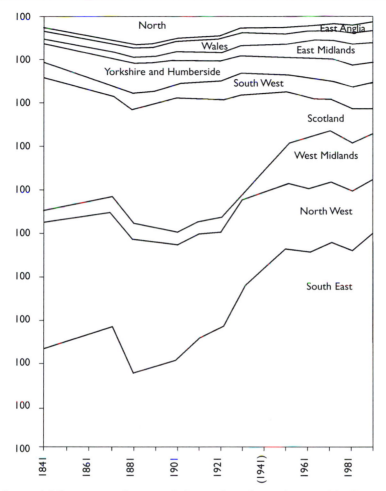

Figure 4.2 Proportional regional share of total population of Irish-born women in Britain, 1841–1991

Source: Census of England and Wales, Scotland and Great Britain, 1841–1991

existing population (Walter 1980). The West Midlands experienced a sharply expanded share between 1921 and 1951 but this declined again after 1961. Scotland, on the other hand, registered a striking drop throughout the period from 30 per cent of the total in 1841 to only 6 per cent in 1991. These changes have important effects on the demographic and social character of Irish communities in all regions. Areas of declining attraction increasingly have

older Irish-born populations, who arrived in periods when education levels were lower and Catholic adherence was stronger. New
arrivals bring attitudes from a more modernised Ireland and a
demographic balance including a younger second generation.

Within these overall patterns, important gender differences
can be traced. Areas of Britain have experienced very varied proportions of women and men in the total numbers of Irish migrants
who have settled there, reflecting local labour demands. On a
national scale, women outnumbered men in Britain in 1861, but
thereafter until 1921 more men were recorded (Figure 4.1). In
fact more women than men left Ireland during this period, so the
male-dominated gender balance in Britain resulted from the
greater preference of women for migration to the United States.
In each decade since 1921, however, Irish-born women in Britain
have outnumbered men, with a particularly sharp increase in the
gap in the Census period 1981–91 when the ratio rose from 1,106
to 1,128 per thousand men. The difference at a national scale,
however, disguises much more marked regional clusters of Irish
women and men.

One way of identifying the varying levels of attraction of different parts of Britain to Irish women and men involves comparing
gender ratios in different regions. These statistical indices are very
simply calculated by dividing the total number of Irish-born
women in the region by the number of Irish-born men and multi-
plying by 1,000. This will show the number of women per 1,000
men and clearly indicate different proportions. Values greater
than 1,000 indicate a region with greater numbers of Irish women
then men, while values below 1,000 are associated with regions
where men outnumber women. The ratios provide a summary of
Irish women's economic and social places in different parts of
Britain, indicating which parts of Britain had specific need of
women's labour and drawing attention to the gendered character
of Irish settlement in those places.

Gender ratios of Irish-born populations by region of Britain 1841–1991

Gender ratios within the Irish migrant population, that is the
balance of numbers between women and men, have fluctuated
very sharply over the last one hundred and fifty years. The long
timespan over which Irish women's work patterns can be traced

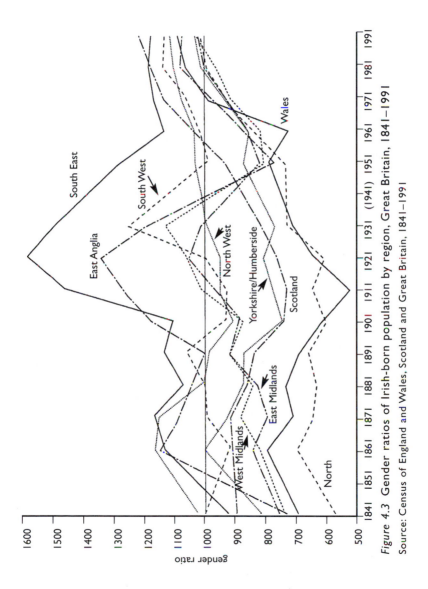

Figure 4.3 Gender ratios of Irish-born population by region, Great Britain, 1841–1991

Source: Census of England and Wales, Scotland and Great Britain, 1841–1991

provides an unusual opportunity to examine changes over time for a migrant group. Despite the upturns and downturns in overall numbers in the Irish-born population in Britain, a migration flow of significant size has been recorded by British Census statistics since 1841.

Figure 4.3 encapsulates this range of experiences with the separate trajectories of gender ratios by region over time, as well as the entanglement of threads. Its overall shape emphasises the complexity of migrant experiences in Britain, but also the continuities, and trends that change over time. This chapter will therefore begin to unravel the complex intertwinings of these threads and explore explanations for these patterns, and their meanings in the lives of Irish migrant women and their families.

Irish women's labour was needed in greater quantities than men's in certain regions. As a result Irish communities in these areas had a larger female component, and this had a number of implications for the social character of settlements. For women remaining within Irish communities, this would mean a smaller choice of Irish-born marriage partners and possibly larger numbers of single women, and for those moving outside, greater likelihood of mixed-ethnicity households. The ongoing ramifications of intermarriage into local British communities include changes in the expression of the Catholic identities with which most women arrived, and the extent and nature of their children's relationship with their Irish heritage. These are issues which have barely been addressed in the literature although there are pointers to differences in the experiences of second-generation Irish people according to the gender of their Irish parent. For example, a survey of Catholics in England and Wales found substantially greater levels of upward social mobility among those with an Irish mother and non-Irish father, though sample size was small (Hornsby-Smith and Lee 1979).

Economic factors also influence Irish women's position within the household. In regions where demand for women's labour has been high, wages were likely to be more reliable and Irish women would therefore occupy a more secure place. Regions with prominent textile industries, for example, drew in large numbers of female migrants including Irish women. Their wages made a significant contribution to household earnings, giving women a greater say over expenditure. Where fewer paid jobs were available, women were more dependent on the earnings of other household members, and relied on work which could be carried on within the home.

Three broad elements of the chronological pattern can be identified in Figure 4.3 as a starting point, before the material realities for
women in individual regions are examined. First, the nineteenth
century can be seen as a period of considerable stability in which
Irish men were conspicuously more numerous in most regions of
Britain. During the period 1841 to 1901 only three regions had more
Irish women than men, with a peak in the 1860s. The two most
important were North West and South East England, also numeri-
cally among the largest Irish-born regional populations in Britain.
The remaining region was East Anglia, with one of the smallest
totals. In the nineteenth century, then, Irish-born women living in
urban areas of Lancashire and in London were in the majority in
their communities, whereas in the North of England they were
greatly outnumbered by Irish-born men. In Lancashire, textiles were
a particularly significant area of work, with smaller numbers of
women engaged in selling and domestic service. In London, on the
other hand, domestic service was the main form of employment,
followed by the clothing and food industries (Lees 1979).

The second element in the pattern is the much greater diver-
gence in gender ratios which can be observed in the first half of the
twentieth century. A striking feature of this period is the high proportion of Irish women settling in South East England. In 1921 there
were 1,630 Irish-born women for every 1,000 Irish-born men in this
region, more than half as many again, mainly reflecting increased
demand for domestic servants as indigenous women found less
arduous and confining alternative types of work. This imbalance was
also reflected in the rest of the southern half of Britain, in East
Anglia, South West England and the West and East Midlands.
Conversely Irish settlement in Wales and northern Britain became
increasingly male-dominated during this period as male migrants
were drawn into heavy industrial sectors such as shipbuilding, iron
and steel working and engineering. Men comprised more than two-
thirds of the Welsh-based Irish-born population, for example.

A further sharp change can be observed following the Second
World War, especially after 1961. The gender ratios of all regions
converged over the following thirty years so that by 1991 there was
remarkably little difference between them. In all regions of Britain
at the end of the twentieth century there were, for the first time,
more Irish-born women than men. Several processes are at work
here. One is the opening up of work opportunities for women in all
parts of Britain and the substitution of part-time 'women's' jobs for

traditional full-time 'men's' paid work. Another is the overall excess of females over males in the Irish-born population in Britain, resulting both from larger number of women migrants and the greater longevity of those who have settled. Thus the ageing process is a major factor in the increased proportions of Irish women in regions such as Wales and the North of England, which recorded a greater number of women for the first time in 1981. In regions which have experienced little new immigration from Ireland for decades women are now a 'residual' population. This, too, is a temporary phase, and the 'bulge' of migrants from earlier periods in the century will die out, leaving populations of Irish descent only.

Irish gender ratios can also be placed in the context of the proportions of women and men in the total population. The overall pattern suggests that there were fewest Irish women in regions where male employment was highest (Figure 4.4). In the North, Yorkshire, and Humberside and Wales, overall gender ratios were low, close to unity, and Irish gender ratios were well below this level. It appears that local women had emigrated from these regions in search of employment elsewhere and that relatively small numbers of immigrant women were attracted in. These were probably 'sequent' migrants, following family members, rather than those actively seeking the best opportunities (Walter 1980).

In North East England, women and children had few opportunities for paid employment in the mid-nineteenth century. Two contrasting consequences for Irish girls in County Durham and Newcastle were longer years of schooling, on the one hand and, on the other, greater numbers working as prostitutes, because of poverty and restricted alternatives for earning money (Cooter 1973). Irish families in these regions were dependent on sole male wage-earners, although relative incomes were higher than in other parts of the country. In 1861 wages of fifteen shillings a week were common in the North East, but rare in other parts of Northern England. Despite the survival of only a 'slender record of Irish life', the evidence suggests that Irish people in the North East were unusually prosperous and well-accepted. However women had few opportunities to earn their livings independently or to make a significant contribution to the household income, and were thus likely to have restricted power within households.

In parts of Scotland and the North West, however, gender ratios in the total population were higher, suggesting a greater demand for women's labour in the economy. Proportions of women in Irish-born

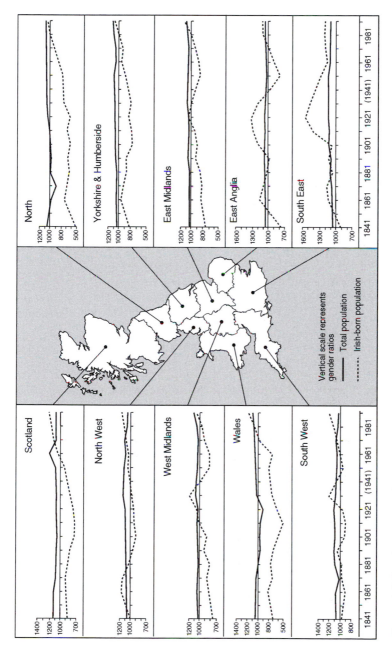

Figure 4.4 Gender ratios of Irish-born and total populations by region, Great Britain, 1841–1991

populations were particularly high in these areas in the mid-nineteenth century, and ratios remained close to unity after that. There
was clearly a specific demand for female labour which had to be
boosted by inmigrants, of whom the Irish formed an important part.

The other major region with long-standing high gender ratios among
both Irish-born and total female populations is the South East of
England, with by far the largest share of the total population of Irish
women. During the 'trough' years of Irish immigration between 1901
and 1931, women were clearly in much higher demand than men. This
unusual pattern again merits more detailed analysis. East Anglia and the
South West show similar trends but involve much smaller population
totals. By contrast the East and West Midlands have low gender ratios for
both total and Irish-born populations, but the trends generally followed
those of the South East and peaked in the 1920s and 1930s.

The demand for female labour in different regions of Britain is
broadly indicated by their overall gender ratios. In many cases the
gender ratios of the Irish-born echo, at a more pronounced level, the
general trend in the total population (Figure 4.4). However at certain
periods the proportion of Irish women sharply exceeded the overall
ratio, indicating a marked shortage of female labour for which they
were acting as a 'reserve army'. In other words when indigenous
supplies of manual labour were inadequate, employers could actively
recruit in Ireland, either directly by sending agents to hire people or
indirectly through networks of existing Irish employees.

The background to all these patterns can be examined in greater
depth in regions with distinctive profiles of Irish women's settlement.
The textile areas of Scotland and North West England attracted
unusually high proportions of Irish women in the nineteenth-
century and South East England has become the major focus of
settlement in the twentieth. In order to explore the implications of
these patterns for the lived experiences of Irish women in Britain I
analyse some occupational and regional case studies in more detail.
This will contextualise women's experiences and show how historical
structures continue to resonate at the present day.

Textile workers in Scotland and North West England

In the mid-nineteenth century, the two regions with the largest
numbers of Irish women were Scotland and North West England
(Figure 4.2). Although Irish men outnumbered women in

Scotland as a whole, in certain towns, such as Dundee and Paisley, women greatly outnumbered men. The North West region of England also had substantially more women between 1851 and 1871 and retained a higher proportion than other northern and western regions thereafter.

A major reason for the larger numbers was demand for female labour in the textile mills, paralleling the situation on the north east coast of the United States in towns such as Lowell and Worcester in Massachusetts. The expansion of the trade in Britain took place at the expense of the Irish textile industry, and at a faster pace than could be met by drawing in local labour. As a result redundant workers from Ireland, who possessed the necessary skills, relocated to the expanding British factories. Domestic industries in Ireland had started to decline in the early decades of the nineteenth century as larger-scale production was concentrated in the Lagan Valley, west of Belfast.

The most striking decline of the cotton trade during the first thirty years of the century was that of the district around Belfast and elsewhere in Ireland. By 1830 English steam factories defeated Irish waterpower, and there was severe distress among both cotton spinners and cotton weavers in Ireland (Redford 1926). Families displaced by the concentration of the textile industry in the north-east of Ireland moved directly to Dundee, following an established route for raw flax exports and spun yarn imports.

In mid-nineteenth century Britain, therefore, rapidly expanding textile towns offered more work opportunities to women, adolescents and children than any other sector of the economy (Collins 1981). In Dundee and Paisley the proportion of adult women (aged twenty and over) in employment was greater than in the Lancashire cotton districts. The majority were engaged in textile-based occupations, with a different balance between handloom weaving and non-weaving textile manufacture in the two towns. More handloom weavers were located in Dundee, comprising 5 per cent of all employed women, compared with only 1 per cent in Paisley, whereas 20 per cent and 27 per cent respectively were employed in the production of non-weaving textiles.

The rates of pay for women were strikingly lower than those for men. In Dundee and Paisley between 1830 and 1855 they averaged about half those of the lowest male earnings within the same textile production unit. Whereas the average male textile labourer's wage was twelve shillings per week, that of all female textile workers was six shillings. It is not surprising that employers greatly preferred to employ women. Even so, women chose manufacturing work in preference to domestic service because its fixed hours allowed greater freedom to enjoy leisure time and greater independence from control by employers.

Mid-nineteenth century Dundee was a town of immigrants, and over half the textile labour force was Irish. The employment of several family members enabled the household to survive. However as well as family employment, of which women and children were the major part, two other groups of migrants, both female, were involved. One comprised young, single women in their teens and early twenties (fifteen to twenty-four), among whom there were more than twice as many women as men. They had been displaced from the textile industry in Cavan and Monaghan and were moving within a familiar framework to mill-work in Dundee. Often sisters migrated together. In total this group comprised 55 per cent of the total female workforce in the textile industry of Dundee. The second group was made up of widows who migrated in order to support their families. Mothers worked alongside their older children or supplemented the family income by taking in lodgers.

The immigration of Irish people to Dundee was closely related to demand. When unemployment rose, immigration declined, even though the overall rate of immigration to Britain remained high. It was not therefore a simple outpouring of relative surplus population from Ireland, but a carefully regulated contribution to industrial expansion. The immigration of Irish women significantly influenced the nature of developments in the textile industry so that the characteristics of the Irish immigrant labour force, such as its domination by young adult women, became the characteristics of the textile labour force as a whole (Collins 1981).

In the later nineteenth century Irish women moved into work in the jute mills. This gave them financial strength in the household and confidence outside the workplace. Walker (1979) describes mill girls in 'Juteopolis' earning more than their husbands or brothers, who fled into the army to preserve their masculine pride. Women had money to spend on themselves and refused to be 'kept in their place'. It was reported that they paraded in the streets as 'over-dressed, loud, bold-eyed girls'. Unusually for women, they were able to defend their interests by joining unions, outnumbering men by four to one in the Mill and Factory Operatives Union. This illustrates clearly the social consequences of demand for Irish women's labour in terms of a reversal of traditional gender hierarchies.

A second case study is that of the cotton textile industry in Bolton, Lancashire. Bolton was a medium-sized Lancashire town with a large Irish population in the mid-nineteenth century, making up nearly 10 per cent of the total in 1861 (6,894 out of 70,395).This included 7.9 per cent born in Ireland and 2 per cent in the second generation with two Irish-born parents (Walter 1979). In 1861 the gender ratio was distinctly skewed, with 1,320 women per 1,000 men. In absolute numbers there were 2,527 Irish-born women above the age of twenty compared with 1,910 men. Demand for female labour was therefore a major factor in the growth of Irish settlement in the town.

An urgent need for female employees in Lancashire mills was being expressed as early as 1836. Mr Taylor, a silk manufacturer of Manchester, reported to the Royal Commission on the Condition of the Poorer Classes in Ireland :

> The moment I have a turnout and am fast for hands, I send to Ireland for ten, fifteen or twenty families as the case may be, and I get the children, chiefly girls of farmers and cottiers. The whole family comes, father, mother and children. I provide them with no money. I suppose they sell up what they have, walk to Dublin, pay their own passage to Liverpool, and come to Manchester by railway, or walk it.
>
> (Parliamentary Papers 1836: xxviii)

Although whole families came to Bolton from Ireland, the main demand was for the labour of women and children. Only 11 per cent of Irish-born men were employed in cotton textile occupations.

The largest group of Irish-born men in Bolton in 1861 was recorded in the Census as 'labourer' (35 per cent). Income among this category of workers was categorised by Anderson (1971) as 'low, or very low, and irregular'. In the nearby town of Oldham in the mid-nineteenth century, unskilled men were increasingly marginal to the economy while demand for women and children grew (Foster 1967). Foster estimated that there was a rise in 'surplus male labour', as measured by the percentage in casual labouring jobs, from 7 per cent in 1841 to 16 per cent in 1851, and as high as 19 per cent in 1861. The pattern of employment of Irish men in Bolton fits this group definition, with a far higher proportion in such jobs than in the population as a whole. A further 29 per cent of Irish men in Bolton were artisans, such as tailors and shoemakers. Although artisans' pay was 'medium and somewhat irregular', according to Anderson (1971), the Irish were clustered in less-skilled artisanal occupations, such as shoemaking, and only seven of these employed others. Most Irish men's income alone therefore was too low and unreliable to support a family.

Significantly Anderson did not attempt a parallel classification of women's work in nineteenth-century Preston. This illustrates and helps to perpetuate the deeply entrenched view, dating from the early nineteenth century, that men's labour is of central importance to the household (Hall 1998), which has disguised the pivotal role played by Irish women's labour in textile towns. Typical of this almost universal tendency to normalise men's work is this description of migration to textile towns in the main textbook on the Irish in nineteenth century Britain:

> *Another dimension for men with wives and children* was found in the availability of employment for all members of the household of an age to be gainfully employed. This proved a major attraction of family migration to textile centres, where employment opportunities were available for women and children, and where men might find employment in building, mining or in a range of assorted trades.
>
> (Davis 1991: 110, my emphasis)

Feminist geographers provide an alternative view to the common-sense assumption of the primacy of men's paid work in these areas. McDowell and Massey's (1984) pioneering account of gender relations in the textile areas of Lancashire in the nineteenth and twentieth centuries showed that although women's millwork was poorly paid, it gave a more regular income than that available to men in the same class. Moreover unionisation was increasingly extended to women workers in the later nineteenth century, giving them more opportunity to resist poor conditions and to recognise their own agency. Indeed this unusual independence among working women was held against them in later twentieth-century restructuring when employers seeking 'green labour' did not locate in the high unemployment areas of Lancashire, but turned instead to regions where women had little experience of paid work, such as County Durham (McDowell and Massey 1984).

The cotton textile trade in Bolton, by far the largest single area of employment for all workers in the town, was indeed dominated by women. Among adult Irish women (aged twenty and over), 54 per cent were 'lower' factory workers, that is the least-skilled and lowest-paid, compared with 13 per cent of men. In the younger age group 85 per cent of girls and 71 per cent of boys also worked in the mills. Irish men, and all women, were of course excluded from the elite positions of spinners, closely guarded by a few local men and their sons. By 1861, in contrast to Dundee, handloom weavers comprised only 0.3 per cent of the total Irish workforce.

By 1900 textile workers accounted for three-fifths of all organised women and received the highest wages in Britain (Lewis 1984). In Bolton, as in Dundee, Irish women posed a threat to male power in areas where they made the major financial contribution to the household. The possibility that this challenge might spread more widely was countered by racism. Irish men were ridiculed in Manchester music hall jokes, represented as weak characters dominated by their wives (Tebbutt 1983). Thus the danger that patriarchal power might be undermined by the strength of Irish women was turned into anti-Irish racism. Irish women were also derided as 'Judy' in contemporary ballads, linking them comically to 'Punch'. This unusual evidence of Irish women's visibility suggests that where women were powerful in the public sphere they became the target of specific stereotyping, though still represented only as counterparts to discursively more central Irish men.

Irish women were as evident on the streets in nineteenth century Lancashire, as they were in Dundee. Although this cannot directly be related to greater financial independence, their participation in street brawls and drinking bouts does not suggest subordination (Tebbutt 1983). *The Bolton Weekly Chronicle* for 1861 reports a number of neighbourhood disturbances in which women were prominent. One was reported under the heading 'Noisy neighbours' described an assault by 'an Irishwoman named Mary Barrett':

> It appeared that the parties were neighbours, but in friendly feeling 'wide as the poles asunder', and much coarse language had passed between them . . . In defence Mr.Flitcroft said if something was not done to protect the English in Blackhorse Street they would soon not be allowed to stir.
>
> *(Boston Weekly Chronicle* 20 April 1861: 8)

Anti-Catholic attitudes inflamed these disputes. In August, Margaret Atkinson was accused by her neighbour, Ellen Ferrimond of making an effigy of her and burning it, shouting to the crowd:

> 'This is the way we'll burn the **** Protestants in ****'. It was stated during the course of the hearing that Mrs Ferrimond places orange flowers in her window when any of the Catholics congregate near, and tells little children what the priests are in the habit of doing to Catholics generally.
>
> (ibid. 24 August: 3)

A clearer link can be made between women's greater financial and political independence in Lancashire textile towns and the working-class suffrage movement in late-nineteenth century Lancashire (Liddington and Norris 1978). Names of suffragists show that Irish women, particularly women of Irish descent, were involved in these movements though their origins are difficult to trace. Prominent Lancashire suffragists with Irish names were Annie Kenney and Mary Callaghan in Oldham, and Nellie Keenan in Salford. A similar background may have influenced those taking part in the Bryant and May matchgirls strike in 1883, who included many Irish women with Irish names (Lennon 1982). However surname analysis understates the full extent of Irish women's involvement where intermarriage has separated them from distinctively Irish surnames.

A combination of experiences probably contributed to the politicisation of Irish women. Family experiences of anti-British agitation in Ireland and Britain, through Fenian activity, gave them a closer experience of direct action. At work their involvement in union activity provided exposure and training in political organisation. Finally, within the family women's greater earning power gave them the confidence, as well as the incentive, to demand the greater rights which suffrage would bring.

Most of the evidence for this is now lost. The generation involved in the Lancashire suffrage movement has died out and can no longer be accessed by oral history techniques. Very few written records were kept, and family origins are unlikely to have been recorded among those that survive. However, by an unusual combination of circumstances, details of one Irish family in Bolton can be pieced together.

Alice and Cissie Foley: political activists in Bolton

This case study of Alice and Cissie Foley illustrates the opportunities for upward mobility for Irish women in the second generation as a result of their political involvement in trades unions and the suffrage movement. It illustrates how forms of political consciousness, including the Irish nationalist cause, union membership and suffragism, articulated with gendered employment, and household labour relations to mediate these women's experiences. However, the story is little known and survives almost by accident, reminding us of the myriad of other stories about Irish women's lives in Britain which have been lost.

The central record of the Foley family is the memoir published in 1973 by Alice Foley entitled *A Bolton Childhood*. This quite brief autobiography of a second-generation Irish woman spans the period from the 1890s to the middle of the twentieth century. It chronicles the careers of two young women who became involved in political activities of different kinds. Alice became the first woman secretary of the Weavers' Association and her sister Cissy was prominent in suffrage activities. The production of the memoir probably results from Alice's long involvement with the Workers' Educational Association and is an articulate and perceptive reflection on her family circumstances. It is supplemented by my own interview with Alice Foley shortly before she died in 1973. The Foley family link with Bolton can also be traced in the 1861 and 1871 Censuses, while Cissy's activities are also sporadically recorded in records relating to the suffrage movement in Lancashire (Liddington and Norris 1978).

In family memory, Catherine and Michael Foley were Famine emigrants believed to have come to Bolton from Liverpool 'because there were too many there'. The earliest official record of their lives is in the 1861 Census, where Alice's grandmother, Catherine Foley recorded as aged 45, and her husband, Michael aged 55, both born in Ireland, were living in the heart of the Irish sector in central Bolton. With them lived their two sons, Thomas and James aged 9 and 5, recorded in 1861 as born in Ireland, but in 1871 as born in Great Bolton. Catherine was described as a housekeeper while Michael was a bricklayer's labourer, the 'low income, irregular work' categorised by Anderson (1971: 26). The family shared its house with boarders, a young Irish couple Margaret and Jeremiah Higham, housekeeper and papermaker respectively, and their daughter Mary aged two.

By 1871 the family had moved house at least once and were living a few hundred yards away in Soho Street. Both sons were working, Thomas as a railway stoker and James as a factory hand. This additional income may well explain the family's move to a house on their own. During the following twenty years the parents died (Michael in 1886), James migrated to Scotland and Thomas married a Bolton woman, Margaret Mort. She was the daughter of an impoverished handloom weaver, who had no formal education and was 'creedless and pewless' according to her daughter. This lack of firm religious affiliation may have made it easier for her to marry an Irish Catholic man.

Thomas alternated periods of unemployment with factory and labouring work. Shortly before Alice, the youngest child, was born in 1891, the family moved to Dukinfield where he had secured a factory job. However he lost the job almost at once, apparently because of his 'Irish' drinking habits, and the family hastily returned to Bolton where there was greater certainty of temporary support from friends and neighbours, as well as credit from local shopkeepers. They moved into Milk Street, close to St Peter and St Pauls' Catholic church, a neighbourhood with a number of other Irish families. The family shared one room in an old farm-house. Thomas's support for the household, which included six children, was thus intermittent, in the ways already described for Irish men's unskilled work earlier in the century. Margaret worked as a washerwoman, eking out a low-paid but more regular living for the family until the children could bring in additional wages.

Thomas was involved in Fenian activities with the Irish Republican Brotherhood, and used to disappear for weeks at a time, apparently tramping around England raising support for the cause. Alice records:

> My childhood was made very difficult by my father. He hated England because of the Irish problems. That entailed a lot of sorrow and misery on my mother, but I could see how he felt. A small group of Irish Catholic friends occasionally came to the house. There was some kind of secrecy about it all. I didn't know about this until later. There was a big box under the bed. My mother said it had firearms in it. She was very upset about it and threatened to reveal it to the police, so reluctantly it was taken away. The others fell away from him then and he became a lonely man.
>
> (Interview 1973)

Alice's eldest sibling, Catherine, known as Cissy, started work as a 'setter-on' in a spinning mill in about 1892 at the age of thirteen. She joined the newly-formed Amalgamated Association of Card and Blowing Room Operatives, started in 1886 with a membership of unskilled workers, mainly young women. It was typical of organisations formed in the later 1880s which were aimed at the large number of poorly-paid workers not previously protected by craft unions. According to Alice 'our father was an ardent unionist and made us join'. Cissy Foley, who moved on to become a 'jack-frame tenter', soon became part of the executive and her sister believed that 'such union experience provided the ideal training ground for her later suffrage campaigning'.

Cissy became an important figure in the Lancashire suffrage movement, speaking at meetings throughout the industrial north west of England. Jill Liddington and Jill Norris (1978) interpret Cissy's political activism as a reaction against 'her mother's hopeless drudgery' and the expectation that as eldest daughter she would share it as soon as she was old enough. However it may also have reflected her early politicisation in an Irish nationalist family. There are strong parallels here with Elizabeth Gurley Flynn's explanations for her own involvement in communist political activism in the United States in the early twentieth century (see Chapter 2).

Alice also recollected that her sister considered their mother 'a poor fool for tolerating such an unsatisfactory husband' who drank, got into debt and frequently left home. Alice herself documents more sympathetically the harshness of her mother's life, which involved keeping the family home scrupulously clean and tidy in very difficult circumstances, taking in washing from other households, and regularly pawning the Sunday best clothes on Monday mornings. She describes her father getting 'the lion's share' of food treats, as her mother shared hers with the children (Foley 1973: 8). Her mother 'plodded gamely on, battling with a feckless husband whom she neither loved nor understood, and succouring her six children whom she never really wanted' (Foley 1973: 9).

Both Cissie and Alice found ways to educate themselves after they left school at thirteen. Cissie joined the Labour Church and found a circle of friends among young women who worked in shops and offices and were interested in socialist ethics and culture. They attended Oxford University Extension Lectures. Although Alice had been unsuccessful in keeping a shop job, being judged unsuitable, and had been forced to enter mill-work at the bottom end of the hierarchy, she won a free pass to study at Evening Secondary School. She too became interested in socialism, and when her father died renounced Catholicism and joined the Labour Church:

> It was, therefore, almost inevitable that under industrial pressures I should become a critical spokeswoman for other fellow-workers in endeavours to steer immediate discontents into more manoeuvrable channels. This activity brought closer contact with the Weavers' Union and broadened attention to the wider issues of industrial organisation and collective solidarity.
>
> (Foley 1973: 63)

She explained how women were slower to become unionised: 'It was never an easy task persuading women and young girls to officially voice their discontents for the fear of victimisation loomed large and there were devious methods of isolating and "picking-out" the so-called culprits'. Moreover pressure from home inhibited women's full participation:

> As trade union negotiation and action became more acceptable to the employers' organisations, recourse to shop-meeting technique developed . . . Time was a main factor, for if talks dragged on married woman grew restless about possibly irate husbands awaiting their delayed evening meal.
>
> (Foley 1973: 64)

After seven years' mill work Alice was appointed to a full-time union post in the insurance section of the Weavers' Association, supervising benefits claimants. Because of the shortage of suitably qualified men she was transferred to the trade union office itself during the First World War. The union was governed by an all-male committee 'and for a long time my presence in the office was tolerated rather than accepted' (ibid.: 82). Moreover the Weavers' Union itself suffered from its largely female membership, having to struggle much harder than all-male 'closed' unions for recognition from local and county employers' associations. Its large female membership was unusual, since many other women factory workers remained unorganised. Robert Roberts (1971) related this to the poverty of their Irish backgrounds. Ring spinners in Salford were among the poorest paid textile workers, lacking social standing on several counts in part because the trade contained a strong Irish Catholic element and unable to give time or energy to participate in union activity.

In 1917 Alice was transferred to a clerkship at the Bolton Weavers' Office, with a significant rise in salary, which still involved work in an all-male environment. She continued to move up through the union movement and actively pursued her involvement with adult education, taking a prominent part at local, regional and national levels in the Workers' Educational Association. She became the first woman to hold the post of Secretary to the Bolton and District Weavers' and Winders' Association between 1949 and 1961, and was President of Bolton Trades' Council between 1956 and 1957.

The Foley sisters' story is thus one of second-generation Irish women in a period from the late-nineteenth to the mid-twentieth centuries in an area of Britain where Irish women's labour was in specific demand. Their father's Irish origins influenced their lives in important ways, contributing to the poverty of their childhoods, the harshness of their mother's life and the limitations of their Catholic education, but also to their awareness of political activism, and possibly their interest in literature and the theatre. Interviewed by the *Bolton Journal and Guardian* at her retirement from the post of Secretary of the Weavers' Association in 1961, Alice attributed some of the success she had achieved to her Irish origins: 'my father gave me the passion, the feelings and the emotion, and my mother steadied me'. But she did not classify herself as Irish when interviewed in 1973. This may reflect the easier identification of people with Irish origins with local industrial communities in the North West of England.

Entry of the children into paid work gave the Foley family a means to upward mobility and this was closely related to spatial mobility. Soon after Cissy started work at the mill they moved to Rankin Street, about a quarter of a mile away. Alice observed that: 'The second house must have seemed roomy after our former cramped abode, yet it was only a two up, two down, dwelling in the middle of a row, with a cobbled yard, privy midden, and earth closet' (Foley 1973: 4). After the youngest child, Alice, entered mill work in 1905 another move was made to Noble Street, close by. Thomas died in 1908 and two surviving sons went to fight in the First World War, leaving the three sisters and their mother who by then had a much larger combined income. Then, 'After a little search in 1915 we moved into a house in Fern Street adjoining an old Wesleyan chapel; this boasted a narrow lobby, tiny parlour, a bathroom and indoor toilet. How happy we were!' (ibid.: 79).

A few years later the chapel and surrounding houses were bought for conversion to a cinema and the Foley family was rehoused in a new housing estate at the edge of the town. From here Alice's two sisters were married to Bolton men and both left the town. Cissie, who had subsequently become a nurse, moved to Grange-over-Sands with her new husband and Emily emigrated to Australia in about 1920. Alice remained in the council house until her mother and remaining brother died in 1932, then made a deliberate break with family memories and bought a small newly-built house in the more affluent north-west part of Bolton. By then she had become an officer in the Weavers' Association and had been appointed a Justice of the Peace in 1931. In 1935 she gained a scholarship to study for a degree at Manchester University. Alice Foley's Irish background was an integral part of her experience. Although she entered higher education as a mature student, she had foregone the opportunity to apply for a scholarship to secondary school because it would have meant leaving her Catholic school.

Irish migration to Bolton declined in the later part of the nineteenth century as the cotton trade passed its peak, although the textile industry did not finally close down until the 1950s. But Irish people continued to settle in Bolton on a smaller scale, often because of family connections with the town. Women interviewed in Bolton in the early 1970s explained how they had still been recruited in Ireland to work in the mills in the early post-war period. They were housed in hostels run by Catholic nuns when they first arrived.

Bridie had been recruited to work in Bolton without any previous connection with the town. She came to work in the cotton mills in the 1950s just before the final closures.

> I came to Bolton through mills advertising in Ireland, in the Irish newspapers. So they caused us to come over and they paid our fare, and found us accommodation, which there is a hostel in Clarendon Street in Bolton, the Cross and Passion, run by the sisters. They put us up like for thirty five shillings a week, which included breakfast of grapefruit, probably, and bran flakes and toast, and we came home from the mills at lunchtime for our lunch. So I had fried meals at lunchtime,

then we came back at half-past five and we said the rosary, half-past five, round the dining-room tables, because there were fifty of us there. And we had tea at six, which included like cold meats and salads and hot broth each day, you know. Saturday we could please ourselves what we did. There were no restrictions. We had to be in by half-past ten. Indeed a lot of the girls didn't adhere to that – they did but they didn't want to do. So we all settled down to our work at the mills, most of us did. But a lot of course, after six months when that time was up, when – you had to stay six months. If you didn't stay in the mill six months you had to pay your fare back. So we all stayed – they all stayed six months anywhere, but then a lot left, you see.

(Interview 1994)

She had arrived at the age of 19 with the support of her mother who felt she would be in safe hands in the hostel. She stayed at the mill for seven years, meanwhile marrying an Irish man who worked in the building trade, and left work when her first child was born. When her youngest child started school, she took up part-time work in the school meals service, entering the other major area of Irish women's work in Britain: personal service.

Domestic service workers in South East England

The single most important occupation for which Irish women have been, and continue to be, recruited is domestic service. Domestic service was given as the occupation of well over 90 per cent of all women leaving Ireland between 1877 and 1900 (Jackson 1963, cited in Rossiter 1996). This area of work expanded greatly in the later nineteenth century as the 'cult of domesticity' took hold. Indigenous women have been unwilling to accept these jobs, because of the hard, demeaning work and low pay, and as a result the demand for migrant women to fill these positions has continued. In the nineteenth century Irish women were the largest group of migrants recruited. There are clear parallels here with their employment patterns in the United States. However, unlike the United States, the lack of data collected on the birthplace and ethnic origin of servants in Britain has made it difficult to trace their numbers and distribution precisely.

Evidence must be pieced together from more localised studies, which can be placed within the larger pattern of Irish women's settlement as a whole.

Irish women's employment in domestic service varied sharply by region (Fitzpatrick 1989). It was lowest in regions where textile towns were situated. Thus no Irish-born women were listed as domestic servants in Dundee in 1851 and only 3 per cent in Paisley. In Bolton 5 per cent of Irish women aged under twenty, and less than 1 per cent of those aged twenty and above were so described in 1861. Proportions of women employed in domestic service were also low in South Wales and the North of England. However even in regions with low overall totals, there were considerable local variations. Despite the low average for North West England, in Liverpool domestic service was the largest single occupation for women, accounting for 29 per cent of the total.

In South East England, especially London, on the other hand, this has been the major occupational category of Irish women's work throughout the nineteenth and twentieth centuries, supporting the rapidly expanding commercial sector. The gender ratio in the total population has also been highest in the South East, suggesting a demand for female labour which has been met by migration from other parts of Britain, as well as from Ireland and further afield. By 1851 Irish-born women in South East England outnumbered men and the imbalance has continued to the present, the only British region where this has occurred (Figure 4.3).

Irish women's place in the hierarchy of domestic servants changed dramatically over the second half of the nineteenth century. In 1851 they were the least favoured and most in need of work. Martha Kanya-Forstner (1997) documents strong prejudice against Irish servants in the wealthier suburbs of Liverpool and argues that Irish women were more likely to be employed by small tradespeople and even working-class families. Thus Irish women were located at the lower end of the employment hierarchy, even within domestic service. British-born servants were much preferred to Irish women, who were forced to take less popular jobs in pubs or with East End Jewish families in London (Lees 1979). In Bristol the 1851 Census shows that the vast majority of Irish servants were in the lowest categories of general servant and maid of all work, rather than in positions which brought them into closer physical contact with their employers such as lady's maid or parlourmaid

(Large 1985, cited in Rossiter 1996). Language may have been a handicap as many Irish women in the 1850s spoke only Irish, but they were also apparently regarded as unruly and unmanageable (Kerr 1938; Wilson 1946). The lack of alternative employment was made starkly clear if they left or were dimissed, the options being prostitution or begging. Particularly at risk from poverty were female-headed households. In 1851 and 1861 over one-fifth of Irish families sampled in London were broken, most with female heads (Lees 1979). Although negative views of Irish servants were also expressed in the United States at this time, there was, by contrast, strong demand for their labour (Fitzpatrick 1989).

Towards the end of the nineteenth century, however, the view of Irish women as servants became more favourable. A number of factors influenced the changed perception. Shortage of domestic workers was a key issue. British women moved into a wider range of work, including clerical and more prestigious caring roles. Thus opportunities in 'white-blouse' work (mainly teaching, retailing, office work and nursing) increased by 161 per cent between 1881 and 1911, while manufacturing and domestic service expanded by only 24 per cent (Lewis 1984). Other women were withdrawn from the labour market into the servicing of individual families as ideologies confining women to the home spread to New Working Class families after the mid-nineteenth century (Mackenzie and Rose 1983). At the same time employment of servants in the increasing number of middle-class homes became an essential mark of gentility.

Young Irish women also came to be seen as more acceptable employees. In part this reflected the rise in social status of emigrant women, especially as they benefited from higher levels of education before emigration (Fitzpatrick 1986). Moreover girls who would have been forbidden by their fathers to take up domestic work in rural Ireland because of the decline in status involved were under no such ban in London. Domestic service became increasingly unpopular in Dublin towards the end of the nineteenth century (Hearn 1989). In 1881 it accounted for 48 per cent of all female employment, but by 1911 this had declined to 29 per cent, as this way of life was increasingly rejected because of its low status and lack of freedom. Irish servants preferred emigration – often simply to do the same work in America or Britain – or even unemployment at home, which increased by 5 per cent between 1901 and 1911. In Britain their urgent need for work made Irish women more amenable than British women, who could afford to reduce their subservience as their labour was more widely sought (Tebbutt 1983). By the end of the century it was London girls rather than Irish ones who were seen as 'saucy' and lacking proper respect.

The Catholic church encouraged Irish women to take up domestic service rather than factory work. Priests could exert greater moral influence on isolated individuals. They presented the work as fulfilling the ideal of Catholic womanhood, preparing young women for marriage and childraising by learning domestic skills and saving money. However Tebbutt (1983) points out that, despite letters of introduction from their parish priest in Ireland, Irish servants found priests remote from their lives and of little practical support. Moreover 'despite its acculturative function, domestic service involved a degree of cultural alienation which was often not resolved until marriage, the experience even then persisting to inform social attitudes' (Tebbutt 1983: 134). She suggests that other service occupations, such as pub work, played a far more valuable socialising role for Irish women in Britain, introducing them to urban working-class life in contrast to enclosure in individual middle-class households.

Nevertheless domestic service had attractions for women. As in the United States, the provision of board and lodging was an important bonus for new arrivals. In 1900 a housemaid could earn £18–20 a year, plus board and lodging, which was close to the annual income of the best paid group of women workers, those in cotton textile mills. The private workplace also protected Irish women from the discrimination that was widely experienced in factories, though not necessarily from exploitation. Thus domestic service persisted as the major area of Irish female employment, contrary to the general trend among the peer group of British women, whose employment in personal service in England and Wales fell from 42 per cent to 23 per cent between 1901 and 1951.

After the First World War, Irish women helped to stem the massive outflow from domestic service in Britain. The increasing age of servants at this period is a reflection of its unpopularity as a form of employment (Lewis 1984). This may explain the sharp increase in the gender ratio, peaking in 1921 in the Irish-born population in the South East and adjoining regions noted earlier. Women who were prepared to live in other people's households were in particularly high demand. One woman confirmed the value of Irish women's labour in service work:

In the thirties things were really bad here. You'd go after a room and they'd say 'Don't take Irish'. I got into Joe Lyons as a nippy (waitress). You had to be nippy and all. The Irish helped each other out. You'd let them share your bed until they got on their feet. Some of the girls I knew cried a lot. They wanted to go back home but they couldn't. The work the English girls wouldn't do, the Irish did.

(Lennon and Lennon 1980: 53)

Another woman described her experience of arriving at Kingston in Surrey after having travelled all night, and being told by a stranger about a woman nearby who wanted a maid to start work immediately: 'At that time – it was the early thirties – in this country, they were really anxious for Irish girls because they were strong and they'd do the work' (Lennon, McAdam and O'Brien 1988: 42).

The other major area of Irish women's work in Britain is nursing, which was closely associated with domestic work in its early development as a profession. Nurses and domestic servants were not differentiated in nineteenth-century Censuses until 1891 when the special category of 'sick nurse' was introduced. Even well into the twentieth century nurses were expected to care for all aspects of their patients' needs, not simply tend to their health. An Irish woman from Leitrim who arrived in East London in 1919 described being required to do all the domestic chores:

It took three years to train as a general nurse. We started at 6.30 am and finished at 9 in the evening and we'd one whole day off every three weeks. The first year I never thought I'd stick it out the work was so hard and food was scarce after the war. We did the medical care, the cleaning and the cooking, in fact if you didn't pass the cookery exam you failed in your finals.

(Lennon 1982: 38)

Another woman who trained in London in the 1920s underlined the high level of demand for Irish women in these jobs: 'Not many English women trained then as nurses – it was too hard' (ibid.: 38).

The period 1939-45 gave Irish women experience of a much wider range of jobs left vacant by the enlistment of British men and women.

At the outbreak of World War Two I thought, this is my opportunity to get out of hotels, so I registered for government clerical work and got sent to work in the Assistance Board in Tottenham Court Road. The war gave me a break too, yes, I do feel that. I would never have got into the Civil Service in peacetime. I wouldn't have had sufficient educational background, but because of the shortages I got in. We were all employed as temporary staff – so that they could push us out when they didn't want us. And they started pushing us out in 1947.

(Lennon, McAdam and O'Brien 1988: 51)

As soon as the war ended the earlier pattern reasserted itself. Women describing themselves as domestic servants dominated the massive outflow of labour migrants from the Irish Free State between 1946 and 1950. In that year 59 per cent of registered Irish women workers in Britain were in domestic work.

Irish women in post-war Britain: workplaces

I now turn to a more detailed analysis of Irish women's patterns of work in post-war Britain in order to locate them within the broader pattern of immigration. Statistical data show that Irish women have continued to play an important role in the provision of labour to meet shortfalls in the economy. Their position in the labour market is a reflection of the needs of the economy, their own values and skills, and views of the dominant society about appropriate areas of work for Irish people. It is necessary therefore to examine profiles of Irish women's paid employment in comparison to those of the dominant and other subordinated groups.

In the post-War period there has been an inadequate supply of British-born women to fill low-paid casual jobs in particular, with additional gaps in less desirable highly-trained areas of work such as nursing. Immigrant workers have been recruited specifically to meet these demands. As I discussed in Chapter 3, the shortage of female labour was partly a consequence of the importance of the home in constructions of national identity in the 1950s. Indigenous white women became the focus of a newly-inclusive form of Englishness which submerged the class and regional differences which had characterised the 1930s. Their place was in the home, particularly in new estates which spread over the suburbs in all parts of the country. They were encouraged to see child-rearing and household management as central to their lives. Middle-class women who had engaged in paid work during the war became full-time 'housewives', while working-class women took part-time jobs which enabled them to provide for the essential needs of their children and households without losing their primary role in the home.

Yet demands for female labour were growing at the same time that women were being withdrawn from the full-time workforce. In part this was due to the very needs of 'housewives' and their families for welfare and educational services to support home-centred life. It also reflected the feminisation of the industrial sector, and increased demand for lower-paid assembly-line workers. Thus the shortage of indigenous women had to be made good by immigrants who did not need to meet the expectations of Englishness. Their own additional roles as mothers and unpaid workers in their households were not seen as needing state support, yet in the same breath full-time working mothers were castigated for failing to care adequately for their 'latch key' children (Webster 1998).

The Catholic church pulled Irish migrant women, especially those married to Irish men, in the same direction as indigenous ones. Those who became mothers and whose partners could provide sufficient income usually left full-time paid work and took on part-time jobs when the youngest child started school. They often had additional caring roles providing hospitality to new migrants from Ireland, especially in light of the difficulty of gaining access to housing in Britain. Buckley (1997) argues that for many Irish women there was also the additional labour needed to socialise children in their Irish background against the grain of its devaluation in Britain and the exclusion of Irish material from the Britain education system.

However many Irish women needed the income from full-time paid work, sharing a place in the British labour market with migrants from other origins. The indigenous/migrant binary is usually overlooked as result of the assumption that it is synonymous with the black/white division. However there are considerable complexities in the nature of the overlap between the two which need to be unpacked.

In this section I examine several components of Irish women's place in the labour force, each of which throws light on their relative position. First, it is necessary to analyse the profile of employment and to explore the issue of change over time, which provides a measure of social mobility both for the group as a whole and between different generations. Second, Irish women's experiences are placed in comparative relationship with those of other ethnic groups, including majority white ethnicities.

Patterns of Irish women's work

Occupational change 1951–91

Profiles of both women's and men's work at a national level, drawing on Census data, provide a series of snapshots of the overall character of employment within the ethnic group. Although changes in recording categories make it difficult to make precise comparisons over time, broad changes in the distribution of women's and men's work among those born in the Irish Republic can be observed. The pattern of work of women originating in Northern Ireland is different in significant respects.

In 1951 Irish women from the Republic were distinctively clustered in two areas of work: the professions (22 per cent) and personal services (40 per cent). They made up 5 per cent and 3 per cent of the total British workforce in these areas. Together the professions and personal services accounted for nearly two-thirds of all jobs done by Irish-born women in Britain, but scarcely one-third of those done by the total female population. Most of the professional workers were nurses and the remainder teachers, while those in the personal service category were engaged in cleaning and cooking jobs.

The distribution was polarised, in terms of qualifications and financial rewards, between women with high levels of secondary schooling and good career prospects, and those with a basic educational background and low income prospects. This was mirrored in Harrison's (1973) observations about the distinct clientele of the Birmingham dance halls in the early 1970s: 'The two main Birmingham dance halls both feature Irish bands on Fridays and Saturdays, but the building workers and shopgirls go more often to the Shamrock, and teachers, nurses and social workers go off to the Mayfair'. By contrast, Irish-born men were more evenly spread by occupation, though there was a marked concentration in construction work.

Irish-born women were thus strongly associated with traditionally feminine types of employment, echoing in the paid sphere the
unpaid caring and maintenance work of the home.

> Overviewing Irish workers in Britain, we see them rigorously
> channelled into hypertrophied gender-stereotypes, with
> millions of women intensely engaged in the feeding, cleaning,
> healing, caring and teaching of Britons and millions of Irish
> men focused into clearing, constructing, and fabricating the
> economic landscape of contemporary Britain.
>
> (Buckley 1997: 109)

The bi-polar distribution of Irish women's employment profile
differs sharply from that of men. It also contrasts with that of white
English-born women, almost a third of Irish-born women being
placed in the professional category compared with a quarter of
the English-born. The largest section of this professional category
is nurses, who are an exception both to the invisibility of Irish
women in Britain and in having a positive stereotype. Whereas in
different circumstances Catholic mothers can be portrayed as
threatening 'others', as nurses their caring qualities, selflessness and
duty, are 'in place' when put to work for the British public good.

Although the principal features of the profile remain, over the
forty-year period 1951–91 the patterns of work of the Irish-born
and total populations have converged to some extent. The
greatest change for Irish-born workers was recorded in the first
half of the period 1951–71, when the proportion working in
personal services fell from 40 per cent to 34 per cent with a cor-
responding rise in the percentage of clerical workers, though this
remained well below that recorded for the total female population. Proportions of Irish-born men in professional occupations
have, by contrast with women, risen very sharply, paralleling and
even exceeding the rate of increase in the population as a whole.

The overall picture therefore appears to contain elements of
both continuity from the nineteenth and earlier twentieth centuries, but also a move towards greater similarity with the total
population. Other statistical sources must be drawn on to assess
the extent to which there has indeed been upward social mobility
among the Irish-born population in the post-war period.

It should be noted that most of the distinctive aspects of
patterns already identified are more strongly associated with the

Republic-born population. Those born in the North are much closer in profile to the average population of Britain. Thus women born in the Republic are more strongly represented in nursing (12 per cent) than the Northern-Irish born (9 per cent), though both groups are substantially above the average (5 per cent). Women originating in the Republic are much more likely to be in personal services (15.2 per cent) than the Northern Irish-born (12.7 per cent) who are closer to the female average of 12.8 per cent. Generally therefore Northern Irish-born women are found in higher status occupations than those from the Republic. The same is true for Northern Irish-born men in categories such as management and administration.

It is clearly important therefore to distinguish migrants by origin in Ireland when considering their place in the British work-force. Whereas both women and men from the Irish Republic show very clear labour migrant profiles, those from Northern Ireland have a more complex occupation pattern. Their greater similarity to the British average may be explained by a number of factors, including the shared education system and its resulting qualifications. Those with higher levels of education may emigrate within common employment structures, such as the civil service. Women in particular migrate within the public sector, often as part of a circulatory movement (Compton 1992). The stereotyped working-class image thus appears to be more characteristic of migrants from the Irish Republic, but the differential employment patterns of Catholic and Protestant migrants from Northern Ireland may be masked by the statistics.

1966 Sample Census: a snapshot of Irish women's regional work patterns

The 1966 10 per cent Sample Census is the only regional statistical tabulation of women's occupations by birthplace, although the method of sampling employed in that Census had severe deficiencies concerning subgroups of the population and can only point to general trends. Nevertheless it provides a useful broad snapshot of the national and regional distribution of occupations, and their groupings into social classes, at the peak of the 'second wave' of Irish settlement in Britain.

The overall national occupational distribution of the total and Irish-born populations shows that Irish women's work was concentrated in far fewer occupational categories than that of Irish men, echoing the gendered pattern of work in the British population as a whole. Thus over 80 per cent of all women were recorded in only six categories of employment.

When the regional pattern of women's work is examined, considerable variations in the mix of occupations can be observed both within the Irish-born populations and between the Irish-born and all women. There were marked differences in employment patterns by area of settlement. Irish women's profile of work in the South East region was distinctly different from that of other regions, especially in the larger proportion of clerical workers, mirroring the higher rate in the total population. In the West Midlands a large number of Irish-born women were employed in engineering and allied trades, substantially higher than among the total female working population.

Finally, more Irish-born women were in professional occupations in the North and East Anglia. These were the two regions with the smallest overall totals, suggesting that Irish nurses, and to a lesser extent teachers, were more widely scattered than the Irish female population generally. For the total population these regions ranked only fifth for their proportion of professional workers. However Irish-born women did not simply conform to the overall patterns of the regions they settled in, but filled particular niches or gaps.

An interesting question posed by these findings is the extent to which Irish women's experience in Britain is determined by the work opportunities available at destination. Do Irish women share common backgrounds which are then diversified by the, possibly chance, factor of their location in Britain? Or are women from particular backgrounds, perhaps based on farm-size and prosperity, drawn to different areas of Britain? More highly educated women may migrate to London, for example, thus influencing the employment profile as they enter higher-paid clerical work.

The result is that Irish women have had very different experiences of life in Britain. The types of work entered affect the nature of relationships with their own and other ethnic groups, for example whether they work as isolated Irish people or as part of a larger grouping. Some kinds of work, for example nursing, involve face-to-face contact with members of the public, whereas others place Irish women out of sight in factories or offices.

Different migrant generations

Migration from Ireland in the post-war period has been at a very uneven rate. Two major 'waves' can be identified, peaking in the 1950s and 1980s respectively. They have had a striking impact on the character of the Irish community in Britain, which is reflected in the occupational profiles of different generations. The 1950s migrants came predominantly from rural Ireland where the economy was stagnating. Acute anxiety was felt at government levels by the massive loss of young people attracted by the 'bright lights' and expanding economy of neighbouring Britain. The Commission on Emigration and Population, which reported in 1956, expressed particular concern about the emigration of women as gender ratios in rural areas became extremely unbalanced. Women were leaving very poor conditions in Ireland and the majority had minimal educational qualifications, completing their education in small rural schools at the age of twelve. The largest proportion of Irish women in Britain migrated at this time and, now in their sixties, are just leaving the labour market.

As the Irish economy industrialised and diversified in the 1960s, following a major policy change in 1958 which opened it up to foreign investment and encouraged branch factories to locate in rural areas, emigration declined to some extent. It fell further in the 1970s after the Irish Republic joined the European Economic Community, though the net immigration experienced in the mid-1970s disguised continuing emigration among the young. In the 1980s very high levels of emigration, equalling those of the 1950s, were experienced again as the economy at home collapsed following redirection of foreign investment to more profitable global locations. At the same time a soaring birthrate accompanying years of lower emigration resulted in large numbers of school-leavers entering the labour force. The young people now emigrating were much better educated than those of their parents' generation. Moreover their availability was matched by demand for highly skilled labour in Britain.

The demographic profile of the Irish-born population in 1991 reflects these differing rates of emigration in the post-war period. There is a 'bulge' of people aged between forty and sixty, who comprise nearly 40 per cent of the total. Women are in a small majority, reflecting their higher rates of emigration and lower rates of return. Higher death rates among Irish-born men because of poorer health and higher accident rates on building sites increase the imbalance. The large numbers of 1950s migrants is also associated with an unprecedentedly large second generation, now themselves in middle age and bringing up a substantial third-generation population. A second 'bulge' of Irish-born people in their twenties comprises the new wave of Eighties migrants. Women outnumber men in the younger age-group (twenty to twenty-four), still leaving home earlier as they did in the nineteenth century.

Among the older working groups, aged forty-five to fifty-nine, Irish-born women are strongly concentrated into the two personal service and catering Census categories, and Irish-born men into the industrial and general labouring groupings. In these age groups married Irish women are much more likely to be working part-time than women in other ethnic groups (Walter 1988). The experience of this large section of the population thus has a major effect on the socio-economic structure of the Irish population as a whole.

The young working age group, eighteen to twenty-nine, has a very different occupational profile. There is much stronger representation in occupations demanding higher qualification levels. Both women and men are overrepresented in managerial and professional occupations compared with the total population. Nearly half of all Irish-born women in the age group are in these categories alone (45 per cent), compared with 27 per cent of all women. Nurses continue to account for an important part of this group and explain the higher representation of women in these occupations. However even if non-health occupations only are considered, the proportion of Irish-born women in managerial and professional occupations (30 per cent) is still substantially higher than in the total population (19 per cent) and the same is true for men. This marks the 'brain drain' from Ireland during the 1980s.

Social mobility

Two studies of social mobility among the Irish in Britain, both over the lifecycle and intergenerational, have been made. The first, examining only male experience, was based on the Oxford Social Mobility analyses (Heath and Ridge 1983), and found a marked downward mobility compared with father's occupational status of Irish men in England and Wales in 1972, compared with English,

Scots and foreign-born whites. Heath and Ridge relate a similar pattern among non-white groups as the result of discriminatory practice on racial grounds, but they attribute the Irish experience to different causes. These include a lack of 'know-how' and an inability to manipulate the necessary network of contacts. In other words they provide a class-based explanation, with the added handicap of migration background. But their grounds for rejecting discrimination as a consideration rest on an unquestioned assumption that racism and discrimination can only be experienced by 'black' people, illustrating the pervasive view, inside academia as well as outside, that Irish people cannot experience discrimination because they are 'white'.

The only other attempt to study the mobility in both first and second generations was by Hornsby-Smith and Dale who introduce their study with the comment that: 'remarkably little is known about the processes and extent of educational and occupational assimilation, convergence of social mobility experiences and patterns of intermarriage of England's largest immigrant community, the Irish' (Hornsby Smith and Dale 1988: 519). Their findings confirm those of Heath and Ridge for the migrant generation. However among the second generation a very different pattern emerges. Both women and men with one or two parents born in the Irish Republic had higher educational and occupational levels than their English counterparts. A striking feature of the employment pattern of second-generation women with Republic Irish-born parents was the high proportion in the category which includes teachers and nurses, 18 per cent compared with 14 per cent for Irish-born women and only 9 per cent for the English control group. Since other evidence points to a decline in nurses among this group, this may point to a sharp increase in the number of teachers. Among second-generation Irish women, there were also considerably lower proportions in semi- and unskilled work compared with both first-generation Irish women and the English control group. For both parts of Ireland, second-generation women had higher proportions in junior non-manual work than the English sample. Second-generation men from Northern Ireland, by contrast, appeared to have declined in social status, and to have much higher proportions in semi- and unskilled occupations.

It appears, therefore, that second-generation women with parents from either part of Ireland show much higher rates of

upward mobility than the English control group. When class
origins are taken into account both women and men with Irish
Republic-born parents have greater upward mobility than any
other group. Hornsby-Smith and Dale offer two kinds of explanation for this finding. One conclusion they draw is that, in
contrast to the situation in the middle of the nineteenth
century, Irish immigrants today report levels of educational
attainment and occupational status, and rates of outmarriage
which suggest little difficulty in social assimilation by the second
generation. However the difference in the experience of
children from Republic and Northern Irish populations leads
them to suggest additionally that 'these migrants may be a self-
selecting group highly motivated to succeed' (Hornsby-Smith
and Dale 1988: 541), presumably through their children using
the education system.

These conclusions are premised within an assimilationist
framework which seeks evidence of conformity to the norms of
the dominant society. There are two problems with this
framework. First, it is based implicitly on the assumption that
whiteness makes this an appropriate concept. Although
Hornsby-Smith and Dale acknowledge that 'the conceptualisation of the processes of assimilation and adaptation is strongly
contested', the 'available concepts' they list are all based on
American theories where a fundamental black/white
distinction is taken for granted. A second problem is the linear
process envisaged, in which the second generation is assumed
to be detached from its roots and considered only in the light of
its relationship with the dominant group. In fact the high levels
of social mobility may have distinctively Irish facets, rather than
simply be evidence of conformity to British norms. The
assumption that the white Irish second generation is no longer
Irish is part of the enforced homogeneity of whiteness, and
contrasts with the parallel assumption that 'black' second
generations are not really British.

More information on change over time is provided by the
Longitudinal Study which permits comparison of individuals'
mobility rates between 1971–81 and 1981–91. The findings strikingly support Hornsby-Smith and Dale's (1988) observations
but add important new detail. They show that the high rates of
upward mobility among second-generation Irish people
increased during the 1980s and were greatest for those with two

Irish-born parents rather than one. The 1970s was the decade during which the children of the 1950s generation of migrants entered the British labour market in large numbers. Thus the 1981–91 period is a better reflection of their experience.

Taken together these findings show that a significant proportion of Irish people born in Britain achieve above-average levels of social mobility by moving from working-class to middle-class occupations both in comparison with their parents' socio-economic class and during their own working lives. Explanations for this pattern must be sought in Irish household strategies and values as much as in the 'tolerance' of the dominant population in allowing the migrant group to assimilate. It has also been suggested that Irish mothers were more successful than Irish fathers in promoting the upward social mobility of their British born children (Hornsby-Smith and Lee 1979: 41). This claim needs further investigation at the qualitative level.

Ethnicity and social class

The distinctive features of Irish women's socio-economic position, compared with those of Irish men, within the British labour market as a whole have been outlined. In this section I examine their relative position in the labour market in relation to other groups of women. The extent to which whiteness explains this positioning can then be assessed.

One summary measure of overall socio-economic position is the Registrar General's index based on levels of skill in occupations. Although criticised for lack of systematic criteria (Prandy 1990) and inadequate representation of women's work this has the advantage of summarising data on occupations. In order to place Irish-born women alongside other ethnicities, including subordinate British nationalisms, the analysis will be restricted to England, using the 2 per cent individual file of the 1991 British Census Sample of Anonymised Records (SAR). Broad patterns can be identified for the main birthplace and Census-based ethnic groups in England. The most striking finding is the clustering of Republic Irish-born women and men in the lowest social category, Social Class V, as would be expected from the high proportion in personal service occupations. The proportions in this class are substantially higher than for any other group, 14 per cent for women compared with 8 per cent for white English-born (the second-highest being Black African women with 12 per cent). For Republic Irish-born men the total is 12 per cent, more than twice the proportion of the white English-born (5 per cent) and closest to the Black Caribbean population (8 per cent). It must be remembered that the Irish are a birthplace group, comprising only one generation, whereas the 'visible' ethnic groups include at least one British-born generation, who may have moved out of migrant niches.

However there is a particularly marked contrast with Scottish- and Welsh-born women and men in England, who share a birthplace categorisation. In fact Scottish- and Welsh-born women are less likely than the English-born to be placed in the lowest ranked occupational groups. When Social Classes IV and V are merged, an approximation to a 'working class' grouping, Irish Republic-born women are second only to Pakistani women in proportion. The greatest contrast is with the internal British ethnic groupings. Women and men from Northern Ireland are also much closer to these British ethnic groupings than to the Irish Republic-born.

At the top end of the class scale a more complex pattern emerges. Irish Republic-born women have low proportions in Social Class I, similar to the English-born total and well below those of the Scottish, Welsh and Northern Irish-born groups. The difference is even more striking when the two highest Social Classes, that is the groups fitting most closely the description 'middle class', are taken together. Women originating in Wales (41 per cent), Scotland (37 per cent) and Northern Ireland (39 per cent) are in much higher ranking occupations than Republic-born women (33 per cent), despite the number of well-qualified nurses. Among men, Irish Republic-born proportions are high in Social Class I, but still lower than those of men from Wales, Scotland and Northern Ireland when the top two classes are merged.

Overall the patterns strongly reinforce the position of the Irish as a labour migrant group which cannot simply be categorised as part of the 'Celtic fringe' with Scotland and Wales. At this broad scale, shared whiteness does not appear to give Irish women a privileged position. Indeed the most striking similarity is with the position of African Caribbean women who are also polarised between the caring professions and 'unskilled' personal service. However at a finer grain within these socio-economic classes, there are important differences between the two ethnic groups.

Irish women are much more likely to work part-time in their child-rearing years (Walter 1988) and there is some evidence that they occupy preferred positions in nursing in terms of payscale, areas of work and career structures.

Conclusions

What emerges most strongly from this detailed statistical analysis of the place of Irish-born women in the British economy is their status as labour migrants. This is often forgotten in representations of Irish people as 'the same' on the grounds of whiteness alone. The construction of Britain as a homogenous nation before 1945 and the conflation of 'black' and 'immigrant' in the post-1945 era have combined to erase knowledge of Irish labour. Irish women's work has been in continuous demand, little affected by swings in the economy which have made men's labouring jobs more cyclical and seasonal.

Many of the differences which are used to stigmatise Irish women as inferior versions of 'the same' arise from their position in the labour market. They have been recruited into low-paid domestic work over two centuries specifically to fill gaps left by changing constructions of indigenous women's roles over time. A central theme, which has taken different forms over the course of the nineteenth and twentieth centuries, has been the 'cult of domesticity'. In the mid- and later nineteenth century, Victorian versions were underpinned by an army of female servants, while its re-figuring in the 1950s as part of constructions of Englishness similarly required the back-up of health workers, teachers, replacement full-time industrial workers and domestic 'help'. Because they fill these undesirable jobs it has been easy to represent Irish women as 'dirty' and 'stupid', unable to manage adequate housing conditions or to take 'proper care' of large families because of low incomes and long hours.

Failure to recognise the migrant status of Irish women in Britain contrasts strikingly with their economic positioning in the United States, where the Irish occupied a conspicuous place as the earliest and largest 'free' labour migrant group. Their cultural specificity was recognised and women were applauded for their roles in the upward mobility of their children. In Britain the apparently higher than average rates of upward mobility of second-generation Irish people has been very little investigated or commented on. Where it has, it has been taken as a measure of 'assimilation' rather than an indication of the unusually low base from which the migrant generation started, because demand for 'unskilled' labour required their parents to continue in low-paid occupations.

The changing labour requirements of regions in Britain over the last two centuries have placed Irish-born women and their descendents in sharply different situations. Women recruited to the textile trades in Scotland and Lancashire in the nineteenth century formed a significant part of the workforce. They contributed to unionisation, both because of their numbers and through politicisation over the issue of Home Rule. Many married indigenous men and after several generations are part of the diaspora space of Britain, intertwined in complex ways but not unidirectionally assimilated into an homogenous British identity. This is part of the unrecognised plurality of Britain which has been squeezed out of popular and academic discourse by failure to acknowledge that it has been a country of immigration for centuries.

More recent migrants have been recruited to London and South East England. The large scale of movement in the 1950s made possible distinct neighbourhood clusterings, often based around Catholic schools (Walter 1986). Cultural differences, unrecognised because of the limited equation of 'ethnic' with 'black', were confined to the privacy and safety of individual homes and community groupings.

Part of the paradox of Irish diasporic experience in Britain is that, although Irish people are forcibly included as 'insiders' through non-recognition of their migrant status or cultural difference, they are simultaneously reminded that they do not 'belong' in Britain. In Chapter Five I examine the social placement of Irish women in Britain, particularly the material consequences of the racialised discourses examined in Chapter Three.

Chapter 5

Everyday encounters

Lived realities of racialisation in post War Britain

Irish women are positioned in Britain both by their construction as outsiders to the British nation and by their class positions in the British economy. In this chapter I explore how these racialised and classed gendered identities structure their experience. How do the discursive positions outlined in Chapter Three affect the everyday lives of Irish women in Britain? How are women identified as being 'Irish'? What strategies are adopted in order to manage the negative consequences of identification?

Being fully integrated into the economy is not the same as being treated as socially equal. Diasporas are often articulated by labour demands but there is a striking mismatch between highly fluid economic movements and extremely restrictive social boundaries. As Lavie and Swedenburg point out: 'Capital requires migrant labor but rejects the person and the culture within which abstracted labor is contained' (Lavie and Swedenburg 1996: 6–7). In the case of the Irish in Britain these social exclusions are masked by constructions of racial discourses around the issue of 'visibility' in the post-war period, placing the majority of Irish people within the 'white' category. However this does not prevent them from being identified as different.

The focus in this chapter is on women's experience of being Irish in Britain. Experience is not simply 'what happens' to Irish women in their everyday lives, but is 'a site of contestation: a discursive space where different and differential subject positions and subjectivities are inscribed, reiterated, or repudiated' (Brah 1996: 116). Women interpret their lives according to their own cultural constructions and the discourses available to them. In turn these interpretations can be analysed in terms of the broader social, political and economic processes in which they are placed.

But there will not be a complete overlap between personal experience and collective histories. Experience is thus a process 'continuously marked by everyday cultural and political practices' (Brah 1996: 117). Although anti-Irish attitudes have been identified as deeply-ingrained in constructions of British national identities, these are not experienced in the same way by all women and women's choices of response in particular situations will vary for many reasons, including social position, personality and the specific context.

I focus here on two aspects of everyday encounters which structure Irish women's experience in Britain. The first is on ways in which Irish identities are signalled to non-Irish people so that constructions of Irishness become part of the social interchange. What meanings are attached to distinctive voices, to audibility rather than visibility? Second, I select a particularly important context in the labour migration process, that of nursing. How is Irishness played out both in the construction of women as nurses and in the responses of British people? Finally I begin to consider the much larger question of intersections between diasporic groups, between people with different 'genealogies of dispersion'. These cross-cutting links are an important counterpoint to the focus on Irish/British relations which continues to centre hegemonic British identities. The discourse of minority/majority structures understanding in a binary way which privileges the dominant group, whereas the notion of diaspora space places all its inhabitants in intersecting relationships with each other.

Voices and language

The prime identifier of Irish people to the British is their voices, labelled as having a distinctive 'accent' (Walter 2000). Irish people may recognise each other through a more varied repertoire of signs, including facial features and ways of walking. British people also make connections between Catholic beliefs and Irish origins, and identify specific groups such as Irish Travellers by appearance and context. But in the oversimplified rhetoric of 'race', Irish identities are overwhelmingly signalled to strangers by speech alone. The overlap between black 'visibility' and Irish 'audibility' was illustrated in a comment made to the anthropologist Mary Kells: 'The thing about being Irish in England, Martin told me, reporting a joke he had enjoyed, is

that they don't realise you are black until you open your mouth'
(Kells 1995a: 33).

Voices are a particularly important part of the process by which
Irish people in Britain are constructed as both 'outsiders' and
'insiders' simultaneously. The 'Irish accent' is distinguished by
structure of language as well as simply pronunciation. This sign of
difference is a reminder of colonial 'mastery', a key aspect of
which was the forcible imposition of the English language. It is
the native Irish language which continues to intrude audibly in
syntax and pronunciation as 'accent'. Sentence constructions
which are dismissed as ungrammatical in Britain, and therefore
evidence of poor educational standards, derive from the Irish
language which was banned from use in schools in the nineteenth century.

At the same time deviations from Standard English are used to
label social classes as inferior within the British nation. The deeply
ingrained acceptance of 'accent' as a measure of class positioning
for the population as a whole makes it hard to disentangle racist
responses to Irish voices from those much more widely related to
social class and facilitates the denial of anti-Irish racism in Britain.
It also restricts recognition of Irish cultural difference, which is
reduced to class alone. Widespread resistance to recognition of
the Irish as an ethnic group for monitoring purposes is a consequence of the insistence on 'sameness' which stems from this
elision of Irish difference.

The confusion between race and class in British people's
responses to 'Irish accents' is brought out by contradictions in the
social positioning of their users as external 'others' and their place
in a hierarchy of preferred speech patterns. Whereas constructions
of Irishness locate these identities in opposition to British ones, the
voices themselves are not the ones least-liked in Britain.
Sociolinguistic surveys show that certain Irish accents are preferred
to a number of British ones. In one study Irish accents were placed
fourth out of ten, after Received Pronunciation, Welsh and
Yorkshire, and well ahead of English urban industrial accents
(Trudgill 1983). However, class and rural/urban inflections are also
at play in the approval of a particular subset of 'Irish accents', so that
working-class urban Northern Irish accents are among the most
strongly disliked and it is the 'soft' rural and middle-class urban
Southern dialects which are considered attractive.

Accent thus plays a distinctive, though ambivalent, role in the race/class positioning of Irish people in Britain, but has received very little academic attention as a sign of difference. In part this results from the unquestioned acceptance of accent as a social marker, but it may also reflect theoretical borrowing from the United States experience, where skin colour rather than voice is the dominant mode of differentiation. Although English-speaking was a distinguishing marker of the dominant group in the United States in the nineteenth century, it did not resonate as an imperial 'master' language in the way that it did in Britain. An Irish 'brogue' was certainly part of the image of Irishness presented in cartoons in the nineteenth century United States (see Plate 2.2), but the centrality of immigrants to nation-building meant that variants of English were usual. Indeed adoption of the English language itself was sufficient evidence of 'Americanization' in the early years of the twentieth century.

The taken-for-grantedness of voices is also brought out in the way Irish people are caught unawares by racist responses when they arrive in Britain. Thus 'Irish women describe the surprise and hurt experienced as newly arrived migrants at negative English reactions to something as central to their sense of identity as their way of speaking' (Kells 1995a). This response emphasises the close relationship between the voice and identity. In particular the homogenisation of Irish accents is unexpected. Those from Northern Ireland may find themselves classed as foreign alongside those from the Republic. Middle-class Irish people become subject to the working-class stereotype when their voices are heard.

The labelling of ways of speaking as inferior undermines the dualism of body/reason, since voices cross the boundary between bodies and minds. Voices are physically attached to bodies, usually heard at the same time that the body is seen. However, they express the thoughts in minds and are thus also intimately linked to rationality. When Iris Marion Young (1990) describes oppressed groups as imprisoned in their bodies, she could also be referring to those linked to particular kinds of voices. Although voices can be changed by deliberate adoption of another accent, this is a difficult and painful process.

Voices are also used in specific ways to express British hostility towards Irish people. The most frequent and open form of racial abuse reported by Irish people is verbal harassment. Physical attacks also take place and are much more hidden from view. These include attacks by neighbours and violent reactions by police officers, usually triggered by hearing Irish accents. But more commonplace, across all social classes, are derogatory comments which draw on a fund of negative stereotypes which are learned from an early age.

Language lies at the heart of one of the most powerful stereotypes associated with the Irish, that of low intelligence and stupidity. The content of anti-Irish 'jokes' frequently relies on misunderstanding through a different construction of language to achieve its humorous impact. This are one of the most common expressions of anti-Irish attitudes, so deeply ingrained in British culture that indigenous people often do not recognise it as racism. The climate of acceptance deters Irish people from challenging this treatment, since they are likely to be further ridiculed.

In the Commission for Racial Equality (CRE) research (see p. 114) 80 per cent of respondents reported hearing anti-Irish comments at work, of which the largest proportion was 'jokes' (Hickman and Walter 1997). Irish men were more likely than women to brush off these remarks as inoffensive or 'a bit of fun', reflecting gender differences in patterns of humour, where verbal banter is associated with male rather than female interaction. Irish women usually understood that a racial slur was intended.

> 'You know when they are in a joke, but then you would know when they want you to pick up from it. You got the feeling they didn't like the Irish very much' (Woman school helper, Birmingham).
>
> (Hickman and Walter 1997: 192)

Two-thirds of the sample always found these 'jokes' offensive, but only one-third always challenged the speaker and made their views known. A high proportion of this latter group, which had equal numbers of women and men, was in white-collar occupations, suggesting that this group of Irish people felt more confident in asserting their rights, or perhaps that they could successfully argue their case. The other third had learned that the safest strategy was to keep a low profile, or select their reaction according to the circumstances. Most of the remaining 20 per cent who said they had not heard anti-Irish comments at work were women. This is perhaps surprising since women tend to be part of more mixed labour forces and to interact with non-Irish people face-to-face. It may reflect a decision to ignore such comments and refuse to acknowledge them.

Nevertheless most respondents could identify specific situations in which they experienced hostility towards Irish people in Britain. Representations in the media were frequently mentioned. Both women and men pointed out entertainment programmes where derogatory images and comments were freely expressed. One woman in her fifties from the Irish Republic, now living in London, mentioned:

> Remarks in the paper. A few remarks on TV and in the papers that I don't like. In the *Express* John Junor said that the Irish were pigs and rolling in muck. I can't think of their names. It's very degrading and I don't agree with it.
>
> (Hickman and Walter 1997: 216)

Abusive remarks were also addressed directly at Irish people or made in their hearing. These occurred in a variety of situations, including work, shopping and leisure, usually unrelated to the context. They had become so commonplace that individual instances could no longer be recalled. The cumulative effect was extremely debilitating, as a woman in her forties from Sparkbrook, in Birmingham, explained: 'I wish I'd never had to leave Ireland in the first place. At home, at least you don't find yourself defending yourself. You have to prove yourself all the time, to show you are worth something.' (Hickman and Walter 1997: 218).

Most anti-Irish comments drew on long-established stereotypes, including stupidity, drunkenness, scrounging and membership of an alien religion. These attitudes are so widespread that they are rarely commented on. Significantly many Irish people responding to the CRE survey (Hickman and Walter 1997) replied 'Oh just the usual' when asked about their experiences of anti-Irish attitudes in Britain.

Contexts of anti-Irish hostility

The situations in which hostile attitudes are expressed have important implications for the social positioning of Irish people. Experiences in the workplace, in neighbourhoods and in contacts with service providers affect the resources available to them and the extent to which they occupy shared space with the indigenous or other diasporic groups or enclose themselves within an 'Irish' environment.

Women are particularly likely to work in situations where their speaking voices are heard. Clerical jobs, where Irish women are underrepresented, place them in positions of contrast with Standard English accents. Miriam Jones left her job as a telephone operator in 1954 because her employer was prejudiced against her accent:

> After a while I learned to operate the switchboard and I used to relieve the girl that was on the telephone but the boss didn't like my accent, so I wasn't allowed to answer the telephone any more. I had been in the job about three or four years, but he didn't like the idea of having an Irish accent at the end of his telephone. Most of his customers and friends seemed to like talking to me, but I think it wasn't good for his image to have an Irishwoman on the telephone. That was the first occasion on which I was rejected as an Irish person, and it was a very salutary lesson. I didn't like it. I was very annoyed and I did complain. 'What's wrong with my voice?' I spoke perfectly good English, I was perfectly polite, and I was reassured – 'Oh no, it's nothing like that. It's just your accent. Mr. Sweetman doesn't like your accent. '
>
> (Lennon, McAdam and O'Brien 1988: 65)

Discrimination in the housing market was particularly marked among the 1950s and 1960s migrants, when overt racism preceded the 1967 Race Relations Act. As Webster (1998) points out this exclusion of migrant women from access to housing stands in stark contrast with the construction of new housing estates to give material support to the ideology of the home in which indigenous women figured centrally in the same period. Una Cooper was given a notice to quit by her landlord in London in 1956 and urgently needed to move. She took on the responsibility for finding new accommodation for herself, her husband and four children:

> I'd have read the local paper for adverts. I'd have gone to shop windows but always – 'No coloured or Irish need apply'. It was Houses to let, Flats to let, Rooms to let, but every one of them 'No coloured or Irish need apply'. So I thought, I'll present myself at their doors. But when they'd hear my accent some of them would say, 'It's gone'.
>
> (Lennon, McAdam and O'Brien 1988: 142)

Even after housing had been found, discrimination could continue in the form of neighbour harassment. Again this was directed most strongly against women who spent time in the local area as principal child-carers. Most frequent reports in the 1997 CRE survey were from neighbourhoods with few Irish people, where the isolated families were reminded about their difference.

Necessary interactions with local shopkeepers could also bring reminders of the 'outside' status of Irishness, even where a familiar relationship had been established.

> There are loads of incidents of a small nature, a constant drip of anti-Irishness in, for example, the media, the police. In the local butcher's a few weeks ago, his comment on hearing I'd just returned from Ireland was 'Like the rest of them, just come back to claim your benefits?' (Woman in her forties, London).
> (Hickman and Walter 1997: 219)

At times of IRA activity in Britain, women avoided using small, English-run shops.

> When a bombing or anything like that happens I say 'Thank God for supermarkets', because you don't have to speak, you don't have to ask for a loaf of bread. I do feel intimidated. I wouldn't want to get into a difficult situation, because I wouldn't know how I'd react. When I buy *The Irish Post* I fold it over when I am in the shop – and I like to buy it in an Indian shop. I notice doing all these things, very much so.
> (Lennon, McAdam and O'Brien 1988: 176)

The strength of verbal attacks increased in the aftermath of these episodes, intensifying an already-established climate of hostility. 'The talk in pubs. They'd say "Look at those Irish bastards". A couple of English said it.' (Woman in her forties, Birmingham) (Hickman and Walter 1997: 217).

Such a 'backlash' is clear evidence of the racialisation of the Irish community in Britain. A common ethnic identity is sufficient for all members of the collectivity to share 'guilt by association'. Thus the stereotype of violence and irrationality is applied to all Irish people and 'naturalises' their support, or at least their presumed culpability, for the actions of an extreme few. However it needs to be stressed that anti-Irish attitudes are not simply responses to violent activities associated with the Northern Ireland conflict. They continue to be the subtext of more everyday experiences.

The mass media in Britain play a powerful role in the reproduction, communication and manipulation of stereotypes of Irish people. In a detailed analysis of British newspapers and television coverage, Sarah Morgan argues that these stereotypes, which are both symbolic ('Irish=IRA') and trait-laiden, become naturalised as 'commonsense' through media portrayal: 'The incorporation of racialised stereotypes of "Irishness" into the cultural fabric of the everyday places them firmly within normative, pedestrian reality' (Morgan 1997: 211). In newspaper reports, Irish people in Britain were constructed as a subversive and 'suspect community' (Hillyard 1993) echoing back to nineteenth-century representations of the politically dangerous Irish population. Trait-laden stereotypes include madness, excessive drinking, aggressiveness and stupidity, which again demonstrate remarkably continuity over time. Morgan notes that women were generally absent from the newspaper reports and television programmes. Where present it was typically as love interest for the Irish male protagonists. Irish people are aware of these representations, and frequently mentioned them when questioned for the CRE survey. But they lack the resources to confront and challenge them.

Apart from these negative images there are very few representations of Irish people in Britain in the media to provide alternative images. Marella Buckley comments on the skewed appearances of Irishness: 'Officially, Irishness is something which happens elsewhere and which periodically irrupts into British consciousness at times when Irishness, viewed like a troublesome, quirky child, is seen to demand a response from the weary, perplexed, benign, elder of Britishness' (Buckley 1997: 97).

This 'active unseeing' contrasts with mythopoetic representations of Irishness in other European countries where it is made to stand for the positive characteristics of 'hospitality, beauty, artistry, naturalness and Celtic mystique'. Buckley contrasts it with the commodification of other problematised identities in Britain such as black, lesbian and HIV+ where the desire/repulsion ambivalence is engaged with. However at the end of the 1990s, in tandem with the rise of the 'Celtic Tiger' and aided by the establishment of the Peace Process in Northern Ireland, there was a significant shift. Old stereotypes of drinking and conviviality were brought together in newly-inflected ways in Irish theme pubs and widely-advertised beer brands, so that Irish imagery now floods city centres and tele-vision advertising in Britain as well as globally. However again these identities are exclusively masculine, though doubtless Irish barmaids are invisibly pulling the pints.

Strategies of avoidance

A variety of strategies for limiting the damaging consequences of being identified by their voices is employed by Irish people, includ-ing staying silent, remaining within an Irish environment, and modifying pronunciation. These actions make Irish people less noticeable and are often mistaken for signs of 'assimilation'. Combined with assumptions about whiteness and sameness, restric-tions on the audibility of people identifying themselves as Irish reinforces their invisibility in the discourse of 'race' in Britain during the postwar period, despite ongoing evidence of undis-guised anti-Irish hostility. Constructions of this invisibility are gendered according to the representational and material places occupied by Irish people.

Irish women have developed ways of reducing the impact of the material practices through which racialising discourses are encoun-tered in their everyday lives. Like Pakistani women in Britain in Brah's study, their 'narratives represent a range of responses and strategies – of accommodation, complicity, resistance, struggle, transgression – as they negotiate the many and varying facets of power in their everyday lives' (Brah 1996: 138).

One of the most common responses by Irish women to negative reactions to their voices is silence in public places. This has been particularly true of 1950s migrants, the majority of whom were working-class people from rural areas of Ireland. Many lacked the confidence to challenge their treatment. Maude Casey, in her auto-biographical novel *Over the Water*, described her mother's crippling fear in London in the 1950s, which she attempted to pass on to her children: 'Mammy knows no one in our road. She is so afraid of scornful glances at her Irish voice that she opens her mouth to no one. She says that we should do the same' (Casey 1987: 2).

The IRA bombings in Britain from the 1970s reinforced this fear of recognition, especially after police warnings to 'watch your Irish neighbours'. As a result Irish people have monitored themselves. Yvonne Hayes describes life in London in the 1970s for her parents:

> For Irish people, there's nothing that distinguishes them from being English, as long as they keep their mouths shut. And if you are trying to bring up a family and build a home, you just try and fit in with the establishment and don't put yourself out on a limb too much, so you don't get into trouble.
>
> (Lennon, McAdam and O'Brien 1988: 220)

Irish accents signified membership of a dangerous 'race', sharing inherited violent tendencies and genetically programmed to support any expression of Irish nationalism. In the CRE (1997) survey, women in London reported:

> When I came over at seventeen [1970s], I think you did [conceal an Irish identity] because there was a lot of trouble. Didn't talk out loud, in case it triggered off. But then I decided I didn't care.
> (Irish Republic-born woman in her thirties, Islington, London.)

> When there was a bombing here, I always kept quiet on buses and trains. I was careful. I knew they would recognise my accent.
> (Irish Republic-born woman in her fifties, Lewisham, London.)
> (Hickman and Walter 1997: 211, 208)

The situation in Birmingham at the time of the bombings in 1974 which killed twenty one people, including nine who were Irish, was extreme. One woman in her forties, living in Erdington, described her experience:

> It was dreadful. I never opened my mouth for a week. We were all glad when they picked up someone to blame for it. It was awful. Thank God I wasn't at work. My sister said it was being discussed all the time. I had a pain in my shoulder from being humped.
>
> (Hickman and Walter 1997: 206)

The imagery used to describe this avoidance strategy vividly links silence with bodily retreat into invisibility. A more commonly-used phrase is 'keeping their heads down' so that they would not catch the eyes of English people and be expected to speak. If they opened their mouths, their voices would be hard to hear. A Northern Irish-born woman in Erdington, now in her seventies, recalled the aftermath of the 1974 bomb:

We didn't get a good reaction from the neighbours. If there is trouble you are all tarred with the one brush. Mr H asked if I would like a brick through my window. We kept our heads down and carried on.

(Hickman and Walter 1997: 206)

Silence represents a complex mixture of accommodation and resistance. On the one hand, it is complicit with the British ideology of enforcing sameness and therefore part of a 'double consciousness' which appears to accept that there is no place for Irishness in Britain (Morgan 1997). On the other hand silence denies opportunities for expressions of anti-Irish attitudes by refusing to provide contexts for them.

However the 'double consciousness' could be more fundamentally deforming when Irish women found it too painful to acknowledge their discriminatory treatment. Yvonne Hayes describes her mother's experience, clearly linking the poor treatment by her employers with anti-Irish attitudes:

A lot of Irish women who did domestic work had very bad conditions and were treated badly by their employers. She talks a lot about that, and that kind of anti-Irish feeling comes up now and again when my parents are talking, but a lot of the time they try and pretend it didn't happen.

(Lennon, McAdam and O'Brien 1988: 220)

In the CRE survey (Hickman and Walter 1997) respondents were also asked a broader question about whether they had ever seen or heard anything directed against the Irish in Britain to which they had objected. The impersonal phrasing of the question was intentional, since people often have greater difficulty in talking about their own lives. Only one-third claimed that they had not heard anti-Irish comments in Britain. However they also made it clear that they organised their lives to avoid painful situations, and chose to ignore them. The majority of these were women.

I keep away from trouble (Woman in her sixties from Northern Ireland, Birmingham.)

I can't think of anything. I just mixed in and took no notice.

If you are looking for trouble you'll find it. (Woman in her eighties from the Irish Republic, Birmingham.)

You get comments, but you'd get that with every nationality going. I think older people might be more anti-Irish. I don't know. You do get comments but you just ignore it. (Woman in her twenties from the Irish Republic, London.)

Well, I've heard 'Irish Paddy' and 'Get back to where you came from'. Things like that. It's upsetting. It is hurtful. I never say anything back. What's the point? (Woman in her sixties, London)

(Hickman and Walter 1997: 213-14, 220)

The last speaker demonstrated vividly Sarah Morgan's (1997) notion of 'double silence'. Not only do women avoid speaking, but they censor themselves by not speaking about Irish issues outside safe Irish environments. This pattern begins in childhood; in Mary J. Hickman's study of Catholic schoolchildren in London and Liverpool in the 1980s, 47 per cent of boys, but no girls, reported discussing the political situation in Northern Ireland with school-friends, although in Liverpool more girls talked about this in the privacy of their lives outside school (Hickman 1990: 419).

The corollary of silence in public places is thus a retreat to the comparative safety of Irish environments, especially for working-class Catholics. This reinforces the silencing of Irish voices in Britain. For women who emigrated in the 1950s and 1960s, the Catholic church has provided such a location outside the home. Anne Higgins' family in Manchester 'mixed mainly with other Irish people. I suppose it was our accents, but mainly our religion which set us apart from the rest' (Lennon, McAdam and O'Brien 1988: 146).

Yvonne Hayes also recalled from her childhood in the seventies that Sunday was the only day when her mother took part in a social life outside the family, meeting Irish friends at the social club attached to the church (Lennon, McAdam and O'Brien 1988). These activities are hidden from sight, especially in the areas of new postwar settlement where Catholic congregations were almost exclusively first- and second-generation Irish in composition. In Luton in the 1970s, for example, half of the Irish women inter-viewed based their social life around Catholic parish clubs, whereas in Bolton only 15 per cent belonged to Catholic social organisations

(Walter 1979). Older Irish women, many now widowed, still focus their lives around the Catholic parish. In Bolton, two friends in their sixties, interviewed in 1994, described their parish as the 'mainstay' of their lives, both spiritual and social (Hickman and Walter 1995).

Self-segregation may also be practised by recent migrants, in this case using the secular space of Irish pubs. A woman in her twenties living in Harrow, London, reported:

> It's great if you are working. I wouldn't raise kids here. One Irish person can get a bad name and they brand the rest of us. We go to an Irish pub – well, there's an English bar, but we never mix with them, it's totally separate. The staff are Irish too. We know most of our friends from the pub.
>
> (Hickman and Walter 1997: 213)

However clustering in Irish communities can also lead to identification. Catherine Ridgeway, who arrived in 1928, and found work as a chambermaid, explained that she avoided contact with other Irish people for fear of being seen as politically involved and facing deportation:

> During that period I didn't mix much with Irish people. Mostly English. I think my uncle and aunt put me off. They said, 'Don't get involved in Irish clubs or anything like that', because there was still the political background all the time. As the years went on and I was learning more about the political situation, I still didn't get involved, because you always had at the back of your mind that if anything crops up and you are involved, you might be deported or something like this.
>
> (Lennon, McAdam and O'Brien 1988: 50)

Many respondents to the CRE survey (Hickman and Walter 1997) gave the same reasons for avoiding contact with Irish cultural groups in London.

A more drastic strategy, available only at considerable personal cost, is concealing the difference of the voice. This can take a number of forms, depending on social and personal characteristics of individuals and context. The most extreme response is for Irish people to 'pass' as British by changing their speech patterns, sometimes going as far as taking elocution lessons to make a permanent change. Even middle-class Irish people recognised that this option might be necessary in order to avoid negative reactions. Caroline, a statistician and lecturer in London, felt that: 'you probably have to change your accent and everything [to] be accepted by a lot of English people' (Kells 1995b: 213).

Such attempts to 'pass' take considerable effort. As Magdalene Ang-Lydgate points out: 'Assimilation on the basis of passing is not only a costly experience psychically but also an exhausting one for it depends on constant negotiation of what response is needed, working out what is appropriate and suppressing the inappropriate'(Ang-Lydgate 1999: 181). It may therefore be only partially successful. Philip Ullah interviewed second-generation children in Birmingham and London in 1980–1, who knew people who adopted an English identity to avoid the stigma attached to being Irish.

> P. U. Do any of you know any kids who hide the fact that they are of Irish descent?
> All Yes.
> P. U. Do you all know mums and dads like that?
> All Yes.
> Girl(1) Well, you know, her mum's standing there – I won't say her name – and her mum . . . it's awful 'cause one moment she's speaking all posh and then suddenly she breaks out into bursts of Irish. You've got to laugh at her. She's just making a fool of herself.
> P. U. Why do you think parents are like that?
> Girl(2) Because they don't want to be classed as Irish. They think the Irish are thick.
>
> (Ullah 1985: 314)

In the 1997 CRE survey respondents were asked 'Have you ever felt the need to play down your Irish identity?' A substantial minority (19 per cent) said that they had, most frequently mentioning changing their accents. One woman in her twenties, living in Islington, London, reported:

> At the beginning [I did] because of people's reaction to my accent, taking the mickey out of the way you say words and you don't want to be seen as stupid. So I changed the way I spoke, but not now.
>
> (Hickman and Walter 1997: 211)

Ways in which racism is experienced in everyday life are strongly gendered. The majority of those in the CRE survey who said that they had played down their Irish identity at times were women, suggesting that their lives may involve verbal interaction with the English population to a greater extent than those of men. Women are more likely to be employed in mixed workplaces and to perform services which require personal responses, whether in a professional capacity as managers, nurses and teachers, or as domestic workers, for example in the catering trade. Mothers have to negotiate state services on behalf of families, areas where their rights may be called into question and the hazards of identification assume added significance. Women who work in the home full or part-time also interact with neighbours to a greater extent than men in paid employment. In all these situations Irish voices are heard directly in contrast to English ones.

The variety of reactions recorded here illustrate a range of the responses and strategies identified by Brah (1996). Accommodation was an important strategy adopted at particular time periods, for example the 1950s when anti-Irish racism was more overt and during periods of IRA bombing activity in Britain between the 1970s and 1990s. It might also be necessary for acceptance over the longer term in particular social contexts, such as English middle-class lifestyles. Newly-arrived migrants, confronted for the first time with negative stereotyping, also felt stronger pressures to conform, but later gained the confidence to assert their difference. Others resisted by refusing to put themselves in situations where they would be exposed to ridicule. Interestingly strong resistance was expressed by the second-generation children, whose own voices classified them as 'English' and who blamed their parents for complicity when they attempted, unsuccessfully, to adopt 'posh' accents.

Second-generation identities

Another absence resulting from the identification of Irish people primarily by their voices is that of their English-born children and grandchildren. Despite the Irish cultural influences in their childhoods, the 'English' accents of British-born children have contributed significantly to the mismatch in perceptions of the place of the so-called second generation. This loss 'proves' their assimilation in all other ways and detaches them at a stroke from the Irish-born population. It is taken for granted that children and grandchildren of West Indian and Asian-born parents in Britain will identify themselves within these 'ethnic' groups on Census forms, because the prime identifier of blackness remains, but the 'lack' of an Irish accent has until very recently restricted official recognition of an Irish ethnic group to the migrant generation. Culture is thought to play a significant role in the continuing construction of ethnic boundaries surrounding 'black' groups, but it inexplicably disappears for those who are 'white'. The 'lack' of an Irish accent among children born in Britain can also be misread as evidence that they have no Irish cultural identity and bolsters the view that Irish ethnicity is limited to the first generation of migrants.

Children's way of speaking is strongly influenced by what they hear outside the home, but even where traces of their parents' voices are retained they may be consciously removed at school. Meg Maguire described the role of Catholic schools in detaching second-generation children from their Irish home backgrounds, which included 'correcting' their accents:

> Although the majority of children in my primary school were of Irish descent, our teachers were not. We never learned about Ireland or our history and culture. Our accents were corrected as was our spelling, notably from Mammy to Mummy. Our parents filled in some of the gaps for us and there were Irish dancing lessons in a local community hall for those who could afford the classes as well as the costume. But we were being schooled to be British.
>
> (Maguire 1997: 92)

A marker which does not so readily disappear is that of names. Many Irish surnames are distinctive and remain attached to children with Irish-born fathers and male ancestors, though they disappear very quickly in families where a mother changes her name on marriage to a non-Irish partner. However the practice of giving children Irish first names may be an even clearer sign of parents' intentional preservation of an Irish connection into several subsequent generations. Irish first names are often less anglicised than surnames and stand out more distinctly against common English ones.

English accents reinforce the diasporic in-betweenness of the second-generation. When they return to Ireland children can be mistaken for English people, or at least have their Irish identities challenged by strangers.

> I think they saw me as Irish until the last time I went back. I had had a gap of about six years, the town had grown a bit and there were people there I didn't know. I had to explain to them that I was Irish and they'd say, 'But how can you be Irish, you were born and brought up in England?' It doesn't annoy me when people just ask 'cause that's fair enough as I've got an English accent, but I hate it when you have to start explaining everything. I think I said to someone, if I was born on a boat coming over, it wouldn't make me a fish would it?
>
> (Lennon, McAdam and O'Brien 1988: 222)

But an English accent may also empower second-generation Irish women to demand recognition in ways not open to their mothers. The increasing recognition of Irish ethnic difference during the 1980s and 1990s was given a strong boost by the generation of children of 1950s migrants who had gone through the British education system, often taking part in the expansion of higher education.

Contexts of work: Irish nurses

The experiences of one group of Irish women are now explored in greater detail to illustrate the importance of contextualising Irish women's experiences of living in Britain. A case study of women nurses draws together many strands of the story of diaspora which has been told so far and connects them with racialised discourses about the Irish in Britain. The choice of nursing as a career is related to dominant images of women in Ireland, to notions of caring and self-sacrifice directly reflecting Catholic values. Nurses are archetypical labour migrants, having been actively recruited in Ireland to fill vacancies in Britain for which there is a chronic undersupply of indigenous women because of unfavourable conditions of work.

The study of nurses' experiences provides an opportunity to examine Irish women's place within the diaspora space of Britain at a number of different scales. At the smallest scale these include workplaces, which may be hospitals, health clinics or patients' homes. Irish women are also residents of the surrounding localities and interact in a wider range of social contexts as neighbours, service and leisure users. Moreover the demand for their labour as nurses is quite evenly spread throughout Britain, providing an unusual opportunity to examine regional and local differences in their working experiences.

Nursing is a major occupation of Irish-born women in Britain, accounting for almost a quarter of those in paid work. This gives Irish women's employment profile a bi-polar distribution which differs sharply from that of men. It also contrasts with that of white English-born women. Almost a third of Irish-born women, compared with a quarter of the English-born, are placed in the professional category. The largest section of this professional category comprises nurses, who are an exception both to the invisibility of Irish women in Britain and in having a positive stereotype. Whereas in different circumstances Irish Catholic mothers can be portrayed as 'others', threatening to 'swamp' state services with the demands created by their large families, as nurses Irish women's caring qualities, selflessness and duty, are 'in place' when put to work for the British public good. The positive stereotype of nurses, and especially Irish nurses who appear to magnify the idealised images of patience, good humour and dedication to duty, also brings sharply into focus the co-existence of hostility to the Irish more generally.

However, despite the widely acknowledged coupling of 'Irish' and 'nurses' in public perceptions, very little information is available. Statistical data on Irish nurses is scattered and partial. Lack of an Irish category in ethnic monitoring procedures means that precise numbers are not available. In 1948 40 per cent of nurses in London were Irish according to an article in the *Irish Democrat* (O'Grady 1988: 12). This high figure may reflect severe national shortages in the immediate post-war period, because the proportion in subsequent years appears to be around 10–15 per cent. Recruits to nursing in South East England between 1961 and 1965 included 11 per cent Irish Republic-born, 37 per cent from overseas and 52 per cent born in the United Kingdom (Knight 1965). In the 1971 Census of the whole of Britain, there were 31,000 nurses born in Northern Ireland or the Republic, constituting 12 per cent of the total. In the Whittington Hospital in east London, known as an 'Irish' hospital, 13 per cent of the nurses were found to be Irish-born in a survey in the early 1980s (Doyal *et al.* 1980 1984). However proportions seem to vary markedly between hospitals, some recruiting extensively in Ireland both through formal means and informally, relying on contacts between existing staff and their home areas when need arises.

These numbers indicate not only the demand for Irish women's labour as nurses in Britain but also their oversupply in Ireland. In 1971 Censuses record 19,000 nurses in Ireland compared with 12,000 in Britain. Mary Daniels (1993: 5) suggests four reasons for this situation: the socialisation of Irish women into caring roles, the narrow range of career opportunities open to women in Ireland, the influence of the Catholic education system in channelling girls into a profession ideologically reconcilable with their future roles as wives and mothers, and the higher status of nursing in Ireland. In Ireland nursing has been associated with middle-class status. A fee for training was charged, which excluded those from poorer families. 'My parents could not afford the training fees required in Ireland. I got a place at St Stephen's Hospital, Dublin, but I could not take it up . . . I was the eldest of nine children'. (Walter 1988: 75) Moreover social networks were called into play, again restricting access. 'You had to know the right people to get in . . . if you were a doctor's daughter or a solicitor's you were all right, or from one of the big farmer's' (Daniels 1993: 5).

Nurses are therefore an example of economic complementarity in migration terms. Their 'oversupply' in Ireland for social and ideological reasons is matched by an 'undersupply' in Britain. Britain is able to draw on a ready-made source of labour which has been educated, and perhaps partly trained, in Ireland. Because the demand is fairly evenly spread, variations in Irish women's experiences as nurses in Britain can highlight a range of contextual differences, especially those of region of settlement. Attention has already been drawn to the absence of a comprehensive analysis of Irish nurses within the British health system, and here evidence is drawn from two surveys which can be brought together to suggest possibilities for a comparative approach.

Irish nurses in London

In 1987 a sample of 148 nurses was interviewed in London as part of a wider study of Irish women in the capital (Walter 1989a). The survey used a structured interview schedule and was wide-ranging rather than closely focused. It was intended as a preliminary data-gathering exercise, with limited opportunities for collecting detailed qualitative material.

Responses showed that the nurses were predominantly young, 80 per cent under thirty-two, and had been recruited during the upsurge in demand during the 1980s. Nearly half came from farming families, though in 1981 agriculture accounted for only 18 per cent of the male labour force. This may reflect both a more traditional Catholic childhood socialisation and the paucity of local work opportunities. The nurses had high levels of education, 45 per cent staying at school to eighteen or over and only 13 per cent leaving before they were seventeen. Most had entered nursing directly they left full-time education, clearly having made a decision while at school. The great majority therefore came to train in England, only a few emigrating after qualifying in Ireland. They saw nurse training as the principal reason for emigration and most said they would have preferred to stay in Ireland. Three-quarters had applied unsuccessfully to train there. Those most eager to return if vacancies arose were the newest arrivals, and in all about half said that they planned to return permanently to live in Ireland. Irish women who enter the nursing profession may be strongly socialised along traditional lines, but appear to be pushed out of Ireland by the lack of opportunities in their chosen profession rather than a desire to break out of a restrictive mould.

The reasons given for choosing a career in nursing bear out the relationship between girls' socialisation and choice of this career. By far the most important reason given was a desire to care for others (47 per cent). A number of nurses specifically described their preference as a 'vocation', with clear religious overtones. These reasons contrast with those given in a study of all nurses at the Whittington hospital (Doyal et al. 1980), where prestige and job opportunities were rated most highly. Second-generation Irish women in the sample were also much less likely to mention 'caring' as a reason for their choice.

A number of Irish nurses stressed the sociability of the work, both with other nurses and with patients. This illustrates the corollary of extreme gender stereotyping, which is the importance of homosocial environment for Irish women and men, replicating the separation of women's and men's lives in Ireland. Over half of the nurses surveyed lived in nurses' homes attached to the hospitals in which they worked. Guaranteed accommodation is seen as a major advantage in attracting Irish nurses to Britain and is prominently used in advertising campaigns in Ireland. It helps to explain the young age of Irish women emigrants, whose families feel that they will be safe in a supervised living environment. Marella Buckley (1997: 107) argues that the association between Irish women and live-in accommodation illustrates the '"enclosedness" formally engineered by a coalition of family, community, clergy and government at home together with Catholic clergy and employers in Britain'.

In fact, the majority (83 per cent) of nurses in the London survey were very dissatisfied with their hospital accommodation. They complained bitterly about the disparity between their actual conditioned and the brochures they had been given in Ireland, complete with photographs of modern, well-equipped study bedrooms and glowing descriptions of the catering, sporting and religious facilities. These views replicated the findings of a wider survey of National Health Service homes in Britain in 1988 where 60 per cent of nurses interviewed criticised the quality of their housing, a figure rising to 64 per cent in Inner London.

The extent to which nurses remained within an Irish world was explored. Nearly half (47 per cent) said that their friends were 'mainly Irish' and only 6 per cent that they were 'mainly non-Irish', the remainder being 'very mixed'. Among the Irish-born, 59 per cent of partners were also Irish. When asked about the advantages of being Irish in London, membership of a large Irish community was most frequently mentioned. Some nurses also elaborated on the positive stereotype of Irish nurses:

> Irish nurses have always been highly respected . . . Most Irish people integrate and become valued members of the com-munities in which they live. Irish workers are greatly appreciated in branches of the caring professions because of their natural empathy, and in other occupations involving hard work. They usually mix well and have a good sense of humour (arrived 1949).

> A lot of respect from English people (arrived 1958).

> Irish nurses are held in high regard (arrived 1986).
>
> (Walter 1989a: 87–8)

Women added qualities of their own to the stereotypes, comparing them to others who did not hold the same traits. These included cheerfulness, friendliness, openness, well-developed oral skills and hard work.

> Irish people are much more friendly and good to work with (arrived 1987).

> Having the ability to communicate unlike the majority of Londoners (arrived 1988).

> Irish people generally are more used to hard work and are usually jolly, happier people (arrived 1987).
>
> (Walter 1989a: 88)

However alongside these feelings of being valued and admirable, more than a third of the respondents (36 per cent) reported hostility towards themselves as Irish people. This is a substantial proportion bearing in mind that many people are reluctant to discuss personally embarrassing experiences of discrimination and the politically sensitive issue of political association with the Northern Ireland conflict. Asked about the disadvantages of being Irish in Britain, a quarter gave examples of racist treatment:

> Condescending attitude towards the Irish from the British (arrived 1985).

> Having to tolerate an ignorant bigoted attitude against the Irish . . . Listening to Irish jokes – people assuming that if you're Irish you're stupid (arrived 1985).

> Stigma of the drunken stupid paddies (arrived 1987).
>
> (Walter 1989: 90)

They also mentioned rejection by British people on the assumption that all Irish people are guilty by association with acts of violence connected with Northern Ireland:

> Because of the Troubles in Northern Ireland, people make you feel uncomfortable and unwanted at times (arrived 1986).

Association with the IRA. If anything happens we're all blamed
(arrived 1987).

(Walter 1989a: 91)

Irish nurses thus occupy a paradoxical position. They are in strong
demand for jobs which are increasingly rejected by the white
British-born population, and their 'Irish' feminine qualities are
highly sought after. At the same time they encounter the racist
hostility meted out to all Irish people, regardless of occupation,
education, class or gender.

The migration of highly-educated young women from Ireland
illustrates the economic benefits to Britain of its longstanding connections with Ireland. Not only is the economy saved the expense of
secondary education, and in some cases nurse training itself, but
the culture in which nursing is a high status and valued profession
contributes a dedicated workforce not motivated solely by monetary
rewards. For Irish women the experience is a mixed one. They are
enabled to pursue careers to which they feel deeply committed,
often in the hope that they will be able to return to Ireland after a
short time. But the conditions in which they work, including pay,
staff levels, working hours and accommodation, do not match up to
hopes or expectations. Moreover the attitudes they routinely
encounter are strongly at variance with their own perceptions of
Irish people, and the knowledge, confirmed by patients and colleagues, of their contribution to the health service.

Irish midwives in the Wirral, Lancashire

The second survey was carried out in the Wirral district of
Lancashire in 1991 (Daniels 1993). This involved in-depth
qualitative interviews with fifteen midwives aged between thirty-
eight and seventy. A number of important differences from the
London survey are therefore immediately apparent. The Wirral
Irish women had migrated at an earlier date and were in more
senior positions overall than the London sample. Moreover they
were living in independent accommodation, and all but one had
married English men. Unlike the London sample, the Wirral Irish
women had entered nursing 'on impulse, or almost accidentally,
attracted by the social life enjoyed by sisters or acquaintances, or
as "second best" where families could not afford the desired
university education' (Daniels 1993: 6).

Despite these differences, however, the two samples were similar in a number of respects. Women from rural farming backgrounds predominated and the majority had high levels of education. Most agreed that they would probably have stayed in Ireland if similar opportunities had been available, although in the Wirral sample none now wished to return to live there. This was also true of the majority of older women in the London sample, perhaps indicating that those who wished to return have already done so or that the wish to return fades over time.

However there were important differences in the experiences of the two samples. The Wirral sample appeared to be much less exposed to anti-Irish hostility than the London one. Only four could recall specifically racist incidents, though the effects of the Northern Ireland conflict had been felt. This probably has a strong regional dimension, reflecting the long exposure of North West England to immigration from Ireland, and high levels of intermarriage over several generations. The middle-class Wirral area is also removed from the 'sectarian' hostilities of nearby Liverpool, where a significant level of Orange Order support continues to manifest itself as anti-Catholicism (Neal 1988). None of the women had felt the need to change their way of speaking, as Daniels comments: 'All the women had marked Irish accents' (Daniels 1993: 6).

The Wirral sample felt that they had retained their Irish identities without any difficulty alongside a sense of belonging in England, which was positively appreciated as their 'adopted home'. In fact they preferred to live outside Ireland, with an option to return on holiday as frequently as they liked. They could thus avoid a number of disadvantages of permanent residence in Ireland, and make the most of the advantages. The same strong sense of an Irish identity had been transmitted to their children, the majority of whom would describe this sense as 'very' or 'extremely' strong according to their mothers. Two of these children had moved to live in Ireland as adults and most visited frequently.

Nursing is a distinctive experience of Irish women in Britain. It places them in a professional career structure and enables them to leave home within a secure framework. Class, and the positive evaluation of nursing as an occupation, protect women from many of the disadvantages faced by women with fewer educational qualifications who are forced to take low-paid casual work in large cities. However outside the workplace Irish nurses in London experienced similar levels of hostility to other Irish-born women when their accents identified them. But the two case studies show that geographical location still influences British attitudes to the Irish, and past levels of in-migration continue to resonate into the present.

Diasporic intersections

The racialisation of Irish women has been explored in the binary context of anti-Irish attitudes associated with constructions of Britishness. These emphasise specific relations between Britain and Ireland. However the notion of diaspora space places all inhabitants in a shared location, without prioritising those who construct themselves as the mainstream or majority. Intersections between the Irish and other diasporic groups need to be taken into account. These may include elements of competition but also co-operation.

The extent to which Irish nurses are privileged as white people in their working lives demands much more thorough research. Anecdotal evidence suggests that Irish nurses are likely to be located at higher levels of the nursing hierarchy than African-Caribbean women, for example. Although when Irish women were recruited in the 1950s they were often channelled into the lower-status State Enrolled Nurse category, without being advised that it had poorer long-term prospects than the more prestigious State Registered Nurse qualification, this practice was even more frequently applied to nurses from the Caribbean. Moreover within the hospital system, black nurses are disproportionately located in undesirable sectors such as mental health care and geriatric provision. Surveys which simply categorise nurses according to a black/white binary division exclude the need to subdivide the white category and establish more clearly the extent to which the Irish benefit from a 'white dividend' or in reality are allocated to an inferior position within the white hierarchy.

There are complexities in the relationships between groups racialised in different ways by British national constructions. As the black/white binary has strengthened in the post-war period, the Irish have been placed more firmly within the white population. However during the 1990s there has been growing acceptance by monitoring bodies, especially local authorities in Greater London, that an 'Irish' category can be included alongside 'white' and a variety of black named groupings. In 1994 the CRE endorsed the use of 'Irish' in addition to 'white' as categories.

There is no doubt that, as in the United States, whiteness protects the Irish from specific kinds of racial abuse directed against 'visible' minorities identified by skin colour. Although this abuse of black people is much more nuanced by the particular origins, age, gender and generation of both perpetrators and targets than is acknowledged in the simple black/white binary categorisation, most Irish people are not subjected to the same intensity of physical and verbal harassment. One consequence is the refusal of many white British people to believe that any form of racial harassment is experienced by Irish people.

The taken-for-grantedness of white privilege extends to Irish people themselves. Both the Irish Republic and Northern Ireland have had almost exclusively white populations until very recently. A woman whose mother was Irish and father from Sierra Leone, described visiting Ireland as a child:

> The second time I went I was about fourteen, and I went on my own to stay with my aunt and cousins who used to come over here. But I always felt like an outsider. I think it wasn't only because I'm black, but also because I'm a Londoner, and they thought of me as English. I think I was kept away from the family in lots of ways, obviously because my father's black and my mother's a bit of an outsider because of it. There was no contact between my dad and my mum's family.
> (Lennon, McAdam and O'Brien 1988: 213)

Outbreaks of racist hostility against non-white asylum seekers in the Irish Republic have occurred on an unprecedented scale in the late 1990s, although extreme racialisation of Irish Travellers has been endemic for centuries (Mac Laughlin 1995).

Racist attitudes towards non-white people can also interact with anti-Irish experiences in Britain to produce hostility towards black people. Yvonne Hayes, a second-generation Irish woman in London who gives an account of her own difficulties in establishing an Irish identity for herself, observed:

> If you look at the National Front, there are kids in it who have got Irish surnames. I'm sure a lot of them are born to Irish parents and must have gone through these changes like me, but they come out of this phase in the end having completely lost their identity and just being English. They get involved with

the National Front through being skinheads at that adolescent stage . . . perhaps anti-Irish feeling and jokes make them feel bad about their identity – but whether they identify as Irish or not, they're white. Maybe being anti-black seems like an answer if they want to build themselves up. But then, to be in the National Front you could end up hating Irish people as well, and not identifying with them.

(Lennon, McAdam and O'Brien 1988: 213)

In other circumstances however, alliances are forged between Irish groups and individuals and other racialised populations. Shared histories of discrimination and deprivation can lead to collaboration. There was an earlier history of co-operation between Irish and other disadvantaged groups in pre-Second World War inner cities. Anne Higgins describes a close relationship between the Irish and Jewish communities, two 'subaltern white' groups in Manchester in the 1930s:

The Jews and the Catholics in Manchester were in the same ghetto in the north, Cheetham Hill Road, and they were very much sympathetic towards each other as minorities. We had Jewish girls at school, I had a friend who was Jewish, my mother worked for a local doctor who was a Dublin Jew and our doctor was an Irish Jew, from Limerick. One of the great Jewish heroes of the post-war years, as far as we were concerned, was Leslie Lever, a Labour MP who had grown up in St Edmund's Parish among the Irish. He was also Lord Mayor of Manchester and made a great issue of being pro-catholic/Irish.

(Lennon, McAdam and O'Brien 1988: 147)

This had some echoes in the post-war period in London where much higher rates of marriage are recorded between African Caribbean men and Irish women than with white British-born women, echoing the partnerships recorded in New York in the nineteenth century (Walter 1988; McAdam 1994; Hodges 1996). In London in the 1980s, Homi Bhabha describes a situation where religious intolerance in the white English majority society was intensifying:

In the aftermath of the Satanic Verses affair in Great Britain,

Black and Irish feminists, despite their different constituencies, have made common cause against the 'racialization of religion' as the dominant discourse through which the State represents their conflicts and struggles, however secular or even 'sexual' they may be.

(Bhabha 1994: 2)

These cross-cutting positions were evident in the responses given by participants interviewed for the CRE survey (1997). Respondents in London and Birmingham, matched with the range of Census characteristics of the Irish-born in the 1991 Census, were asked 'Do you think the Irish should be recognised as an ethnic group?' The majority, with equal proportions in London and Birmingham, answered 'Yes' (59 per cent). A minority (28 per cent) gave a firm 'No' and the remainder (13 per cent) were ambivalent.

The reasons given in the follow-up question throw important light on the attitudes behind these responses. People giving a positive answer underlined the similarities they perceived between the situation of the Irish and those from the 'visible minorities'. Their comments could be grouped into four categories. The largest group (50 per cent of those favouring an ethnic label) drew attention to the similarities between their own position and that of others, especially African-Caribbean and Asian labour migrant groups and their descendents. They made the point that Irish people are treated as outsiders, but not given the recognition that can be claimed by other groups. Irish experience of racialisation was excluded from public discourse, leaving no mechanisms through which it could be countered.

Because there's an awful lot of comments, racist remarks, discrimination. With the black person, it's 'You're racist', and why not for the Irish? Had to put up with an awful lot of abuse and racism. Should be like any other nationality, any other culture. (Woman from the Irish Republic, Islington, London, aged 30–39).

(Hickman and Walter 1997: 223)

A second category claimed entitlement to benefits now accorded to 'visible' minorities, which were also needed by Irish people because of the similarity of their socio-economic position. Again the problematic situation of the Irish arising out of the 'myth of homogeneity' of whiteness underlay the comments made. Inequality in the British response to the specific needs of migrant workers and their families was the underlying theme.

> There's an awful lot of benefits given to ethnic groups that the Irish don't come into. There are those missing out on benefits. In comparison to other groups the needy Irish miss out.(Woman from the Irish Republic, Erdington, Birmingham, aged 50–59).
>
> (Hickman and Walter 1997: 223)

Third, a sizeable group of respondents favouring recognition felt that the contribution of the Irish as labour migrants was not acknowledged. They believed that the positive value of Irish manual work was taken for granted, while English people were quick to condemn Irish benefit claimants as 'scroungers'.

> Why not? They built the hospitals and the roads, so they should get something. I said it to somebody. They are naming roads after Asian people, I said 'Why not Irish people – they built the roads! McAlpine Way!' (Woman from the Irish Republic, Erdington, Birmingham, aged 60–69.)
>
> (Hickman and Walter 1997: 225)

Finally, a number of respondents believed that Irish cultural difference was not understood by the British. This illustrates the incorporation of Ireland within a 'British Isles' or 'Celtic fringe' framework in which Irish characteristics are seen as an inferior variant of the metropolitan norm, rather than culturally distinct.

> We have huge cultural differences from the English. We are a totally different race and should be recognised. More councils should recognise this. It's not a hate thing of the English – I have grown to like the English. (Woman from Northern Ireland, Islington, London, aged 30–39).
>
> (Hickman and Walter 1997: 225)

In contrast to these positive demands for an ethnic identification, a number of respondents were uncertain whether to support this view. Some mentioned that the large numbers and long residence of Irish people in Britain had reduced their feelings of difference, perhaps reinforcing the earlier observation that those living in Irish neighbourhoods are less exposed to harassment. However another strand to this ambivalence was a reluctance to take on the negative connotations of the 'ethnic' label.

Attention should also be paid to the reasons given by those who would definitely prefer not to identify themselves as Irish. Just over one quarter (28 per cent) of the respondents in the survey did not support the idea of a separate 'Irish' category. However only a very small proportion (6 per cent) said that there was 'no problem' and therefore no need to record such information. Many more feared that identification would cause difficulties and preferred the strategy of keeping a low profile and integrating into British society.

> Because when people are recognised as such it causes problems and other things come up (Woman from the Irish Republic, Islington, London, aged 30–39).
>
> (Hickman and Walter 1997: 227)

The issues raised by these interviewees question any quick dismissal that the results are inconclusive. They illustrate the contradictions experienced by Irish people who are denied recognition yet constantly reminded that they are outsiders. A desire to remain anonymous can be a strategy for protection rather than a denial of difference.

Conclusions

Racialisation is experienced by Irish women in very varied ways. As Ruth Frankenberg (1993) explains, 'the word *experience* describes the production of meaning at the intersection of material life and interpretative frameworks' (author's emphasis). Women not only live in very different material worlds, but interpret their situations differently. Indeed experiences are re-interpreted in the telling.

Individual women's interpretation of attitudes and events depends on a range of factors. There are complex interconnections between time and place which structure both events and the discourses used to explain them. Time is a key variable in many ways, including the historical period in which Irish women have lived in Britain, which has affected the specific forms taken by the political relationship between Britain and Ireland and the presence of other diasporic groups. Age, length of residence and generation are significant variables. The diaspora space of Britain is also highly differentiated. Nurses in London had different experiences from those in the Wirral, though class and period of arrival added more complex differentiation. Women living in Birmingham in 1974 were subject to an extremely hostile 'backlash' after the IRA pub bombings.

The issue of whiteness has had a largely unacknowledged impact on Irish women's experiences in post-war Britain. It has signalled a sameness, which has ruled out discussions of racialisation. The lack of recognition of hybridity of Irish identities in Britain is related to a linear view of the migration process in which Ireland no longer plays a part. Integration of Irish women through their labour is taken as a sign that placement is complete and that displacement has no relevance in their lives. Locating Irish women in a diaspora framework, however, provides a space within which social complexities and ambiguities can be explored. For Irish women in Britain, interpretative frameworks draw on discourses and material lives in both Ireland and Britain, which continually collide, intersect and change. Because of Irish women's 'double silence', evidence of displacement remains largely hidden. In the next chapter I examine ways in which Ireland has ongoing relevance in women's lives.

Chapter 6

Meanings of home
Identities and belonging

The notion of 'home' brings together key themes of this book. It has specific resonance for migrant women who are simultaneously linked to a homeland of origin and to settled homes at places of destination. Ways in which ties to these connected but contrasting places are represented discursively and negotiated materially are central to diasporic identities. Homes imply places of belonging at different scales, from the global to the local. Some aspects of belonging are actively chosen by women to express their feelings of identity, but others are imposed on them by constructions of their gendered positionings in society.

Two sets of ideas are brought into relationship by an exploration of the meanings of home for Irish women in the diaspora. The first involves the place of home in conceptualisations of diaspora. Although dispersion is foregrounded in the notion of diaspora, home is implicit, a necessary counterpart rather than a binary opposite. As Brah argues: 'The *concept* of diaspora places the discourse of "home" and "dispersion" in creative tension, *inscribing a homing desire while simultaneously critiquing discourses of fixed origins*' (Brah 1996: 192–3, author's emphasis).

Dispersal must be from somewhere, however distant or mythical, and the names of diasporic peoples usually highlight this connection. The 'Irish diaspora' firmly foregrounds Ireland as a homeland even for fifth and sixth generation Irish-Americans. But diaspora also involves the creation of new homes, an entitlement to claim the area of settlement as one's own and a state of 'feeling at home' (Brah 1996). Clifford's (1994) definition of diaspora as 'dwelling-in-displacement' emphasises the coexistence of these two forms of home. The 'place' which is present in the notions of both placement and displacement is 'home'. Lavie and Swedenburg describe the 'doubled relation-ship or dual loyalty that migrants, exiles and refugees have to places – their connections to the space they currently occupy and their continuing involvement with "back home"' (Lavie and Swedenburg 1996: 14).

The coexistence of two places of identification is thus a key facet of diaspora which fundamentally challenges hegemonic notions of inclusion and exclusion based on assimilation. Assimilation is a concept based on binary categories of belonging which involve identification with the society of the destination. It invokes fixed boundaries between place-based cultures which represent the gradual termination of relationships that are deemed threatening to the unity of the centre. Those who are seen as unassimilated or unassimilable are told to 'go home', clearly signifying that only one home is assigned to them, that outside the nation. These understandings of home as bounded and unchanging reflect traditional definitions of place: 'The most common formulations of the concept of geographical place in current debate associate it with stasis and nostalgia, and with an enclosed security' (Massey 1994: 167).

Massey argues that ethnicity and gender are deeply implicated in the ways we inhabit and experience place. She asks whose iden-tities are supported by definitions of place which emphasise stability, oneness and security, and suggests that the answer is pri-marily white western males. In societies where genders are constructed as highly differentiated, boys need boundaries to separate themselves from their mothers and it is masculinity which is particularly threatened when boundaries dissolve. Colonised peoples have not known their homelands as safe, stable places but have experienced invasion by imperial violence, and even been displaced by slavery and involuntary emigration. However Massey's reference to 'white' once more excludes the Irish experience of colonisation and its consequences.

There are thus strong overlaps in understandings of place and home, in which women stand as a metaphor for continuity, reliabil-ity and authenticity and from which men can make journeys, but expect to return to a comforting base. These overlaps seem to imply that the term 'women migrants' is contradictory, which has con-tributed to the overlooking of women in migration studies.

As Massey points out, there are other ways of imagining places; 'Of course places can be home, but they do not have to be thought of in that way, nor do they have to be places of nostalgia. You may indeed have many of them' (Massey 1994: 172). This chimes with Brah's (1996) ideas about the 'multiplacedness of "home"' which is not anchored in the place of settlement but combines the local and global, and is an important aspect of diasporic identities. The concept of diaspora thus re-orientates conventional notions of place and exposes their ideological underpinnings. Homes and places could be thought of as meeting-places where the outside and inside intersect in ever-changing ways, rather than fixed containers of particular groups of people whose characteristics need control and surveillance.

The second set of ideas focuses more directly on connections between homes and particular kinds of identities. The most widely recognised is that of gender. The phrase 'a woman's place is in the home' denotes simultaneously a social position and a geographical location, and implies the binary opposite for men. Massey argues that 'the attempt to confine women to the domestic sphere was both a specifically spatial control and, through that, a social control on identity' (Massey 1994: 179). It prevented women from having access to an independent income, but also restricted women's knowledge of alternative ways of living in worlds not defined by husbands and families. At the same time, women were needed to manage the home as a place of security and safety for men, which explains its characterisation as a stable, symbolic centre rather than a place of control and labour. Masculine definitions of both the home and its opposites – the street and the city – have been accepted as universally applicable. In reality 'the characterization of place as home comes from those who have left', usually men (Massey 1994: 166). Similarly, more anxiety about the uncontrolled aspects of city life, that is life outside the home, has been expressed by men than women. Escape from home may therefore represent freedom for women, but a frightening loss of boundaries for men.

But 'race' and ethnicity also cut across these gendered meanings. Whereas homes may signify control and imprisonment for women in dominant societies, they may represent places of safety for racialised groups whose physical and cultural integrity is threatened by the dominant group outside. They can also provide subversive sites where valued aspects of the culture, disallowed in the dominant culture, are maintained and passed on to children (hooks 1991: 42).

These gendered and racialised meanings of home are explored here in the context of the Irish diaspora. Meanings of home for women in the Irish diaspora can be examined by connecting their senses of identity with particular places. As Katherine Woodward points out, the construction of identities links wider social structures with individual experience:

> Identities draw on a multiplicity of sources, including nationality, ethnicity, gender, sexuality, generation and locality. For individuals, identity links the subjective and the social, giving 'a sense of who we are and how we relate to others and the world in which we live'.
>
> (Woodward 1997: 1)

These identities are 'always plural and in process' (Brah 1996: 196). They change over lifetimes and configure differently in different contexts.

Diasporic women are thus placed in a paradoxical relationship to home. It can be a source of containment and fixity, rendering women invisible,and linking them to the mundane and routine. But it can also be the basis for challenging dominant cultures both outside and inside their own ethnic group. Issues of identity and belonging are thus raised for diasporic women by their relationships with home. These relationships are different for migrant and later generations of Irish women.

Identities of displacement: Ireland as 'home'

In this section I examine ways in which Irish women's identities in Britain are constructed around continuing connections with Ireland. All those living outside Ireland who identify themselves as 'Irish' are in some way displaced. There is a continuing tie which connects them significantly to a place of origin elsewhere. The tie may take a variety of forms, including physical presence in Ireland before migration and during subsequent return visits. There may also be indirect contact, such as sending money to sustain family members who remain there, maintaining personal connections through writing letters, telephoning, electronic communication or reading newspapers and providing hospitality for visitors from home. Finally, ties may be maintained through memory, drawing on real or mythic events which took place in Ireland, including national and family histories.

These ties cannot easily be disentangled from each other but to help to analyse them, themes which link them can be identified. They are distinctively gendered in ways which reflect the place of women in Irish society, as well as in areas of destination. Ireland is experienced as home at several scales, most frequently as family space at the household level, as a neighbourhood peopled by kin and neighbours, and as national space.

Displacement takes very different forms for Irish people living in the United States and Britain. Whereas until recently the move to the United States has been seen as likely to be permanent, the closeness of Britain means that Irish people can make frequent visits and need not make a commitment to remain. Many post-war migrants give this as a reason for preferring Britain, and it strongly influences ways in which Ireland figures in the lives of Irish-born people, their children and even their grandchildren. Marella Buckley argues that the:

> unshakeable sense of continued belonging to their native neighbourhood in Ireland must be recognised as a distinct feature of the Irish community in Britain, particularly those from rural areas in Ireland. Geographical proximity to Ireland may foster this nostalgia with a vividness which the Irish in the United States or Australia must do without.
>
> (Buckley 1997: 112)

Another contrast is that the tracing of family histories is much more strongly pursued by Irish-Americans than by British people of Irish descent. This is evidence of the acceptance, and indeed celebration, of hyphenated identities in the United States as well as the recognition of immigration as a central part in American non-First Nation identities. It reflects the higher esteem in which Irish origins are held in those countries and greater retention of knowledge in families, as well as a symbiotic relationship between ethnicity and national belonging. The absence of a category of Irish-British and the assumption of assimilation after the migrant generation, make tracing Irish ancestry more difficult and problematic in Britain, if it is desired.

Family homes: childhoods in Ireland

Family and home are two interlinked notions which feature strongly in the nationalist discourse of Ireland. They were used symbolically to represent the independent nation as self-sufficient and bound by close common ties of heredity and support. The ideal form was the farm family, which stood in stark contrast to the anomie of urban Britain. Ireland was represented by the rural west, where images of places as stable, bounded and unchanging were underpinned by generations of the same family 'keeping the name on the land' by passing it from father to son. Both notions were thus strongly gendered, while appearing to combine groupings of women and men in mutually beneficial relationships.

Ciaran McCullough (1991) argues that the ideology of the family was promoted in order to stabilise a society which was in reality full of tensions, including land disputes between neighbours and family disputes over inheritance. What appeared to be a well-functioning system which led to continuity and order, and was presented in this way in the classic work of the United States anthropologists Arensberg and Kimball (1968), was in reality one where gross inequalities between siblings were disguised. Children worked without pay on the land 'for the family' when only one son could ulti-mately benefit. In particular women were disempowered through a set of interlocking patriarchal traditions, that included inheritance, work patterns, food consumption and social interactions.

In the case of emigration from Ireland, this is reflected in the greater ease with which women leave, and the smaller numbers who return (Brody 1973; Walter 1991). Women's looser attach-ment to the family land has contributed to their leaving Ireland at younger ages than men. Girls have been able to find live-in jobs in Britain as nurses, domestic and hotel staff, and therefore leave with parental agreement. The commonest age group is fifteen to nineteen, whereas among men it is nineteen to twenty-four. In rural areas there has been no role for girls in helping fathers on the farm when they leave school, though boys may continue the pattern for a few years, often uncertain about which son would inherit the property. According to the Commission on Emigration and Other Population Problems (1956) young women were also more determined to reject stifling rural life and find independence as soon as they could support themselves financially outside their family.

Even for urban populations in Ireland, the ties between family and home are given special resonance in the teachings of the Catholic church, to which the overwhelming majority of people belong. The model is 'the holy family' whose most prominent parent is the Virgin Mary. Through exhortations to model themselves on the self-sacrificing, undemanding example of Mary, mothers are therefore given the greatest responsibility for the welfare, spiritual as well as material, of their children. Women who do not become mothers are given no place in the picture of acceptable national life (Byrne 1997). Yet permanent singleness among both women and men is a distinctive feature of Irish demographic life. Although it declined from 28 per cent of women aged thirty-five to forty-four years in 1851 to 12 per cent in 1992, these are high proportions by European standards.

Family homes therefore resonate strongly for Irish migrants in their images and memories of Ireland. This is reinforced by the stage in the lifecycle at which most emigrate, that is as young adults at the start of their working lives. Displacement from Ireland coincides with displacement from the childhood home as they reach adulthood. The majority of migrants will have lived in only one part of Ireland before leaving the country, and rural children are likely to have lived in only one house throughout their childhood, leading to an intense involvement with a small local area. Mary Kells, in her ethnographic study of young Irish middle-class migrants in London, counts early formative experiences in Ireland as one of the two 'most basic consensual emphases' of Irish identity for her informants, the other being a shared cultural heritage. She found that childhood was a key source of Irish identification: 'the aspect that seemed the most compelling for my informants is the fact that this ethnicity is woven in with early, formative experiences in Ireland, which are not easily forgotten' (Kells 1995a: 19).

These childhoods are strongly marked by gender. As well as the norms conveyed by family roles, schooling has emphasised highly gender-differentiated expectations. For some girls and women, homes have also been sites of sexual abuse and other forms of domestic violence. This has been hidden behind doors with the added connivance of the Catholic church, and is only very recently being brought into the open (McKiernan and McWilliams 1997; Meade 1997). Taboos on discussion of these issues, and of the wider question of abortion, have meant that the extreme measure of emigration has been the only means of escape (Kelly and Nic Giolla Choille 1995; O'Carroll 1995).

A relationship defined most intensely in childhood to one's place of origin has important consequences. As time passes, memories become increasingly detached from the contemporary character of the places one knew as a child. When asked whether they intend to retire to Ireland at the end of their paid working lives, women often say they would not want to go back because it is 'no longer the same place'. However, many continue to pay frequent visits, especially to visit their mothers and to keep up family contacts for their own British-born children.

Much of the work of maintaining contacts between Britain and Ireland falls on women's shoulders. Telephoning relatives in Ireland is usually done by women on behalf of families. King and O'Connor (1996) found that over three-quarters of their sample of fifty Irish-born women in Leicester called at least monthly, and half called weekly. This is costly, especially for women on low incomes. Maintaining connections is 'another layer of their everyday life in England' (Gray 1996c: 25) which is often invisible to the outside observer. It may involve Irish women in 'complex and emotional processes of translation as one culture comes into contact with another', for example explaining and justifying family commitments in Ireland when a crisis means that women have to ask for leave from work (ibid.: 26).

Visits to Ireland: second-generation women in Britain

Many Irish-born women migrants also have a phase of intense relationship with Ireland if they have children of their own. Thus the importance of childhood memories also affects the formation of the Irish identities of the second generation, through holiday visits to Ireland when they are young. Migrant women who marry in Britain and give birth to children, return to their own families and relatives in Ireland, often for a long summer holiday period. Margaret Collins recalls the effort required to organise such visits.

> We had four children altogether and they were brought up very conscious that they were Irish. I brought them to Ireland every year, I never missed a year, and we'd go for the whole six weeks. That was no joke – it was such an ordeal – the train

> journey to Heysham and then all night on the boat to Belfast,
> with small children and two suitcases! I had to bring summer
> clothes, winter clothes, wellies, the lot.
>
>   (Lennon, McAdam and O'Brien 1988: 107)

Fathers often joined the family for part of the time, but the
requirements of paid employment have usually limited the time
they could spend. Only families which have migrated as a unit,
leaving no close relatives in a homeplace in Ireland, lack sustained
periods of return to Ireland.

These visits may be among the most positive reinforcements of
their Irish identity for second- and subsequent-generation
children. They are associated with holiday periods and summer
weather (always an important consideration in rainy Ireland).
Moreover they are underpinned by the welcome offered by relatives, who feel that their way of life is validated by migrants' choice
of return visits to their home area (Brody 1973: 41). Meg Maguire
describes the difficult journey from London on the 'cattle boat',
which was followed by time when the children were 'freed to
spend days wandering in the fields and playing in the hay and
barns of neighbouring families . . . At these times we "knew" powerfully that we were Irish' (Maguire 1997: 91).

Children may even be sent to live with their Irish grandparents
for longer periods, perhaps to ease financial burdens on large
families in Britain but also in the belief that they will have a safer,
healthier childhood. Anne Higgins described the complex web of
family relationships which meant that as a child she spent various
periods of time in Ireland as a child.

> My mother and us children visited Ireland almost annually. I
> spent a year there when I was four years old because my grand-
> mother was very ill and my mother went to look after her. Then
> I spent a year there at the outbreak of war, as an alternative to
> evacuation. I loved being in the country . . . I rather wanted to
> stay in Ireland. I became very fond of my aunt when I went to
> stay with her on my own, and I was spoilt there you see.
>
>   (Lennon, McAdam and O'Brien 1988: 149–50)

But the 'English' accents of second-generation children can cause
comments outside the family, as Yvonne Hayes described (see
Chapter 5). There is a very different reaction to American-English

accents heard in Ireland, where it is immediately assumed that the speaker is of Irish descent.

Frequent return to their Irish roots is only available to the children of migrants settled in Britain (their cousins in the United States have had few or no opportunities for this high level of contact). The very naming of these children as the '*second* generation' implies that they have a primary relationship with Ireland rather than Britain.

National belonging

Childhood ties to home are to specific houses and neighbourhoods rather than to the notion of 'Ireland'. Although the experiences are specifically Irish, reflecting a particular constellation of ideologies, in the absence of an 'other' against which to compare them, they remained unnamed. Migrants recall their surprise at learning they were 'Irish' when they arrived in Britain and first encountered British constructions of Irish stereotypes. This labelling may be particularly acute and unsettling for those originating in Northern Ireland whose official nationality is British.

However, discourses of the nation – which are embedded in a range of public debates – inevitably structure senses of belonging at the national scale, whether this is explicitly recognised by individuals or not. Formal education imparts a strong sense of what it means to be Irish (Johnson 1992). In fact Mac Laughlin argues that in Ireland young people have been socialised in a climate which devalues the sense of national belonging by presenting emigration as a positive choice for the young and enterprising. This contrasts with the situation in other small nations in Europe where 'the nation still anchors young adults in the national economy' (Mac Laughlin 1997: 205). He shows that after a period of intense nationalist expression from the 1920s to the 1950s, in which emigration was linked to the colonially-deformed economy of Ireland, a sharp change took place in the 1960s when a revisionist view began to represent emigration as voluntary, individualised activity. The current representation of emigration as 'global' similarly devalues Ireland as a place to live.

Irish women have also had a particularly problematic relationship with the notion of homeland. Although women are apparently identified with the country and nation through the trope of Mother Ireland, the image can be read as that of a mother who has failed her daughters. Those who have had an economic or social need to emigrate have not been given an appropriate role model. Whereas boys need to separate themselves from their mothers in order to construct their independent masculine identities, so that for them emigration from Mother Ireland is an appropriate metaphor, women are abandoned by a nurturer with whom they could identify and should expect to remain connected (Hartsock 1983: 296).

A specific example of the lack of support and protection offered to women by the Irish state is the restricted range of reproductive choices available. Significantly this has been in the very realm of choices about motherhood, which continue to be claimed as religious and national rather than individual prerogatives. Marella Buckley shows that whereas Irish men could retain a strongly bounded sense of Ireland, Irish women's map has always included Britain:

> Large proportions of Irish women 'complete' their inner picture of reproductive life choices available to them in Ireland by 'supplementing' them with the possible option of availing of British social services and climates. Thus, most Irish women know that if they needed an abortion or a non-accusatory climate or childbirth or a relationship, one available option is to try to get to England to find it. This means that mainland Irish women's inner mapping of their country's relationship to Britain is silently, but urgently, different to that of Irish men. Britain, or more usually England, fringes their experiences of their own country with a sort of virtual reality of possible escape-hatches in case of reproductive crisis. This unofficial, inner map shades in an extra, politically-loaded dimension which utterly differentiates their potential or actual migration from those of their male counterparts.
>
> (Buckley 1997: 122)

Hegemonic discourses of nation and national identity in Ireland are apparently ungendered making it difficult for women to locate their own experiences within them. Drawing on her interviews with Irish women in London in the 1980s, Breda Gray (1997) argues that these narratives are so powerful that they 'overwhelm' migrants' particular experiences as women. These are left as 'silences, gaps and tensions' in the accounts they give of their experiences of Irishness and emigration. She identifies three dominant stories arising from her research with Irish women: bodily relocation, emigration as a normal part of Irish life, and the representation of reasons for leaving in terms of career opportunities. But these narratives leave out parts of women's lives which can hardly be talked about.

Among these missing elements are the experiences of women who find they can belong outside Ireland, preferring the anonymity of a foreign city and freedom from interference in their lives. Another set of experiences which is not acknowledged in the dominant view is the 'ongoing pain, loss and re-configuration of family and friendship relations that emigration brings about' (Gray 1997: 219). Hegemonic constructions of Ireland as 'the only place you can belong' limit the identifications open to migrant women and clash with the reality that many need to leave.

Whatever women's own feelings about belonging to Ireland, it is also an identity constructed for them in Britain, where there is always a possibility that they will be told to 'go home'. The threat of forced repatriation, mooted at times of high unemployment or political conflict, is a reminder that nationality can dictate the 'homes' in which people are entitled to live (Glynn 1981).

Memories and stories

Memory reproduces connections for migrant women and allows information and feelings to be transmitted, especially to children and friends, largely through conversation. Both family and national histories are passed on in this way.

> My father was a republican, so he told me lots of stories about 1916, the Civil War, Michael Collins and other people he'd met while he was in Dublin. That was the high point of his life probably, that exciting period between 1912–1928 and he talked a lot about it. He was a great storyteller naturally and he told us stories every night when he took us to bed . . .
>
> Looking back on it, I suppose there was a difference in the kinds of stories my mother and father told. It's only since I've thought about it that I've realised this difference. My father's stories were mainly about the 1916 and 1922 events and Irish history from way back, whereas my mother's stories were about her family, her brothers and sisters, her aunts and

uncles, her great-aunts and grandmother. She talked about what great-aunt Lucy did and what Aunt Julia did and her stories were all concerned with families. It was she who kept close contact with our relatives and who invited our cousins to stay when they first came over to find work. My father relied on my mother even to send cards to his relatives at Christmas.
(Lennon, McAdam and O'Brien 1988: 148)

Family accounts may be the only source of Irish history available to Irish people born in Britain. Very little Irish history is taught in British schools, and what is taught is usually from a British perspective (Hickman 1995; Maguire 1997). Hickman (1990) also found that fathers were a particular source of historical information in discussions about Northern Ireland in Irish homes in London and Liverpool.

Ancestor-searching is a specific form of recontructing family narratives, drawing on documentary evidence and oral histories. The conscious seeking of links with Ireland represents yearnings to be connected with an imagined past. By far the largest numbers are from North America, Australia and New Zealand. Nash (1999) argues that at first sight this movement appears directly opposed to the increasing academic and political popularity of ideas about diaspora, which emphasise fluid relational identities rather than the 'blood and soil' of genealogy. However overseas visitors have discovered greater complexity through their searches which replaced the simplified and romantic versions of Irish history with which they had begun.

Identities of placement: homes outside Ireland

Diaspora involves feeling 'at home' in the area of settlement while retaining significant identification outside it. Catherine Ridgeway summed up the ease with which both senses of belonging could be experienced without ambivalence: 'I never wanted to leave London. I went home regularly, but I saw England as my home' (Lennon, McAdam and O'Brien 1988: 50).

Feelings of at-homeness outside Ireland are gendered. Irish men often express a stronger desire to return to Ireland than women. In a sample of 132 people I interviewed in Bolton and Luton in the early 1970s 76 per cent of women but only 60 per cent of men saw themselves as permanently settled in Britain. Indeed in the 1970s when there was a net immigration to Ireland from Britain, significantly more men than women returned. This reflects the positive benefits which have accrued to women through migration, including the freedom to develop a better sense of their gender and sexual identities and to find paid work outside the home (Gray 1997). Women also regard themselves as permanently settled in Britain once their children are established in schools and working lives, the more so when there are further generations.

Placement is at a number of scales, from the smallest that of the individual household, through the locality and finally to a sense of belonging to the country in which they have settled. Senses of belonging interact at these different scales in a number of important ways.

Family homes in Britain

Households of Irish women in Britain are the sites where different aspects of diasporic identities are brought together. They are the physical expressions of placement, of settlement in Britain. At the same time they are places where Irish cultural difference can be most fully expressed. Moreover hybridities, which develop over time are worked out in the home, especially as subsequent generations negotiate their different relationships to the different types of home with which they can identify. Homes also locate Irish women in relation to social groups in the neighbourhood, including Irish, indigenous and other diasporic collectivities.

The themes link across the generations, demonstrating the inclusivity of the concept of diaspora. Migrant women have a different relationship to home in Ireland from their daughters, but their own ties are handed down to their children in a directly personal way. Because these are family linkages which take place within domestic contexts, they are hidden from the view of the dominant society which fails to acknowledge the strength of the bonds which are forged. Assumptions about the 'assimilation' of second-generation Irish children draw only on stereotypical public indicators such as accent, and not on the content of fundamental formative experiences. Anne Higgins, who was born of Irish parents in Manchester in the 1930s and later moved to St Albans in Hertfordshire, concluded:

> My religion, political beliefs and national identity were all
> inter-related when I was a child. I've had to rethink my position
> on all of these over the years but I'm glad I have been able to
> carry with me much of what was important to me as a child.
>   (Lennon, McAdam and O'Brien 1988: 155)

The very large generation of Irish women who settled in Britain
in the 1950s and raised families had a distinctive relationship both
to the ideology of home, which was brought from Ireland and reinforced by the Catholic church, and to the English homes which
were being promoted as icons of English national identity. This
combination often produced a parallel, but hidden, Irish world for
children of Irish parents. Meg Maguire describes the invisibility of
this way of life:

> My experiences of growing up as a working-class girl/woman
> of Irish Catholic descent are rooted in a specific historical
> moment and a particular locale – south London. Growing up
> and being schooled in the 1950s and 1960s in a deeply devout
> Catholic Irish family has a uniqueness and a specificity which
> have to be recognised and which are as yet undocumented.
>   (Maguire 1997: 89)

However there were also differences within this distinctive
pattern. Meg Maguire uses the categories of 'rough' and
'respectable' to describe internal Irish working-class categories,
terms which resonate from discourses of the nineteenth century
when the 'rough' were most thoroughly racialised (Davis 1996). An
important ticket to 'respectability' was acquired through a Catholic
grammar school education. Although the religious aspects of school
life provided continuity with home, in class terms the move represented a major disruption. An English middle-class ethos was
imposed with rigour and Meg learned to 'pass' on a class basis as she
had learned to 'pass' as a white English person. She took the classic
route to higher education for working-class girls: a teacher-training
course rather than a university degree.

A different path was mapped out for working-class girls of Irish
descent who went to secondary modern schools, where children not
selected for grammar schools were educated. Heidi Safia Mirza
shows how second-generation Irish schoolgirls in South London,
whose parents had migrated in the 1950s, valued home-making and

child-rearing more highly than careers, in contrast to Caribbean girls in her sample. She relates this to their strong sense of an Irish identity which ensured 'the maintenance of their traditional values about work and marriage' (Mirza 1992: 150). This specific cultural concept of femininity gave them only a partial and often transitory commitment to the labour market, which they saw in terms of 'work' rather than a longer-term career. In other respects, however, the second-generation girls had moved on from the values of their mothers' generation, and did not want to repeat the self-sacrifice they observed. Transplantation of Irish domestic ideologies into British situations was illustrated by Russell King and Henrietta O'Connor's (1996) research in Leicester, an industrial city in the East Midlands, where women with Irish-born husbands had much more traditional gender roles than those with non-Irish husbands.

The importance of Irish homes as places apart from racist society has parallels with bell hooks' (1991) writings about African-American homes as places of resistance where positive identifications can be nurtured. Discourses surrounding Irish women and their individual homes highlight the different positionings of Irish women within the United States and Britain. In the United States, Irish mothers became respected as 'civilizers' of their families, that is agents of change towards the formation of 'Good American' citizens through their unpaid work in the home. In Britain Irish working-class homes in London and Liverpool in the 1950s were still represented as 'dirty' and 'overcrowded' with too many children (Spinley 1953; Kerr 1958).

Private expressions of Irish identity within the home counterbalance the low public profile adopted by many Irish people, especially those who arrived in Britain in the 1950s when overt expressions of anti-Irish hostility were common, and during the more recent phases of the Northern Ireland conflict. Mary J. Hickman (1990) describes the 'synonymity of family life and Irishness' in London, summed up in the phrase 'brought up Irish' which Catholic school pupils used to describe their home lives. They contrasted this with the absence of Irish cultural expression in Catholic schools. Hickman interprets this as part of a strategy of incorporation and denationalisation, by which the Catholic church established its own respectability in Britain by neutralising the threat from ongoing political dissent in Ireland. She suggests: 'Whereas education has been a prime way in which the public mask of Catholicism has rendered Irishness invisible in Britain, the family has provided an effective counterweight to the school and its incorporating strategies' (Hickman 1995: 253). A mismatch in attitudes between home and school environments was brought out sharply by the treatment of the Northern Ireland conflict. At home pupils were exposed to accounts of Irish history which diverged from the dominant consensus in Britain, but at school there was silence about the issue.

However the strength of expressions of Irish identity in the home varies for many reasons, including class, religion, region, extent of participation in Irish social and cultural activities and period of arrival. In Liverpool, for example, Hickman (1995) shows that Irish roots are masked by the local identity of Liverpudlianism. This 'Scouse' identity includes Irish Catholic experience as a major ingredient, but merges it with others from a broader range of indigenous and other migrant working-class origins.

The home-based quality of Irish ethnicity in Britain contrasts with the high visibility of African-Caribbean street life and youth culture. Buckley (1997: 96) argues that this has 'rendered the racial trajectory of the Irish a relatively safer one'. However she also discusses the distinctive targeting of Irish homes in Britain under the Prevention of Terrorism Act introduced in 1974. This campaign aimed to demoralise the Irish community in the 1970s and 1980s through night-time raids on homes in which women and children were seized and taken to police stations. Sister Sarah Clarke visited families who had been arrested under the PTA.

> It was terrible from 1975 to 1981. That was the worst period; I call it the 'bad time'. Police with dogs, guns and vans swooped on houses in the early hours of the morning, frightening young children, damaging property and making innocent, law-abiding citizens targets of suspicion in their own streets and neighbourhoods. If they were anyway involved, and when I say 'involved', I mean anyway Irish at all, they were raided or taken in. After these raids the families were stunned and isolated.
>
> (Lennon, McAdam and O'Brien 1988: 196)

Large numbers of people were taken from their homes in these raids which intimidated the Irish population in Britain (Hillyard 1993).

It would appear that under a rising, hysterical pressure from provisional IRA operations in mainland Britain, the authorities lunged about blindly for a comprehension of what the relationship could possibly be between Irishness itself, including Irish political violence, and the millions of individuals who quietly, anonymously laboured in Britain's own cities.

(Buckley 1997: 115)

Homes were targeted because of the symbolic stereotyping which linked all Irish people with IRA activity. In contrast to the indigenous population who could regard their own homes as a place of safety and retreat from external control, Irish families were being identified through their homes, which were arbitrarily broken into in ways which could not be challenged.

Irish community life in post-war Britain

In areas where there are substantial Irish populations, it has been possible for women to remain encapsulated to a large extent within Irish worlds. Irish cultural activities are often invisible to the outside world, reflecting both the British lack of acknowledgement of Irish difference and Irish anxieties about hostility. It has many consequences, both for individual Irish women and for British perceptions of Irishness.

For Irish women there may be a sharp divide between Irish identities with which they can feel 'at home' within Irish contexts in Britain and an almost complete lack of recognition of Irish cultural difference in English contexts. Yvonne Hayes, a second-generation Irish woman growing up in London in the 1970s, explained: 'although I always knew I was Irish, there was a complete gap between the sense of Irishness within the Irish community and any other way of being Irish' (Lennon, McAdam and O'Brien 1988: 218).

On the other hand, lack of knowledge about Irish community life contributes to an assumption of 'sameness' and assimilation in the English population. In the 1960s there was a large Irish population in Luton, comprising over 10 per cent of the population of the town, but the main local newspaper the *Luton News* did not carry any reports about the many and various church-related and cultural activities of the Irish (Walter 1986).

Many Irish women, especially in the older generations, participate extensively in Catholic church activities. It represents continuity with their earlier life in Ireland. A second-generation Irish woman in London said of her parents: 'For them there was no separation between being Irish and being Catholic . . .Maybe my parents felt it was a grip on their background in this country' (Lennon, McAdam and O'Brien 1988: 220). Church attendance has offered a point of contact with other Irish people as well as a place where news from Ireland can be exchanged. It also provides support and a means of coping with a hostile environment. Maguire suggests that: 'For many women of my mother's generation for whom birth control and divorce were non-starters, their religion provided a shelter from the storm' (1997: 92). This was made easier by the attitudes of acceptance and passivity which the Catholic church encouraged women to adopt. The importance of religion in the lives of many older Irish women is hard to over-emphasise and marks a strong cultural divide from English women of their generation. In Leicester 74 per cent of King and O'Connor's (1996) sample said that religion significantly affected their lives, though the association was weaker for more recent arrivals.

Cultural activities also include music and dancing, especially classes for children, which mothers in particular supervise and provision. Ullah (1985) argues that girls are more strongly drawn into these activities than boys, which he links to their stronger senses of Irishness. A large number of Irish community organisations now exist throughout Britain providing social, cultural and sporting facilities. The weekly newspaper *The Irish Post* carries several pages of notices and reports about events and there are large annual gatherings, such as the Roundwood Park festival in London. There may still be an input from the Catholic church, but these activities are now largely secular in character.

Local British identities

Although no name exists to describe the hybridity of Irish and British identities in the diaspora at a national scale, different generations, including migrants, often describe themselves as belonging to localities within Britain. The identities of 'London Irish' and 'Birmingham Irish' can be adopted without the irreconcilable binary clash that national hybrid names would entail. This process parallels that of other diasporic groups in Britain. Brah (1996) describes this as evidence of resistance to the processes of exclusion.

Young African-Caribbean and Asian women in Britain seem to be constructing diasporic identities that simultaneously assert a sense of belonging to the locality in which they have grown up, as well as proclaiming a 'difference' that marks the specificity of the historical experience of being 'black', or 'Asian', or 'Muslim'. And all of these are changing subject positions. The precise ways and with what outcomes such identities are mobilised is variable. But they speak as 'British' identities with all the complexity, contradiction, and difficulty this term implies.

(Brah 1996: 176, author's emphasis)

There are important regional variations in the form taken by local Irish identities, as shown by Hickman's (1995) comparison between the choices of 'London Irish' identities by second generation school children and 'Scouse' by those of more distant descent in Liverpool. These underline the complexities of articulations of ethnic identities with generation, class and religion over differing time periods.

Conclusions

Diasporic relationships involve not simply dual allegiances between two sets of homes, but an active remaking of identities which are continuously in flux. Such populations are 'enmeshed in circuits of social, economic, and cultural ties encompassing both the mother country and the country of settlement' (Lavie and Swedenburg 1996: 14). In the case of Irish women in Britain these include return movements to 'home areas' in Ireland, achieved with great difficulty in the early post-war years when travel was difficult and expensive. For more recent migrants, movement and other forms of communication have been far more frequent. As a result direct links with life in Ireland 'prevent the ethnicity of the Irish in Britain from closing into a reactionary nostalgia' (Buckley 1997: 99).

At a collective level the two homes have been linked by the overarching presence of the Catholic church. This institution has had a distinctive impact on women's life in the diaspora through its prescriptive models of mothering and 'home-building'. It has also played a complex role in constructions of the Irish diaspora in Britain, in some ways complicit with the political project of enforced assimilation. For migrants its church services and priestly community involvement have contributed to the provision of a 'home from home', but for the second and third generations the Catholic edu-cation system it has denied opportunities to children to retain cultural and political Irish identities alongside religious ones.

Although homes at different geographical scales, from the national to the individual family, have been separated analytically, they are also closely intertwined. For example, conflicts over national identities, notably those involved in conflicts in Northern Ireland, are played out at the level of private homes during police raids under the Prevention of Terrorism Act. Irish homes in Britain thus repre-sent IRA activism to law enforcers, despite the almost unanimous rejection of political violence by their occupants.

The discursive positioning of Irish women by the ideologies of both the Irish and British states structures the material realities of their lives. However these positions are also negotiated by individ-ual women on a daily basis as they contruct identities in different contexts, while their Irishness also intersects with other identities including those related to gender, sexuality, age and geographical location. Lavie and Swedenburg (1996: 18) call for more specific recognition of these material intersections through 'a reconcep-tualisation, from the standpoint of lived identities and physical places as well as the texts of expressive culture, of the multiplici-ties of identity and place'. I now turn to the specificity of detailed narratives of ten Irish women in Bolton, Lancashire in the 1990s in order to trace the mechanics involved in the negotiations and transformations of these identities.

Chapter 7

Doubled relationships of displacement and placement

Irish women in Bolton

Although identities of displacement and placement have been separated for analytical purposes, it is central to the concept of diaspora that these are simultaneous, 'both/and', forms of identification for individuals. In this chapter I explore the ways in which these doubled identities are experienced in the everyday lives of ten Irish-born women interviewed in Bolton in 1994. Detailed examination of their experiences throws light on the commonalities of shared places of origin and destination, but also the rich range of variations according to age, generation, class, religion and motherhood. While clear themes can be identified in the collective experiences of diasporic groups, these cannot simply be 'read off' as applying to individuals. As Brah (1996: 124) points out:

> Each 'I' is a unique constellation of shared collective meanings. Thus the relationship between personal biography and collective history is complex and contradictory. While personal identities always articulate with the collective experience of a group, the specificity of a person's life experience etched in the daily minutiae of lived social relations produces trajectories that do not simply mirror group experience.
>
> (Brah 1996: 124)

The ten women cannot be seen as representative of all Irish women in Bolton, but each of their lives is woven into the collective story and together they provide a rich set of insights into the complexities of the wider picture. They were introduced to me by people connected in different ways to the Irish community in the town. The spread of the women's geographical origins, their ages and the time periods in which they arrived echo quite closely the pattern of Irish settlement in Bolton (Walter 1979, OPCS 1993).

The size and regional location of settlements play a central part in the experiences of Irish women. This medium-sized Lancashire mill-town offers a different perspective from published narratives of Irish women in Britain which have largely focused on London (Kells 1995a, Lennon, McAdam and O'Brien 1988; Gray 1997). Women who arrived in London, or even Glasgow or Manchester, would have had access to larger Irish communities, perhaps more specific provision of welfare and cultural facilities, a different religious mix among their neighbours, and a different history of interactions between Irish people and the regional/national dominant group as well as with other diasporic groups. Those who settled in smaller towns, or regions with fewer people of Irish descent, might have encountered more hostility and incomprehension of their cultural background.

Bolton provides a distinctive historical and geographical context in the 'diaspora space' of Britain. It is located in North West England where there is a long history of Irish settlement (see Figure 4.2). This means that, as in Liverpool, the 'entanglement of genealogies of dispersion with those of staying put' has developed over several generations, resulting in social mixing and intermarriage between Irish people, other diasporic groups and local English people on a wide scale (Walter 1984). Many 'English' people in Bolton have at least one Irish ancestor. Identification, however, depends on Irish surnames which have survived in a haphazard manner among male lines long detached from their origins, or on family memories. One indicator is Catholic allegiance, at least at the nominal level, which is now widespread so that Catholic education is an important component of the overall pattern. In the nineteenth century Bolton was a cotton-spinning town, and the textile industry remained an important area of employment until the 1960s. As in other Lancashire mill towns, however, unemployment has been at high levels in Bolton since the 1970s, so few people have chosen the town for work as they did in the past.

Specificity of place and time also relates to the place of origin within Ireland of women who settle in Britain. The cultural and material conditions of different parts of Ireland provides marked variations in reasons for leaving, the nature of family networks, experience of paid work and religious beliefs and practices. The origins of the ten women in the sample reflect the pattern of Irish origins of women in North West England. Half came from farms in the rural west of Ireland. These women all emigrated in their late teens or early twenties, needing paid work to support themselves. Four married Irish men, also born in the west of Ireland, and three of these met their partners in Bolton. All had strong pre-existing networks of relatives in Lancashire and elsewhere in Britain. These are very common patterns for Irish women in Britain, especially for the large numbers who arrived in the peak years of the 1950s.

Two of the interviewees originated in or close to Dublin. Again this smaller number from large urban areas and eastern counties is typical of the emigration pattern as a whole, especially in the earlier part of the post-war period. These women differed in important respects from the first group. Both came from families with very little experience of emigration and both married English men. One met her future partner when he went on holiday to Ireland and the other married a Bolton man after she had lived in the town for a year.

The third group comprises three women who were born in Northern Ireland, in Belfast, and left either directly or indirectly because of the 'troubles'. Two of these had an English-born mother who had been taken to Belfast as a child because of family connections there, illustrating the long-standing diasporic connection between Lancashire and Ireland. Two women were Catholics and one was from a Protestant background, again typical of the differing levels of migration of the two religious groups. More Catholics than Protestants have left Northern Ireland because of their higher levels of unemployment and a greater incidence of displacement by the political conflict (Compton 1976).

The interviews focused on women's relationships with Ireland, their working lives in Bolton and their feelings of belonging. There are underlying similarities in the stories they told, but individual specificities in their personal situations and their reactions to events in their lives. An important reason for bringing Irish women's lives together, both individually and collectively, is that for a variety of reasons they are not spoken about in Britain. These are the stories ten Irish women chose to tell. Although the women interviewed 'speak for themselves', they do so in response to an agenda largely set by me. Unlike the authors of *Across the Water* I have given them new names, as well as commenting selectively on the transcripts. My aim in this book is to provide an interpretative framework and I am using the stories to illuminate and add detail to the analysis so far.

Women's stories

Stories reintegrate lives prised apart by analysis. I have chosen parts of the much longer biographies offered in interviews with me by the ten women, in order to examine the contexts in which they spoke about their feelings of belonging both to Ireland and Britain, and to specific localities within each. These individual accounts illustrate ways in which the discursive and material positioning of Irish women in Britain in the mid to late twentieth century is experienced. The longitudinal perspective of each lifetime brings together the multiple, changing and ongoing relationships between Ireland and Britain which weave through their lives. Moreover memories and intimate family relationships mean that this time-frame is extended both backwards into their parents' generation and forwards into the lives of their children.

Rural women from the West of Ireland: Mary, Eileen, Bridie, Kathleen and Nora

Mary

Mary's story is that of a labour migrant who entered live-in domestic service in Lancashire just before the Second World War. She was born in 1914 on a 50-acre farm in County Galway, one of eight children in a family where emigration was part of everyday life. However she left Ireland because of an unexpected series of deaths in her family which meant that she was displaced from the family farm and therefore from the home area in which she had expected to stay to become a farmer's wife. 'I never would have come to England if my mother had lived. Mother died when I was twenty. I would never have left, probably would have got married over there.'

In fact, the train of events was begun in the United States, when two older brothers and a sister went out to an aunt in America. The sister fell ill with tuberculosis, said to have been contracted from a 'black cook' in the household where she worked as a domestic servant, and the disease then ravaged Mary's family, killing four siblings. Their mother died soon afterwards and Mary herself moved to Britain to allow her younger brother to 'bring in a woman' to the family farm.

Working life in Britain

More distant family members were already established in Lancashire and Mary's father had spent the summers as a hay harvester there. Mary took over the job of an Irish woman from her home area who had gone back to live in Ireland. After three years in Glossop, she spent a summer with relations in Bolton and looked for a job there. She found one in a large house with five servants, but the employer then visited her to withdraw the offer because one of the other 'maids' refused to share a room with an Irish woman.

> The others were all English, and because they had to share – well, that's what she told me. She came to see me where I was staying out at Moses Gate, on the Saturday, because I should have started on the Monday, and she said, I'm very sorry, through no fault of your own, she said, we have four – no, five – no, five, I would be the fifth, because the other one had left, she said, and she said, unfortunately you would have to share a room with this English girl and she doesn't want to share a room with an Irish girl. But that was the only nastiness I ever – well, it wasn't nasty even, when I came over. And then I went for another job at Moses Gate, but they were Jews so my cousin's wife wouldn't let me take it, wouldn't let me take it because they were Jews. So anyhow, I went to an Irish dance and I met this Irish girl, and she said, well, I can give you an address, she said, she's gone home because of the war. She's frightened and she's gone home and she hasn't come back.

This experience illustrates the complex placing of different social groups in Bolton in the 1940s. Mary was excluded by an English woman who was also a domestic servant. The employer recognised this behaviour as discriminatory but felt unable to counter it. Mary also saw the incident as racist and had already mentioned it in a general discussion about Irishness at the start of the interview, but here she dismissed it lightly. She then found a job in a Jewish household but her relatives in Bolton refused to allow her to work there, because of their own racisms. They could do this because demand for Irish women as servants was high and indeed Mary had no trouble finding another job through an Irish network.

During the war she was drafted into munitions manufacture and married an Irish man from the neighbouring county of Mayo, a miner, whom she met at an Irish dance in Bolton. They had five children, and Mary did not have paid work when her children were young. However her husband died from a coal-related disease when the children were still at school. This was one of two instances Mary mentioned which illustrate her lack of knowledge of the British welfare system and anxiety to protect her family, even at great personal cost. She did not seek compensation for her husband's death from an industrial disease, misunderstanding the meaning of an inquest and fearing one of her family would be blamed for her husband's death. Later she refused to apply for welfare payments to enable her to stay at home and look after her children because an Irish friend in similar circumstances had described a negative experience. In that case the welfare officer had mistaken washing water for beer when he visited her house to assess her needs, probably applying an Irish stereotype. Mary was anxious that she would also be misjudged if she applied for benefits.

Consequently Mary took on several paid jobs in addition to bringing up four children alone, one child having died.

Mary: I always cleaned, so I didn't go out until they were gone to school, and then I finished at twelve till one, then I was home to get an evening meal ready for them, and then I used to go on a snackbar after my husband – well, I didn't go to work until after my husband died.

Author: So you did two jobs?

Mary: I did three some days, I went to three houses. Then weekends I worked on the dog track two nights a week, I worked on a football ground Saturday afternoons, I went onto the dog track at night. Everywhere there was money to be earned.

This is typical of work done by labour migrants who take whatever low-paid jobs are available and make few demands on the state, even those to which they are entitled.

The major connection with Ireland for Mary was return visits to stay on her home farm every summer.

I went back, we went every June, well, during the holidays. Poor daddy, when I think of him, five – he used to have a case here and two here. And then we had – we went a fortnight, yes. And you look forward to that. And then you see, it cost you nothing when you got there because my dad wouldn't take anything for our food or anything, and these, there were so many of our relations and neighbours, they were thrilled to have them, you wouldn't see them. My brother used to say, what are the neighbours going to say? They'll say you're bringing them home and they're feeding them. And I used to say, well, they will play with their own children their ages, you know, they were thrilled to have them, you know. As a matter of fact, was it Joseph hid when we were coming back once? We had such a good time.

Both for Mary and her children, summers spent in Ireland reinforced ties with the extended family and the home area.

In Bolton, Mary's social life has focused almost exclusively around her immediate family in the town. The other major activity in Mary's life is participation in the Catholic church, which she attends daily.

Home and belonging

Mary had no difficulty in calling Bolton home. The main reasons she gave were its comfort and convenience compared with the isolation of the family farm in Ireland. Perhaps most important, her children were settled there. It was also the place where her husband was buried. But she still spoke of going 'home' to Ireland.

Author: Do you feel homesick for Ireland ever?
Mary: No, not any more. Two of my best pals have gone. Well, I've a brother there, there's only him left now, but you miss it, and I don't know, there is something. When the Irish music comes on, there's something. And when you put your feet in Ireland, you seem to get that atmosphere, I don't know what it is, but I do feel very happy and that kind of thing. But I'm always very glad to come home because it's so handy. Mind you, it's not so bad now because of the care and all that, you know, what we didn't used to have.
Author: So this is home, is it?
Mary: This is home now. Well, I still call Ireland home, they

laugh at me, I still say I'm going home to Ireland, you
know, but yes, this is, and I've had a good life here...

Author: So you've never felt you wanted to move back to Ireland?

Mary: Oh no, no, no way.

Author: What particularly makes you say that?

Mary: Well, I suppose I've had so much comfort here and that
kind of thing. I've always had a good life here, and I've
always had plenty of friends. I suppose this is it. To me
life is what you make it. And then my family have all –
they all like Ireland, don't you?

Son: Yes.

At the end of the interview she reaffirmed her dual sense of
identity, and the impossibility of making the either/or choice which
my questioning was trying to impose:

Author: So I've really asked you this – where do you feel you
belong?

Mary: Well, I suppose I'd always say Ireland. I don't know. It's
where you were born and reared, isn't it?

Mary's family clearly illustrates the ways in which Irish homes in
Britain are places where aspects of Irish identities are passed on to
subsequent generations. She said she had not consciously tried to
pass on a sense of Irishness, but that her children were very aware
of their background. Her son said:

I think we'd say we were Irish in England and English in
Ireland, or that's how we're perceived. She has actually –
what she's done, she's taught us some expressions that we
actually use. We use things like *mearadh* for mess, and we say
Gaelic phrases which are meaningless to other people. Even
my own wife now uses them, you know. So there has been
some influence from her.

Mary is firmly placed in Bolton and has strong positive
feelings about the town. The main ties are the better material
life it still offers and the establishment of her adult children and
their own nuclear families in the vicinity. Her links to Britain
are very local and revolve around her own and her children's
households. But this is also to some extent an Irish world,

centring on the Catholic parish and Irish friends. Moreover Irishness continues to be a significant component of both her children and grandchildren's identities. After fifty years in England, displacement is part of Mary's everyday life. She found no difficulty in retaining two places called 'home', although to her children this was incongruous.

Eileen

Eileen also came to Britain just before the Second World War, worked in domestic service and married an Irish man. However a major contrast with Mary's life was that Eileen's husband lived longer and provided a wage which supported the family. She has not had paid work since her five children were born and her life has been intensely focused around the home.

Eileen was born on a twenty-five-acre farm in County Galway, one of five. Her father died young, echoing Mary's experience of premature mortality breaking up the nuclear family in Ireland. One brother stayed on the farm and one sister married a farmer nearby. Another brother emigrated first to England and then settled in Canada. Eileen's other sister came to work as a house-keeper to a Catholic priest in Bury, near Bolton, where she had an aunt. When she was eighteen, in 1937, Eileen joined her there as a live-in domestic worker for the priest. She had helped out at home for four years after leaving school but 'there was nothing much for us, really, you know'.

Working life in Britain

About 1941 Eileen moved to Bolton to work as a cook in a hostel for munitions workers. She returned to Ireland for two years after the war to nurse her dying mother and keep house for her brother, but he was planning to marry and Eileen had to make way for his new wife just as Mary had done, so she returned. In Bolton both sisters married Irish men, Eileen's husband coming from the neighbouring county of Sligo. Like Mary's husband, he was a miner, also invalided out because he contracted tuber-culosis in late middle age, continuing the story of poor health in both parents' and respondents' own generations.

Eileen had five children and her life was very closely bound up with theirs. She described a very private world which revolved around provision for their needs and included very few other people, especially when they were young.

Author: What have been the good things for you about leaving
          Ireland?
Eileen: I don't know really. The best thing I enjoyed was my family.
Author: Over here?
Eileen: Over here, my children, and they go back to Ireland as
          well. I never went out, I don't go out a lot here, and to go
          in pubs and that, I was never interested, you know. My
          husband went sometimes for a drink and very occasion-
          ally I would go. But I enjoyed teaching my children and
          watching them, you know, grow and that.

She invested a remarkable degree of effort in the physical wellbeing and education of her children, strongly rejecting the idea of
sharing their care with anyone else.

Author: Do you think you look after your children – or you did –
          in the same way that your mother looked after you, or
          do you think you did things very differently?
Eileen: I didn't do them that much differently. I mean I wanted
          to dress them and feed them well. I taught them, I bought
          books for them, I taught them at night.
Author: Did you?
Eileen: Oh yes, I taught them in the evening, oh, very much so.
          I never held with them running round the streets at
          night, no. And my husband worked shifts as well, some-
          times he worked at night and he didn't want them out
          while he was gone. We always had a lot of games, played
          games, Monopoly and all these games, and we were
          always happy.

Eileen's enclosure within the world of her own family was reinforced by the hostile attitudes of some Bolton women she
encountered in the 1950s.

Eileen: When my children were going to school, some of the
          people at school, they weren't very friendly and actually
          there was one woman at school and she did everything
          she could to humiliate me. She – I suppose she thought

she was better off and I had those five children, they were all young together, I had twins, and she said one day, children of big families aren't properly looked after. And then her daughter, who was the same age as my daughter, she bullied my daughter at school, and bullied her very much. . . . But I realised after my daughter was cleverer and better than her and she was jealous, she was jealous of her. But I used to take my children and I wouldn't go near the woman at school, if I was standing outside the school, because she was there.

Author: So this was about large families?

Eileen: I don't know, I suppose she thought, this woman with all these children, and perhaps being Irish as well, shouldn't be in a higher position in class than her daughter. Yes.

Eileen felt excluded from school social events, although these were some of her few sources of contact with the local community. The school was Catholic but this did not protect her from the anti-Irish racism of the other mothers.

Eileen: I remember I once went to the school with my children, they had started going to school, the two eldest, and I brought them to the school one evening, and I didn't know them – I knew some of them but I wasn't very friendly with many of them, so I sat down at the table to have my tea, and she poured everyone's tea except mine.

Author: So what happened?

Eileen: Another very nice lady came along and said, Mrs Concannon hasn't got any tea, and poured it for me. I really don't know, she really treated me very badly.

She was also hurt by the way another neighbour described her.

There was a woman lived near me, in fact I helped her a lot, she was always coming to the house, I was the only one that helped her, she used to go drinking a lot, and she'd say, oh, that Irish one, you know, she'd be talking and she'd say, that Irish one.

Eileen's five children achieved remarkable upward mobility. They gained scholarships to the Catholic grammar schools in Bolton and all went on to higher education in the 1960s. Four have continued to work in education: a university lecturer, a college lecturer, a college administrator and a teacher.

Home and belonging

Eileen's focus on her children meant that she had no doubts about where she would choose to live. Unlike Mary she said 'England' rather than 'Bolton' perhaps reflecting her encapsulation in the house rather than the locality. She may also recognise that her children, who had become socially mobile, might move. Indeed her eldest daughter already lived in Cumbria.

Author: Where do you feel you belong? Where do you feel at home?

Eileen: Oh, I belong to England, England's my home now, and my children – my home is where my children and my grandchildren are. I mean I still say I'm going home when I go to Ireland, but my home is here, yes, and my happiness is with my children.

Author: So you feel you belong in England?

Eileen: Oh yes.

Author: You don't feel that you're an outsider?

Eileen: Yes, I feel happy and my children are happy, yes. That matters to me more than anything else, if you can live a good happy life I don't think it matters where you are. It's nice to go back to your own country, it's nice to hear your own Irish songs and Irish music and all that, but we're happy here. We'll be buried here. Yes. I mean some people – why don't you come back and live in Ireland? I'd never leave my children, no, nor my grandchildren. I mean we could sell this house and get a house like it cheaper in Ireland, but we wouldn't do.

Eileen's unintentionally ambiguous response to the question about whether she felt she was an outsider may be revealing. England was 'home' in the very specific sense that it was the location of her children, although she explained that 'as I got older, as my children got older, I found some very friendly people'.

However Ireland provided a wider sense of belonging to a group of family and friends.

Author: What particularly is it that you like about Ireland?
Eileen: I don't know really. I feel I've got a life over there, you know. I love seeing the people. When I went to this wedding I saw a lot of the people I hadn't seen for a long time, and I enjoyed that . . .
Author: But when you think of Ireland . . .
Eileen: Oh yes, yes.
Author: What is it that comes into your mind?
Eileen: Well, I feel, you know, I feel so at home, and you always meet people, you go out and you meet people that knows you, people that grew up with you, so pleased to see you.
Author: You wouldn't consider going home to live?
Eileen: Well, I couldn't. I couldn't – I wouldn't leave my family, no. No. I mean there's no hope for me going back. But I mean I'm quite happy here, yes. I have sixteen grandchildren, and we enjoy those children and grandchildren.
Author: So you think if you hadn't children and grandchildren you might have gone home?
Eileen: Maybe. I don't know. I should perhaps be – I suppose if there was only the two of us we may have done. I don't know.

Eileen's children have retained a strong sense of their Irish identities which in turn they are passing on to their own, third-generation Irish, children. Three married partners with some Irish ancestry, one is married to a Polish Catholic and one daughter to an English Protestant. One daughter takes her small son to piano accordian lessons to learn Irish music

Author: Would they say they're Irish, do you think? If people ask, your children, do you think having Irish parents means that they think of themselves as Irish?
Eileen: Oh yes, they do, yes.
Author: If someone said to them, are you Irish or English, what would they say?
Eileen: Some of them, I think the boys rather than the girls, would say they're Irish. One of my daughters, she'd say she was Irish.

Eileen was displaced from Ireland. As the daughter of a small farmer in the west of Ireland she could not remain on the land and there were no other opportunities for her to earn a living. She was able to move to England within an intergenerational network of close relations and live within an Irish circle of labour migrants. Irish social activities enabled her to meet and marry an Irish man, from a very similar background. She recreated a close family life revolving around motherhood, with little reliance on outside support except from the Catholic church and school, as her farm family of origin had done. Encounters with anti-Irish attitudes among English neighbours when her children were young reinforced her belief in the need for self-reliance. Although Eileen now talks positively about English people she knows, especially her daughter's non-Catholic English husband, she is still embedded in close personal relationships in Ireland and feels comfortable and 'at home' when she is there.

Bridie

Bridie came to England to find more highly-paid work than was available in Ireland in the 1950s. She was born into a sixty-acre arable farm in County Tipperary, one of six children, three of whom emigrated to England, though no others settled in Lancashire. One of her parents also died young, in this case her father. She described her mother as 'very poor, of course, just poverty-stricken really, all she had was a few cows and the profits from the milk and what not'. Bridie left school at fourteen and like other farmers' daughters where 'there was too many of you on it', went to the town to work as a 'housemaid cum shop assistant'.

Working life in Britain

In 1952, at the age of nineteen she answered an advertisement in the newspaper for workers in the textile mills in Bolton.

Bridie:　The money sounded much better anyway, from ten shillings a week to four pounds ten shillings a week and expenses paid. So we were sent our tickets and we had a medical with a doctor before we left. I always remember it. And then we were put on the boat and sent. Somebody met us in Liverpool and put us on the train for Bolton.

Someone met us here and took us to the hostel, and the following morning some representative came from the mills and took us to the mills and showed us where we were going to work.

Author: Did you go with friends?

Bridie: Oh, I did – no, I came from Tipperary on my own. On the boat that day there was three more coming, one – a lady from Mayo, and two from Kilkenny, I met up with.

Author: And so you met them and you found out that you were all coming here?

Bridie: Yes. They had answered the same advertisement at the time. But a lot more came after that, a couple of years later they were still coming to that. They came from every county. At the hostel there were representatives of every county, really. . . .

There were quite a few women working at the time. And then of course it was near the hostel, we hadn't far to go to work each day, which avoided bus fares and travelling too far into town and with being new here, you know. And we were registered with the doctors and the dentists through the hostel as well. The sisters looked after us really and made sure we were settled in, you know. So we were fixed up after that, but a lot of people had left the hostel and got flats or whatever, and left the town eventually, and a lot got married and that's how it went, really. You know? There's quite a few in the town still that I know of, you know.

The recruited women had to stay six months. Many then moved on to other jobs. Bridie stayed seven years, until after her marriage when she had her first child. She also married an Irish man from Clare whom she met at an Irish club in Bolton. He was in the building trade. When her four children were older she entered the schools meals service, where she still works. Bridie's pattern of full-time work followed by part-time domestic work while her children were at school was typical of many Irish women who became mothers. Ancillary work in schools was particularly popular because holidays coincided with times when their own children needed supervision.

Bridie has been back to Ireland for a month every summer to stay in the family home with her brother. When the children were younger she took them. She points out how much harder it was to maintain ties in the 1950s.

Author: Did you feel homesick when you came?
Bridie: Oh yes, oh yes. I did, yes. We all did. Very much. It's a big wrench. When you're only – I'd left home when I was fourteen but I was only sixty miles from home which wasn't too bad, but when I came here at nineteen it was a different kettle of fish. I was much further away, and then you didn't go back as often, whereas now, it's much easier to go and come now, of course. You can fly and what not. But them days you just went back for a few weeks every year and that was it. You didn't see your mother then for another twelve months, and you only wrote like, you didn't ring then, at that time, you know.

Bridie took her children home each summer when they were young, but only one daughter still visits Ireland.

She's the only one in the family that's still interested in going over to see her people in Ireland, because she loved Ireland, she went every summer with me and she used to stay with my cousin a few miles away, and she used to spend her summers like with this lady while I was in my homestead with the other children. But she enjoyed being there, and she likes going over there. But that's as far as it goes really. But she doesn't class herself as Irish, no. . . .
The other three, no, they're not interested. No, full stop. I take the grandchildren over instead.

Her main social interactions are with other Irish people of her generation. She describes her relationship with English people as one of 'acceptance' of her, but reveals that they express hostile attitudes towards, and low levels of knowledge of, Ireland.

Author: Do you think your good friends are Irish people?
Bridie: They are, yes. . . . But I mean we've English friends as well, of course. We find they all accept us. I work with plenty of English women, they don't mind, I don't bother any more, you know. They can't just understand the troubles in Ireland still, but I tell them that it's only

in one part of Ireland, that is. It doesn't affect the whole country. But they imagine it's all over the country, which it isn't. That's their impression of Ireland, that's a bad country, that we have this trouble all over the country.

She describes her husband as even more tightly connected with a male Irish social world.

Bridie: I mean we know a lot of Irish in the town, Joe does especially, he seems to mix more with the men than I would with the women, you see.
Author: Why is that?
Bridie: Well, he goes to the pub and he goes to Manchester, to the Irish centre, and they meet all the men there. I don't go as much as he goes. He goes off on his own from time to time.

Bridie feels much closer to indigenous British ethnic groups than to members of the other major post-war diaspora in Bolton, the Indian population. Talking about ethnic change in her neighbourhood she showed undertones of anxiety, and a clear homogenising of 'whiteness' over 'migrant' status.

And I still like it here, but there's been a lot of Indian influx now into the street and into the area. But as neighbours I find them all right. I don't bother. And we've more and more of them coming, of course, and more and more white people are leaving the area.

This was also the subtext to a discussion of the desirability of categorising the Irish as an ethnic group.

I think you're better off integrating, I would think so. If people try to keep in little group to themselves, they end up being pinpointed then.

Home and belonging

Bridie says that she belongs in England, and then more specifically Bolton. However the sense of exclusion from Ireland also comes through strongly in her response.

Author: Where would you say you belong?
Bridie: I belong to here. I'm here now.
Author: Where is here?
Bridie: England. Bolton. My home is here, my family are here. I
          don't think I belong to Ireland. I feel – I know if I go back
          to Ireland I feel an outcast, for instance . . . So your home
          is where you make it, here. I'm too long here to go back.
          You see, I was very young when I left and didn't experi-
          ence much over there in the line of work. So I'm here too
          long now.

Although she says she has not regretted coming to Britain, the
benefits she mentions are material ones, as Mary did. Behind these
there is also a sense of yearning for the family she left behind and
the land itself.

Author: Do you look forward to going on holiday?
Bridie: I do, yes.
Author: What do you particularly look forward to?
Bridie: I like the countryside. I like to be in the country. Yes.
          And with like with people, my own family, you know,
          brothers and their families, aunts and uncles are still
          surviving there, you know, and cousins, extended
          families that you know, really. Oh, I do like to go and see
          them all, yes.

But she also recognises the material benefits of living in Britain.

    I've never regretted coming here. I know I wouldn't go back
    to live there. I'll go for a holiday, but I wouldn't go back to
    live. No, it's not the country I left. There's a completely dif-
    ferent generation there altogether.

However her children, to her disappointment, have moved away
from or rejected, their Irish identities. In her experience this is
common and she links it with going on to further education and to
the lack of an Irish family club in Bolton.

Bridie: No, no. They don't want to know. A lot of the offspring
          do not – like my own family, they don't want to know
          anything about the Irish.

Author:	So if you said to them, are you Irish? what would they say?
Bridie:	No, they would – no, they would say their parents are Irish. They would not admit to being – they are not Irish, which to me they're not, they're English citizens really, all born here. So they're not, they're of Irish descent, that's as far as it goes.

Bridie was a labour migrant recruited directly in Ireland to fill shortages in the textile mills, part of a pattern which had continued from the mid-nineteenth century. Unlike either Mary or Eileen, she had no family already settled in Bolton and had to substitute friends, initially young women living in the hostel, for the close family she had known in Ireland. Her account of her life in Britain expresses a strong sense of loss, starting when she first arrived with homesickness which could only be assuaged once a year by a visit home. It continues with the falling away from a strong sense of Irishness she perceives in her own children. Bridie is displaced between Ireland and Britain and feels fully 'at home' in neither. When she returns on holiday to Ireland, she also feels a stranger there and knows she could not resettle. She has no choice but to remain in Bolton where her Irish identity, which remains very strong, is sustained only by a few friends of her own generation.

Kathleen and Nora

Kathleen and Nora are friends in their sixties who chose to be interviewed together. They became close when they moved into the same neighbourhood in Bolton and attended the same church, which they both agreed was a central part of their lives. They also worked together in an old people's home before they retired. Their husbands had established a very good relationship and spent time together while their wives worked. Both women were now widows.

Working lives in Britain

Kathleen came to Bolton first in 1946 to work as a barmaid. She was following her older sister and left because the family farm in County Mayo was to be sold. Her father had died some years earlier when she was thirteen, yet another early parental death.

Her mother moved in with her married sister. Earlier there had been a suggestion of matchmaking for Kathleen with a postman 'but that didn't appeal to me, certainly'. She wanted 'to earn money, really, to have a job and to earn money and make some headway in life'.

The sisters came to Bolton because of strong family connections. Their father and his brothers had been there many times in the past as seasonal labourers. The two women became part of a large Irish female labour force working in the hotel trade because they could live in.

Kathleen: There were quite a group of us Irish girls who knew one another and we used to meet in the afternoons and on Sunday afternoon we used to go to Jackson Street in Manchester dancing. Yes, so . .
Author: So how did you know other Irish girls?
Kathleen: Well, my sister had already known a friend who – that was why she came, and, um, then you get to know them through church and of course through going to the dances, you know. And there was a group of us in the same type of jobs, which meant that we were free in the afternoon between three and five, and we sort of got together then.

Kathleen met her English husband, a Bolton man, in the pub and they took up work together in a succession of pubs and clubs in the Manchester area. Her husband loved to visit Ireland. They had seven children. Her mother came over to live with her, as Kathleen said 'she was quite fit at seventy, and she settled in quite well in this country'. The family then moved back to Bolton and rented a shop.

Nora's story was rather different. She too came from a farm in the far west of Ireland, in County Galway. However, none of her family had emigrated to England and, unlike the other rural women who met their partners in Bolton, Nora met and married Joe in her home area. His family had a shop as well as a farm and could afford to educate their son for longer. He planned to train as a teacher, but the training college closed during the war and he found a job as an electrical goods salesman in Dublin. Nora and Joe married and moved to Dublin, but in 1950 Joe was made redundant. They decided to come to Britain for a short time, while waiting to find a better job in Ireland, and chose Bolton where her husband's brother was living. They moved back briefly to Galway when Joe was offered a good job with an expanding Lancashire printing firm, but the branch was never established and they had to return. Joe went back into clerical work in Bolton.

Nora and Joe had five children, all of whom achieved high educational qualifications. They gained scholarships to the Catholic grammar schools in Bolton and the four boys went to university. Their sister trained as a solicitor.

Neither Kathleen nor Nora said that they had experienced any ill-treatment because they were Irish. In fact they believed that the Irish were strongly in demand because they were known as good workers. They did not support the idea of placing the Irish in a separate ethnic category, thinking it 'best to mix and not to keep as a group in themselves'. Kathleen revealed her anxiety about the underlying thinking behind proposals for an Irish category in the Census. When I suggested that welfare groups believed it would help Irish people gain resources they needed, she was wary.

> Was it that or was it the other? It was definitely that, was it? Or could it be possibly that they wanted to – because at one time there was an initiative to deport the Irish.

Home and belonging

Kathleen remembered the pleasure of going back to Ireland after she had been in Bolton for a year and a half.

Kathleen: I went back home, that was absolutely fantastic.
Author: What, lovely to go home?
Kathleen: Oh, the lovely feeling, the lovely feeling of getting back there.
Author: Do you remember, what did you feel?
Kathleen: I don't know, just riding down on the bus from Dublin and the fields and the deep sense of belonging really, you know. And back home, you know, the people, seeing everybody.

Both Kathleen and Nora would say they now belong in Bolton, but they are clear that the main reason why they stay is that their children live there.

Kathleen: I belong in Bolton now because my family are here, because family, as I said, I've no close relatives in Ireland.

Author: This is home, is it?

Nora: Oh yes.

Kathleen: It has to be, you see. That's why.

Nora: Although funnily enough, if I was going over to Ireland I'd say I was going home. It's habit. You say, oh, I'm going home this year.

Kathleen: We call it home, yes. . . . for us, you never lose it all. I don't think you do. Do you, Nora?

Nora: Oh, no, you don't, and I think it gets a bit stronger really as you get older.

Both families had returned in the summer to Ireland when the children were young. Kathleen's children did not visit Ireland now, but she felt they would do so again. However only one cousin now remained in the home area so it would be more difficult for them to stay. Nora's children had closer relationships with family in Ireland and still returned frequently. The two older ones had lived in Galway with their parents for six months and had expected to move back there. They call themselves Irish and frequently go back to stay with cousins. There are very large numbers of relatives still in the home area, partly because both parents' families lived there. They had also become more prosperous over time, which freed them from the need to participate in migration networks to the same extent as many rural families. Nora describes a very large area as 'home', including many neighbouring farms. When she returns she has a very busy time as each relative has to be visited.

> They all want you to call. And they'd be disappointed if you were at home and you didn't call on them. Well, what did I do on them that they were home and never called to see me like? You know? And they all make you so welcome. They all want to make tea and all sorts and bring it, and you're to come for a meal and all the rest of it.

Nora and Joe had not intended to settle in England. They saw their stay as temporary while they earned money. Their life was built around saving, so they bought 'the smallest house we could get and everything that was the cheapest'. They took extra work whenever it was available. But when they came back the second time they decided to settle in England to give the children an undisturbed education.

Both women said that the reason they came to England was to find work.

Nora: We came for work. It was work brought us all. It was
           work brought us all.
Author: But it's been all right?
Kathleen: Oh, of course it has, oh yes. [N is agreeing too] But I'll
           tell you, only for work.

For both women the price that had to be paid for living in England was that their own children would settle there permanently. Outside the family their own lives were sustained by their friendship and their church membership. These three elements, family, religion and Irish friends, made up an Irish world in Bolton which allowed them to continue many of the activities and values which would have characterised their lives if they had remained in Ireland. For Kathleen, who had no close kin left there, they represented a displaced society now totally removed to England. Nora, on the other hand, could still re-enter an active family life when she visited each summer.

Two women from the Dublin area: Margaret and Bernadette

Women leaving urban localities in the Irish Republic have a very different set of experiences from those raised in the rural west. Although emigration has affected all parts of Ireland,until recently fewer left from cities and Dublin people are not enmeshed in such strong networks of family and neighbourhood moves to the United States and Britain. Moreover they already have experience of urban life and do not face the initial disorientation of moving from an isolated rural area to a town. 'Going home' for holidays also has a very different meaning. There is no family farm to absorb children and provide a summer's entertainment at low cost. However, until quite recently it has been much cheaper and easier to travel back to Dublin than to make the long journey to remote farms in the west.

Margaret

Margaret's story is of an individual move to marry an English man who lived in Bolton. She met him when he went on holiday to Butlin's holiday camp near Dublin in 1953. She was eighteen and had a summer job as a waitress to make a change from her low-paid regular job in domestic service. They kept in touch and married four years later.

Margaret was one of five children and the only sibling to emigrate. The others all found work locally, the sisters in service and the brothers in market gardening and lorry driving. She says: 'we were never really out of work'. However both her parents had worked in Liverpool when young, her mother in service and her father as a docker. Her mother encouraged her to marry and go to England, even when she herself was unsure. Margaret felt very hurt that her mother said to her 'if you go, I still have all the rest'.

She has two children and from the outset worked in Bolton as a part-time daily domestic 'home help', work involving cleaning and childcare. Her husband was a joiner. Margaret also took on public service jobs, first as a Labour councillor and then as a magistrate. She was surprised and angry that her family in Ireland were not more pleased by these achievements. They did not think women should, or could, take on this kind of work outside the home.

Margaret: When I first actually – which disappointed me really – when I first become a magistrate, I phoned them up at home and told them, you know, and they didn't seem interested at all, only – how are you going to manage? And, what would you know about that? You know? Which aggravated me, you know, because I was willing to learn about the job, you know.

Author: It wasn't women's work?

Margaret: No, no. When I become a councillor they didn't seem to be – it quite disappointed me really. I thought they would have been pleased that I was trying to improve myself as such, you know.

Author: Been proud of you?

Margaret: Yes, but they didn't seem to be interested at all.

Margaret's encounters with English people in Bolton were presented positively on the whole. She puts this down to her outgoing personality. She feels she has equal numbers of English and Irish friends. When she first arrived 'they were lovely with me. Yes, I made great friends. Mind you, my daughter said, mum, you'd talk to the devil.' She did experience anti-Irish hostility but was able to challenge it with more confidence than the rural women, partly because of her experience of public work. On one occasion she went to the police station to hand in a wallet she had found. The sergeant 'joked' that she could use the student pass 'to gain admittance to the college and plant any little thing'. When she protested he threatened her: 'He kept opening and closing this little gate as if to say, I can arrest you, you know?' Margaret's sister and daughter who were with her, were terrified.

> I came home and I was trembling. I was so annoyed that he could even think that I would do such a thing. Soon as he heard my accent, you see, he thought, here we go.

She made a complaint, which had to be notified to the Magistrates' office. Within half an hour the Chief Inspector came round to apologise and promise disciplinary action, excusing the sergeant on the grounds that he might have served in Northern Ireland.

Home and belonging

Margaret has no doubt that Bolton is now home.

Author: Where do you feel you belong? Where is home to you?
Margaret: Here.
Author: Where's here?
Margaret: In Bolton.
Author: Bolton as a town?
Margaret: Yes. Yes, I like Bolton, I think it's a lovely place, yes. Especially with all the improvements they've made to it, shopping and . . .
Author: So what is it that you like about Bolton, would you say?
Margaret: I like the people. I find the people very friendly. And I like the shopping, of course.

Although she calls Ireland 'home' she now rejects the way of life there.

> Oh no. I will never live at home again, even though I miss my son and my grandsons now living in Dublin. . . . I wouldn't live anywhere in Ireland. I find them very frustrating, you know. I want to be saying, oh, for goodness sake, get on with it – you know? This business of, there's always tomorrow – you know? I can't go. It takes me nearly a week to get into their way when I go home.

Margaret's son moved to Ireland when he was eighteen. He married a woman from his mother's home village who had visited Bolton when she was a child.

Author: You had often been as a family, had you?
Margaret: Oh yes, oh yes, we went over from when they were babies, and he always said he always loved Ireland and he would live there if he could.

Margaret followed the pattern of full-time domestic service before marriage, followed by part-time paid domestic work when her children were young. However, unlike the women from the rural west, she became politically active outside the home and moved into much more mixed social networks. She now sees herself fully settled in Bolton, ironically returning to visit her English-born son in Ireland. The strong sense of an Irish identity was experienced by both her children, especially her son, despite the English origins of their father.

Bernadette

Bernadette was born in Dublin, in the inner-city area known as the Liberties, but the family moved to the newly-built Crumlin housing estate when she was six. She left school at fourteen, and went to work in the button factory next door to the school, like all the girls in her class. At sixteen she went into domestic service, but pay was very low and she and all her siblings, five girls and one boy in total, moved to England in the 1950s. Gradually, as the economic situation improved in Ireland, four went back. They married and settled in Dublin. Her brother stayed in London and Bernadette married an English man in Bolton. Her husband had an Irish surname and was a Catholic, but had no knowledge of his Irish ancestry.

Working life in Britain

At seventeen Bernadette answered a newspaper advertisement for a live-in job in a café in London.

> Living in, yes. I always lived in. I liked living in, because at the time like, I always used to think to myself, well, you get your food. You were sure of your food, you were sure of a clean bed, and you were sure of your money. And they were the sort of jobs – well, that you did.

She moved on to find work in the Lyons' chain of restaurants, which led her into an Irish network in London. Three women from Limerick were already working there and they rented a flat from an Irish woman.

> We used to go to the Irish clubs, to dance halls and that, together. We used to go dancing, to the Irish clubs, you know. But they were smashing. Yes, but I would say London on your own, yes, very, very lonely. It can be the loneliest place in the world unless you know people and you have friends. It's a big place and like I said, Londoners, they don't go out of their way to make you feel at home, you know. Not like the Bolton people. The Bolton people will knock themselves out to make you feel at home, but Londoners don't.

She described the entirely fortuitous way in which she arrived in Bolton where she had no personal ties. There was a newspaper advertisement for hotel work in Dumfries and Bolton.

> So I picked Dumfries, but as I was walking down O'Connell Street with my mother, for some apparent reason, it was twenty past four in the afternoon and the boat used to go out then at eight o'clock. I said to my mother, I said, I don't think I'll go to Dumfries, I said, I've a feeling I should go to Bolton.

While there she met and married her English husband. After her children were born she had a wide variety of jobs while they were growing up in the 1950s and 60s, including hotel work, mill work, engineering, and delivering cars.

Bernadette: Anywhere I could make money, I was. In between
             having my children and bringing them up I've always
             worked, always.
Author: This is full-time work, is it, or part-time?
Bernadette: Full-time, yes, full-time.

Bernadette contrasted the attitudes she encountered in London
and Bolton.

Bernadette: I've lived in Bolton ever since and I've never
             looked back. I've been happy. I've been happy
             living in Bolton. I love the people. They're friendly,
             they're homely, they make you welcome. I've never
             had any problems, living in Bolton. . . . And of
             course in them days, in them days if you lived in
             London, and there used to be adverts in the paper
             shops – rooms to let, no Irish and no coloureds – at
             that time. You know? I mean it was like that – no
             Irish and no coloureds.
Author: So when was that, when did you come, what year was
             that?
Bernadette: 1952.
Author: You've never seen those signs in Bolton?
Bernadette: Oh no, no, no.
Author: It would be unthinkable, would it?
Bernadette: Oh, I've never seen anything like that in Bolton. It
             was unheard of.

However she spoke about the anguish which she and her Irish
friends felt about the Northern Ireland conflict.

> And they all stopped like when you walked in, and I just turned
> round and said, carry on, I said, I agree with you. I agree with
> everything you said, just carry on. Which I did agree with.
> Because I mean I think one of the things with me is, I think it's
> the most embarrassing thing in my life when these bombs and
> that – it's so humiliating for you. Yes, yes, I would say it's one of
> the most embarrassing things I've ever had to cope with, that.

Bernadette described herself as a 'lapsed' Catholic although she
married a Bolton Catholic man and brought up her children as

Catholics. She stopped attending church after two incidents when she felt the priest showed no understanding of her circumstances. She had accidentally put a christening fee in the charity box, but he demanded a second payment, which she could not afford. He also criticised her decision to have only two children. She continued to hold her religious beliefs, 'but I don't have to go to church to pray'. Her grandchildren were not being brought up as Catholics.

Home and belonging

Bernadette recognised that she called both Ireland and Bolton 'home'. She spoke very positively about Bolton, but gave priority to Ireland.

Author:	So where is home to you now? If I were to say to you, where do you really feel at home?
Bernadette:	Well, if I had the choice it would be Ireland.
Author:	That's where you belong?
Bernadette:	Yes, well, I – yes, deep down in my – yes. I'm passing through. I keep saying to my husband, I'm just passing through. Forty-odd year on, like, I'm passing through, you know. But I don't know. I love the people here. I do love the people. I've nothing against Bolton. I love Bolton, I love the people. But it's just something with me. I don't know, I've carried it all my life, that I would love to end my days in Ireland, strange as it seems.

In contrast to all five rural women, Bernadette placed her sense of belonging in Ireland above her attachment to her immediate family in England.

> Yes, but at the end of the day you've got to live your life too. There is life after your grandchildren. There's life after your children, if you think about it. No, I love my children dearly, but it's only twenty minutes from Manchester to Dublin, it's only twenty minutes, if you look at it like that. You know? But I don't know. I like my own people, yes. Yes, I do really.

Despite their mother's very strong feelings of belonging to Ireland, her own children did not recognise an Irish identity at this point in their lives.

Bernadette: But my own boys don't go to Ireland all that much. They have been. I used to take them when they were little. But as they grow up they don't want to.

Author: Would they say they were Irish if anyone said to them, what are you?

Bernadette: Oh no.

Author: They'd say they were English?

Bernadette: Oh no, they're English. Their mum's Irish. . . . They are part-Irish but they class themselves as English, you know.

Bernadette saw herself as close to her children, 'always there for them', but she did not devote herself exclusively to the home. She enjoyed paid work because 'I like meeting people' and 'because I'm not the type of person that can sit around all day doing nothing'. Although she felt a strong affinity with Bolton and said that her own parents regarded it as 'home from home', her sense of displacement was uppermost so that she still saw herself as 'passing through'.

Women from Northern Ireland: Deirdre, Teresa and Anne

There is a stronger representation of women from Northern Ireland in Lancashire than in South East England. Moreover Northern Irish women have been less likely to cluster in large Irish groupings. Their distribution is closer to that of the population as a whole, with some tendency to stay closer to the Irish seaports in Scotland and North West England. The three women interviewed in Bolton had very varied histories of travel and settlement. The two Catholic women had left during the height of the troubles in the 1970s in order to find safety in Britain. Although the conflict also underlay the decision of the Protestant woman to leave, she had also moved for career reasons and had not felt personally threatened.

Deirdre

Deirdre was born in Belfast in 1962 into a Catholic family. Her father was a barber and, unusually, her mother also worked outside the home, as a book-keeper. Deirdre was an only child, but part of a large, close family on her mother's side, including cousins, aunts, uncles and a grandmother. A few family members had migrated to England for short periods, but none was living there when Deirdre and her husband left.

She left school at eighteen and went to work in a college library. She had not seriously considered emigrating when she was single, although she and a friend had idly speculated about going to London.

> I know I did have a friend who always said, oh, we'll go to London or wherever, we'll kind of fly, and we'll do this, and I wasn't particularly bothered. I was quite happy, I was feeling quite happy to stay at home really. That was before things really got so bad. But it wouldn't – I don't think if the troubles hadn't started I don't think I would have moved. I think I probably would have stayed.

Deirdre married in her early twenties. Within a short space of time her husband's family had moved to Bolton and was urging them to follow. She and her husband left Belfast in 1974.

Author: And why did you leave?
Deirdre: Well, really because of the troubles. Things were quite bad in Belfast and Northern Ireland at that time, and we – well, I was expecting a baby really, and we just didn't feel that, um, it was a very good place really to – to live at the time, really. Things were quite – the situation was quite dangerous. My husband's family had moved to Bolton, his brother – and I think there were a brother and two sisters still at home at that time, and they moved to Bolton really, so that was one of the pressures as well, you know – why don't you sort of come and live with us, or come over here and, you know, stay over here, and we'll – you know, it's a lot easier to live, and things, you know, obviously there's nothing – you're not getting in a sort of a war situation really.

Her husband's brother had come to Bolton with a friend to look for work and had encouraged his parents and siblings to follow. She described the benefits of the move.

Um well, probably just from the safety point of view, you

weren't worried that anyone would come to the door and, er, you could go about your business and no one was really bothered about what religion you were or anything like that. And just – well, really that I suppose no one – you could – you sort of could come and live anywhere, you didn't have to worry about religion or what area was safe to live in or anything like that really. And obviously there wasn't a presence, an army presence, on the street, things like that. You couldn't walk into a riot or in the shops and things like that you weren't worried about bombs or anything like that really. All those sorts of things.

They thought at first that they were making a temporary move and would be going back to Belfast quite soon. Although she and her husband talk about 'going home', they have no plans to do so. Now their son was nineteen and Deirdre felt that it would be difficult for him to settle back in Northern Ireland even if he wanted to. He was five years old when he last visited grandparents there.

Author: Does he show an interest? Does he want to go?
Deirdre: He has more recently, really, because he sort of shares an interest in Irish music, things like that, and if we're watching something on television he'll say, well, I don't understand this, why are they doing that, or whose side are they on, or that kind of thing, explain to me how this came about, or something like that. And that's come more recently. Before that he wasn't really interested in Ireland.

Unlike her own mother, Deirdre stayed at home when her son was at primary school. She then had several part-time jobs before taking up a more permanent job as a library assistant. Deirdre felt that it had been easier for her to live in England as an Irish woman than for her husband as an Irish man.

Deirdre: I don't know whether I could say that perhaps women are accepted, or easier accepted, perhaps, than men, or um it may be because of the jobs that women do really, that they – they sort of blend in a bit more perhaps than men, depending on what they do, really.
Author: Has anyone ever called you a Paddy?
Deirdre: Um, no, but I have heard my husband being called that

or my brother-in-law really, and I think – I just want to say, well, I'm sorry but that's not their name and, you know, why do you think everybody Irish is called Paddy really?

Neither Deirdre nor her husband and son had kept up regular Catholic church attendance in Bolton. Although they had chosen a Catholic school for their son, neither parent felt they would necessarily do so if they had to make the choice again.

Home and belonging

Deirdre felt that she was now settled in Bolton and regarded it as her home.

Author: Where is home to you now?
Deirdre: Um I think probably this is home. I know when I went home to visit my parents I'd call this home. I'd say, oh, back home and such-and-such . . . . I think probably now I feel that Bolton is home. I think probably when my parents were alive, I possibly still felt that Ireland was home, or Belfast was home. But I think I'd have to say it's mostly here really.

She was unsure of how her son would regard his identity.

Author: Does he say he's Irish if you ask him, or . . . ?
Deirdre: No, I don't think he would really. I don't really know what he'd say, actually. I'd have to ask him that. I don't know what he regards himself as being. Perhaps English with Irish parents. I don't really know.

However she still had a positive sense of her Irish identity.

Well, I think Ireland was a good place really, that the people really – I think in general leaving aside troubles and things like that, I think most Irish people have a fairly good outlook on life really and they're fairly generous, you know, friendly. And I mean I think I had quite a rich childhood and a happy childhood, a happy family and things like that. So I suppose that came into it as well. I think I was quite lucky in a way.

Deirdre left Ireland directly because of the political conflict, which made her husband's family anxious about physical safety. Once her parents had died she stopped going back to Belfast or regarding it as home, although her sense of an Irish identity continued to be very strong.

Teresa

Teresa's family had a long history of movement between Bolton and Belfast. Her great-grandmother on her mother's side was from Belfast, and her daughter, Teresa's grandmother, moved to Bolton. However the daughter died giving birth to Teresa's mother, who was then sent back to Belfast to be raised by her grandmother. The other siblings stayed with their Bolton-born English father. Teresa's mother married a Belfast man, and kept close ties with her siblings in Bolton. Teresa herself came over to Bolton to live with an aunt for a year when she was sixteen. Although the family was split between the two places, there was frequent contact between them. Teresa had lived in Bolton for fifteen years at the time of the interview but she had very close family ties to her niece in Belfast whom she often visited.

Teresa had travelled widely in Ireland as a child, having entered show business as a singer at the age of nine. She came from a Catholic background but her family had a very open attitude to other ethnic and religious groups.

> With me being in showbusiness, everyone was at our house, black, white, everybody, they all came to our house, and religion even was never a thing with us. We were never taught, you know, you're different from that other, you know. No, or Irish, no, no.

She married a Protestant man, but had no problems from the mixed marriage. 'We never saw anything, and I lived in a mixed community, no problems. Best people, [no] problems at all, great neighbours, good friends. Still my friends.' In fact Teresa had stopped attending church altogether because she was angry at the openly pro-nationalist stance of the local priest at the time of internment in Northern Ireland in 1971.

She had one son and her final move to Bolton was on his account rather than her own. As a young man of twenty he had been shocked and frightened by a violent incident he witnessed in Belfast in 1979.

> My son managed a record shop, and it so happened they were throwing bricks at the army and one hit an old lady and he took her into his shop and washed her face and gave her a cup of tea. He came home that night and he said, can you get a house in Bolton?

Teresa's husband died at about this time and her son went to the United States for a few months on a long-planned visit with friends. While he was away Teresa came over to Bolton and arranged bar work for herself, a mortgage on a house and a job for her son in a record shop.

Home and belonging

Teresa felt very strongly that Belfast was her home. She had very close social relationships in both Bolton and Belfast and continued the family pattern of moving between the two 'homes'.

> But as I say, I like Bolton, you know. I always say, my heart's over there and the rest of me is in Bolton. And my niece is always asking me. I went home last year and she had my bedroom done up beautiful with my wedding photo enlarged on the – you know? And she's more like a daughter that I never had, than a niece. She really is. . . . I really do miss them. No, I love getting home. I really do.

She contrasted her own feelings of belonging in Belfast with those of her son who did not want to return.

Teresa: I think when you come younger you don't miss so much. He hasn't been home from when he came here. He said this is his home here. But there is my home, no matter what's happening, you know. And you'd finally finish up over there, you know. I always want to go back. . . . But I always have this – I was always going to go home. I went home for five weeks every year, and that five weeks is never long enough. I started with two weeks, three weeks, four weeks, five. My other boss said to me, some year you'll go and you'll not come back. That will be it. I was always able to get off five weeks. I think the last one was six.

Author: You'll miss your friends in Bolton when you go back?

Teresa: Oh yes, I'll miss this, in the bar, as well, you know? I've made some good friends. I have really made some pretty good. And I have a very special friend here, my friend I was with today, and oh, she stands up every time she thinks of it, saying, oh, I miss you, Teresa, could you not come over once a week?

Teresa also mentioned the importance of her husband's and parents' graves in Belfast to her decision to return there permanently.

She explained her son's reasons for cutting himself off from his earlier life in Belfast.

> He never liked me going back, even for my holidays. He used to say, keep your mouth closed when we go back, because I had this habit of saying what I had to say.

However in accepting Bolton as his only home, he had by no means rejected his Irish identity.

> No, he knows he's still Irish, but this is his home now. Yes. I don't think he's any thoughts either way. He lives in England and that's it. That is it. Yes. And he's made a lot of friends here as well, he has.

Teresa gave an example of her son's strong reaction to anti-Irish attitudes. He was lecturing in a college when he overheard trainee teachers making remarks about the 'thick Irish'.

> I said, if that had been me I'd have beaten the jaws off them. No, mum, you don't do that. I get my own back. So he was teaching them something and he says, by the way, this thick Irish man has two degrees and this thick Irish man is teaching you, and this thick Irish man doesn't need right and left on his shoes – it worked in with what he was teaching.

Teresa's story illustrates the close links between the north west of England and Northern Ireland. Moves between the two provide generational ties which are activated as changes occur over the life cycle. Her life has some similarities with that of Deirdre. Each had one child, in contrast to the much larger family sizes of the women from the Irish Republic, particularly those from the rural west. Each had given up attending services in the Catholic church. Their sons were also alike in their current attachment to Bolton. However, unlike Deirdre, Teresa herself felt a stronger tie to her friends and extended family in Belfast where she had 'her own room' in her niece's house. The distinction between holidays and resettlement was becoming blurred and might finally be resolved by her return to live in Ireland.

Anne

Anne was also born in Belfast, but her story is sharply different from those told by all the other women. She was a middle-class Protestant woman, who would not describe herself as Irish.

> Well, I'm not quite sure what you mean by Irishness, because I have a problem, because I'm an Ulster Protestant, and so when you say Irish, really it's a very particular kind of Irishness, it's not like – it's not the same sort of Irishness as being brought up in Dublin or in Eire, because my education was very British, and so when you say Irish, I don't actually feel particularly Irish. It sounds strange though.

Her mother was born in Liverpool, but went to live with her grandmother in Belfast when she was fourteen. Again there were longstanding links between parts of the family in Lancashire, this time because of the linen trade. Her father was born in County Monaghan, before the partition of Ireland, and belonged to a farming family, though his own father was a Royal Irish Constabulary officer. But 'his memory or knowledge of family matters is minimal'.

Anne's mother had worked as a secretary for Harland and Wolff's shipyard, a major Protestant employer, but gave up paid work when she married. There were two children, Anne and her younger brother. Her father was a journalist, later working on the Protestant newspaper, *The Belfast Newsletter*. When Anne was fourteen the family moved to Belfast. They lived in a 'good area' but middle-class Catholics were beginning to move in when she

was at school in the early 1960s. Anne described her parents'
strong disapproval of her becoming friendly with Catholic girls on
the same housing estate.

> Oh yes, the fear of meeting Catholics, that was the thing, you
> see. You hoped nobody would meet Catholics, because then
> once you met them that was the thin end of the wedge and I
> mean that was a major, major problem, and there were active
> blocks put on me being friendly with a Catholic girl and that.

She illustrated the scale of her parents' feelings by relating a
family incident involving black/white difference.

> But I mean I had a cousin who married a Nigerian, this will
> perhaps give you a measure of what it was like, and he's a
> Nigerian doctor, she was a nurse, very nice bloke actually, and
> subsequently in the Nigerian civil war, we think he was killed
> but we don't know. He was an Ibo. But I mean that was –
> anyway, they had a – I was asked to be bridesmaid at this
> wedding, and oh, the dilemma the whole thing caused,
> because of course he's black, and everybody thought this was
> totally and absolutely shocking. It was not something you did
> in those days, you just didn't. It was not only rebellious but I
> mean it was foolish and a terrible thing, and her mother said
> at the wedding to my mother, well, she said, it could have been
> worse, it could have been a Catholic! And that was the measure
> of where Catholics came in the order of things.

Anne went to Queen's University, Belfast and then taught in a
school in her home town. But she was very unhappy as a teacher
and decided to go back to university, this time in Manchester
where one of her lecturers from Queen's now taught. This was in
1968, but her decision was not related to the renewed outbreak
of the 'troubles'. She had already been to England, as well as travelled abroad, a number of times so it seemed very familiar to her
and she did not see it as emigration.

After completing a postgraduate degree Anne spent two years
on a university teaching exchange in the United States, where she
had to confront a new set of issues about her Irish identity.

> I was a bit more aware of being Irish, I suppose, of the dilemma,

if there is a dilemma, of being Irish and British, in the States, because there was such an Irish identification, and as soon as you said you came from Ireland, then you were latched onto as having some kind of, you know, Irish connection. Well, that was very difficult because I didn't have an Irish connection as such.

Anne returned to England and took a job in Bolton where she married and has remained ever since. Her husband is English, nominally Protestant. Anne stopped attending Protestant churches in England after a sermon in Manchester in the early 1970s when the minister had preached about the Northern Ireland 'troubles' and suggested everyone bore some guilt. 'I got very irate and I thought, that's nothing to do with me, why should I feel guilty?' She used to return twice a year to visit her parents, but was anxious about safety and had not taken her son since he was very small. When her father retired, her parents moved to Bolton.

Home and belonging

Anne responded very differently from the other interviewees to the question of belonging. In contrast to their very strong ties both to Ireland and to Bolton, her response showed an unusual measure of detachment.

> That's a good question. I don't really feel I belong anywhere, actually. I don't mean in a negative sort of way, but it's an interesting question because although we've lived in the North West now for a long time, if we found somewhere else that, you know, economically we could go to and survive and that we liked, we would go. I don't think either of us is very rooted at all.

Her idea of home focused around her immediate family and belongings, 'where everything is'. The place, even the house, is therefore a temporary part of what makes up 'home'.

Author: So if you think of home, what springs to mind?
Anne: Oh, the house.
Author: Just the house?
Anne: Yes.
Author: Your present house?
Anne: Yes, just where everything is, you know. No, I don't think

> of home as Ireland as people do, you know. Oh, I'll go
> home – and then they use the word home still for – no,
> no, I've given up using that one a long time ago.

When she considers her feelings for Northern Ireland she talks
about detaching herself from her past with a sense of relief. The
only slight regret is for the landscape she left, which could be
replaced: 'we've been looking for places that were similar'.

> Um, I think I've sloughed a lot of it off. I mean I think that I
> no longer have any great interest in what happens in Ireland,
> and I mean I think that I don't have any particular nostalgia
> for the roots. I haven't been back since my parents left.

The only thing she misses about Northern Ireland is the landscape, particularly the coastline and empty beaches. The absence
of any mention of people to whom she is attached presents a stark
contrast to all the other interviewees. She blames her parents for
this lack of attachment, because of their extremely restricted
acceptance only of 'true blue Irish Protestants'. They remain in
contact with the few remaining relatives in Northern Ireland 'but
it's only a very tenuous link' and she feels it will break when they
die.

When asked about her son's identity, Anne felt there was no
Irish dimension.

Author: Does he have any sense of Irish background?
Anne: I don't think so.
Author: Any interest, does he show more interest than others in
          the political situation or anything like that?
Anne: No, no. He's your usual sort of rock-mad teenager really,
          there's not much – and to be honest I haven't actually
          actively encouraged it, because it doesn't particularly
          interest me and I've not really thought about encourag-
          ing it, to be honest. So perhaps I should.

However Anne is also fascinated by the Ireland which was forbidden to her as a child. She feels that she would now like to
holiday in the west of Ireland.

Anne: But I would be going as a tourist really, as somebody

	coming to a foreign country really, rather than somebody Irish.
Author:	Would it be the scenery, do you think, mostly, that would take you there?
Anne:	Oh yes. Well, hopefully the people might be quite nice as well, but I mean, you know, it would be getting to know them as a foreigner really. Because that's the way we were brought up, they were foreign, they were different, they weren't like us. It's stupid really.

Anne's story illustrates axes of difference which include the inter-locking dimensions of political allegiance, class and religion. Anne came from a background of middle-class Unionism in which religion was a badge of difference, but the political identity of Britishness was uppermost. When Anne's parents retired to live in Bolton they stopped attending church, even though a Protestant one was nearby. Anne's move to Britain was part of a rite of leaving the parental home, although her relief at 'sloughing off' her Northern Irish past suggests there was also a strong desire to 'escape' from it. Nevertheless she moved effortlessly into middle-class English life and saw no major discontinuity between Ireland and Britain.

Commentary: difference and belonging

The ten biographies provide a counterpoint to the homogenising category of 'Irish women' produced by stereotypes and statistical analysis. There are striking variations in the identities and experi-ences of diasporic Irish women in Britain. My categorisation initially highlights differences by place of origin in Ireland, iden-tifying three contrasting environments. But in addition to the commonalities of different 'home places' in Ireland, women's individual circumstances and subsequent trajectories also diverge, placing the women in a variety of relationships to those with whom they share the diasporic space of Britain.

One of the sharpest contrasts is between women from farming families in the west of Ireland and indigenous Bolton women. Rural women, especially those from the West, were constructed as iconic by the Irish nationalist project in the early twentieth century, promoting characteristics as different as possible from those of England (Nash 1993). In the immediate pre- and post-war period, when the five rural women left Ireland for Bolton, they described a way of life which was still congruent with this image, characterised as rural, Catholic, focused on children and home, and enmeshed in a complex web of extended family relationships. This contrasted fundamentally with the suburban, secular life of women in Britain, based on single-generation households with small numbers of children, which was being projected as the essence of the English way of life in all regions in the post-war period (Webster 1998).

These two contrasting gendered discourses of nation intersected in the diaspora space of Britain. In reality they also interlinked in fundamental ways. Despite their iconic status, Irish farm mothers were only a small proportion of the rural female population and their continued presence depended on the emigration of most of their daughters when they reached adulthood. Emigration was thus a powerful subtext to the 'difference' of Irish life, allowing it to portray an apparent stability and timelessness in contrast to the fast-changing modern industrial world of Britain. The stories of the five women illustrated the material consequences of this discourse. Both Mary and Eileen had to leave their own family farm to allow the inheriting brother to 'bring in' a wife. Thus the women who stayed literally displaced them. All the women spent long summers on the home farm with their English-born children, recreating for a short time each year the lives they might have had. In Britain they retained many characteristics of the lives they would have led, placing child-rearing at the centre and continuing a very close relationship with the Catholic church. Each had at least four children, well above the English norm. None of the rural women mentioned any discordance between their religious practices in Ireland and Britain. This was in contrast to four out of five of the urban women who had severed their connections.

The major difference between the lives of mothers in Ireland, and their daughters in Britain was the paid labour of the latter. The nature of this labour again links to the discursive position of women in the two nations. In Ireland representations of women as home-based carers restricted their educational background so that they were qualified only for 'unskilled' work in Britain, especially domestic service. In turn this meshed neatly with the need to support the home-based image of English mothers through paid help, and through a replacement female labour in factories and mills.

Rural women thus occupy a distinctive representational place in the Irish diaspora. They are also foregrounded in stereotypes which focus on large families with a strong Catholic allegiance. Perhaps ironically, snippets of information about the rural women's English-born children suggested exceptionally upward mobility through the English education system. They had benefited from the system of selective Catholic grammar schools in the 1960s, through which they had gained scholarships at 11 and then fully-funded university places. All five of Eileen's children went to university and four were working in higher or school education. Similarly in Nora's family, four out of five children gained degrees and the fifth qualified as a lawyer. Mary's son, who was present at the interview, was a teacher.

However the category of 'Irish women' in Britain is much more heterogeneous than this stereotype allows. The biographies of the women from farms in the West contrast strikingly with the histories of the two women from Dublin. Neither had any connection with Bolton; they arrived there by chance, Margaret because she met an English man in Ireland, and Bernadette because she answered an advertisement. Both married English men, and although they became mothers this was not the central focus of their adult lives as it had been for all of the women from the west of Ireland. Each had two children, a much smaller family size than that of the rural women. Each took on roles which were non-traditional, particularly for women in Ireland. Margaret participated in the public civic life of Bolton as a Labour councillor and magistrate, while Bernadette had done a variety of full-time paid jobs, including millwork, engineering and van-driving. Neither Margaret nor Bernadette saw their future lives as revolving around their children and grandchildren despite the closeness they felt to their families and indeed they planned to live in different countries. Both had a strong Catholic faith, although Bernadette had separated herself from the institutional organisation because it clashed with her own principles.

In addition to rural–urban differences, the political division between the Republic and Northern Ireland added further complexities to the category. Indeed one interviewee did not recognise the description of herself as an 'Irish woman' at all. All three of the Northern Irish women interviewed had city childhoods in Belfast, and two of the three were Catholic, but their lives contrasted strongly with those of the Dublin women. Employment prospects for Margaret and Bernadette in Dublin of the 1950s were bleak, so emigration was a move which brought greater economic security. However Deirdre and Teresa, and their families, were quite well-established in employment in Belfast. They left very suddenly because political violence in the early 1970s made close members of their families fear for their lives. In fact neither woman expressed this fear for herself, and both felt that they would have managed to stay if the decision to leave had not been made for them. Each woman had only one child, but their lives were strongly home-based. Deirdre described herself as unusual in Bolton for waiting until her son was at secondary school before she looked for paid work, although her own mother had been 'unique' in her home neighbourhood in Belfast for having full-time employment during her own childhood.

The most starkly different story was told by Anne, the middle-class Protestant woman from a staunch Unionist background in Northern Ireland. Anne's biography also brings to the fore the issue of class, which was submerged in the similarity of the working-class backgrounds of the other interviewees. In doing so it also highlights the clustering of the Bolton women's stories in the years immediately before and after the Second World War. More recent emigration from Ireland, especially during the 1980s, included larger numbers of middle-class women who had benefited from the expansion of free secondary and higher education, especially in the Republic of Ireland. These younger women were not found in Bolton in the 1990s, however, their migration flow being directed almost entirely towards London and the South East (Kells 1995a).

The stories reflected important aspects of the heterogeneity of the experiences of Irish women living in Bolton in the 1990s. However, the sample does not tell the full story. It excludes women who were single, were not mothers or were economically insecure. None of the women mentioned coming to England for an abortion or to escape censure with an illegitimate child, and none had been divorced or separated. No Traveller woman was interviewed. But even among those who have been grouped together for analytical purposes, there are individual constellations of life-events and responses. The friends, Kathleen and Nora, were brought together by shared cultural understandings and many similar experiences, but their individual locations in patterns of diaspora diverge quite strongly.

Negotiating 'homes' in Ireland and Britain

The central experience of diaspora is that of negotiating ongoing displacement with the choice or necessity of permanent settlement outside the 'homeland'. The ten Bolton Irish women managed this dichotomy in a great variety of ways. Breda Gray (1997) points out that women's conceptualisations of diaspora are circumscribed by official narratives about emigration from Ireland. She argues that the need to present it as a positive part of Irish national identity has distorted women's personal experiences by limiting the categories into which they can place themselves. Her analysis relates to the specific historical period of the 1980s and 1990s, but earlier migrants have also developed frameworks for explaining their life choices which are similarly constrained by the discourses available to them.

Two women had rejected Ireland as a place to live and said they had greatly improved their lives by settling permanently in Britain. The most extreme example of this was Anne who, although not seeing herself as a migrant, had distanced herself psychologically as well as physically from the country where she had lived for the first twenty-two years of her life. Although she says she does not have 'any particular nostalgia for the roots' and speaks with distaste about her parents' Unionist views, she misses 'the landscape' although she did not feel that was 'hers' in any way. Anne has been displaced by being cut off from her own childhood and a specific form of Irish culture which she no longer values. She feels 'placed' in England, but shares the lack of place-specific roots associated with university-educated middle-class women whose career is a central part of their lives.

Margaret had also rejected Ireland and felt much more strongly 'placed' in England. In her case she had chosen Bolton as her new 'home', on the grounds of the town itself and its amenities, its people and specifically 'very good friends'. She retains strong links with Ireland, through visiting her son and his family, but in her narrative the different homes were reconciled without difficulty. Gray (1997) points out that for Irish women migrating in the more recent period the option to reject Ireland has been removed. Because it is now portrayed as 'the best place on earth', other explanations have to be offered in order to keep intact an idealised sense of the Irish nation. But Margaret left in the 1950s when national morale was at a low ebb and the difference in economic opportunities between the Republic and Britain was undeniably large.

These are stories of progress, which Swirsky (1999) argues fit with the narrative structure of archetypical autobiography, and therefore rarely include mentions of displacement and loss. Both women presented their current lives in positive terms. However there are underlying losses which are hidden in the construction of a coherent life story. As Eva Hoffman points out in conversation with Elena Lappin: 'Even in the case of people who are very positively disposed at first, some sense of loss or mourning comes upon them later, because there is no getting away from the huge fact of being severed from the past' (Lappin 1995: 11).

Anne has been displaced by being cut off from her own childhood and a specific form of Irish culture which she no longer values. Her attempts to revisit the landscape by finding similar places and her fantasies about visiting the west of Ireland may be ways in which these suppressed feelings of attachment are finding expression. Margaret's rejection of Ireland may also be related to her mother's lack of concern at losing her and the family's failure to celebrate her achievements in England.

By contrast, two women had a clear preference for returning to live in Ireland. Although there were family ties to Bolton, both intended to move back. Bernadette described herself as only temporarily resident in Bolton after forty years: 'I'm passing through'. But to return to Dublin would be very disruptive of her friendship patterns and she would lose her daily contact with her children and grandchildren. Despite many positive aspects of her life in Bolton, the largest part of her life has been spent away from the place she regards as 'home'. Teresa also felt that she belonged in Belfast and was gradually starting to return by staying longer on each visit. She explained that she missed her friends. Again the unspoken subtext is of years among family and friends which have been lost. Even if she resolves the tension by returning to live in Belfast, she will leave her son behind in Bolton. Again, despite the positive way in which Bernadette and Teresa speak about their resolution to the problem of displacement, by recovering the original place, displacement will continue to be part of their lives.

Much clearer awareness of the inevitability of ongoing ambivalence, and recognition of the pain of displacement, is shown by the responses of women who feel that they are tied to Britain by their children and grandchildren. All five women from the rural west said that home was now Bolton. But as they elaborated on their feelings, they revealed the regret they still felt at leaving home in Ireland. Mary, who left Ireland nearly fifty years ago, said 'you miss it' and that 'I suppose I'd always say I belong to Ireland'. There was an element of compulsion about her statement that 'home to me now has to be here'. Eileen, who declared with passion that home was where her children and grandchildren were, also said 'I feel so at home' in Ireland but 'there's no hope for me going back'. Bridie said 'I'm here too long to go back', revealing a yearning which could never be answered. Nora also agreed that Bolton was home because 'it has to be', but said that if all her children went abroad 'I think you'd find I'd be going back'.

These stories illustrate ongoing displacement among women who all stated that they felt contented with Bolton. There was no doubt that they felt 'at home' there. Mary said 'I suppose I've always had so much comfort here and that kind of thing. I've always had a good life here, and I've always had plenty of friends'. Bridie said she would miss the shops and the town that she knew. Although a few instances of anti-Irish attitudes could be recalled, all the interviewees spoke very highly of the friendliness of the town. As Nora said: 'because when you think of down south now, Bolton and round here is very friendly, they are very, very, very friendly, aren't they?'

However, although they considered their relations with English people to be good, the women were attached to an Irish world in Bolton. Their primary focus was on their immediate family, and the Catholic church also featured very strongly. Their closest friends were Irish women. Bernadette worked providing school meals with twenty-four women, but although 'I'd sit with anybody' she also noticed that 'strange as it seems there's always three or four of us sitting having our lunch every day and we're all Irish'. The most enclosed world was described by Eileen whose one point of contact with English society was her children's school, which was blocked by the anti-Irish behaviour of a Bolton mother. But her children later brought her into a wider social environment: 'when my children got married like, I met more English people then, and they were all very nice people'.

This enclosure was mirrored by the different attitudes expressed by the rural women towards anti-Irish hostility. Whereas the urban working-class Catholic women had confronted it openly, by

challenging the comments or agreeing with expressions of anger
about violence, the rural women had avoided situations in which
they would be exposed to it, often at great personal cost. Mary
worked very long hours in addition to caring for four children rather
than claim welfare benefits which might subject her to hostile
scrutiny. Eileen had been almost literally confined to the house by
racist comments of a neighbour. The three other women insisted
that they had no experience of unequal treatment. Nora said:
'People say that has been happening lately, with this Northern
Ireland problem, but we didn't suffer it, Kathleen and I, no we
didn't, there was none. We couldn't say anything like that, no'. Bridie
also denied having any problems: 'I've been treated well over here,
by everybody, you know, by doctors or anybody that you meet
anywhere, wherever I've been. I've never been – had anybody say, oh,
you're Irish, and been put down by it'. However these denials may
mask treatment which is ignored and responded to by silence or
withdrawal. Bridie also revealed ways in which she overlooked
negative attitudes in order to keep good relations: 'I work with plenty
of English women, they don't mind, I don't bother any more you
know'.

Multi-generational identities

A key facet of diaspora, which marks it out from a migration perspective, is the lack of a time limit on the significance of
displacement. Migration is a narrative of progress, which implies
replacing old with new, loss of the old being seen as necessary to
acquiring the new. From a diaspora perspective, however, the old
continues in parallel with the new until it is no longer salient. Some
aspects of the old, such as family memories, may continue over
generations and carry personal significance to individuals. Viewed
in this way, the notion of Britain as a 'diaspora space' becomes
easier to imagine. Entanglements are much deeper and more
complex if the lives of 'indigenous' people are not only shared with
those 'from elsewhere', but their own identities include elements
of 'otherness' when account is taken of their family background
extending backwards over several generations.

An important theme which emerged from the interviews was
the continuity in identifications of Irish identities among British-
born children. This was not universal and showed many
variations, but the notion of automatic 'assimilation' in parallel

with the acquisition of an English accent was shown to be false. The discourse of assimilation, a correlate of the migration perspective, is differentially applied to white and black groups. Whereas it is imposed on white groups in order to shore up a dangerously diverse population, it is denied to black groups so that the boundary between 'same' and 'other' is maintained. Thus blackness continues to signify difference over generations even when income and education have produced strong commonalities. The consequence for Irish people in Britain is that Irishness is not recognised beyond the migrant generation. However Irish people in Britain may also collude in this denial of difference. The name 'Plastic Paddies' is an ironical name for second-generation Irish people used by the Irish-born, at once accepting the British stereotype of 'Paddy' and simultaneously turning it into a badge of authenticity. Mary Kells (1995a) shows how her middle-class informants placed an Irish birthplace alongside religious and class allegiances in identifying 'real' as opposed to 'counterfeit' Irishness.

In all but one case Irishness featured in the identities of the English-born children of the interviewees according to their mothers. Only Anne, the Protestant woman from Northern Ireland, said she thought that her son had no sense of Irishness as part of his own identity. She had not 'actively encouraged it' though she felt 'perhaps I should', so did not dismiss its relevance to him. The other Northern Irish-born mother of an English-born son, of a similar age in his late teens, was more unsure about how he saw his identity: 'I don't know what he regards himself as being. Perhaps English with Irish parents'. For both these children the issue of their Irish identity was bound up with the political conflict, a major aspect of which is precisely the nature of national and ethnic identities in Northern Ireland. Although they came from different political traditions, this must underlie the absence of discussion of the issue in both households. The children themselves had not been to Ireland since early childhood. Their mothers had been displaced by the conflict, either indirectly or very directly, and neither felt that she would return.

Swirsky, discussing the lives of Jewish migrants in Britain, points to the very different experiences of political and economic migrants.

> Economic migrants leave a home which continues to exist, with
> kin and community continuing to have a concrete presence

which acts as a reference point, a focus. Indeed in these more affluent times of accessible international travel, 'home' can be visited to provide reassurance and help to dispel the longing, assuage the emotional loss, and indeed the guilt at having left. This is not to say that physical accessibility mitigates the sense of dislocation and the unhappiness of displacement. However as mobility, migration and exile have become more common-place, they may also have become less traumatic, albeit still involving loss.

(Swirsky 1999: 201)

She argues that political migrants may have to 'turn their faces more resolutely forwards', which would describe the narratives given by Deirdre and Teresa's son, and in a more complex way by Anne.

The meanings for economic migrants of temporary returns 'home' resonate with the accounts given by the rural women inter-viewed. One consequence has been the immersion of English-born children in the family networks of the 'home' area. Margaret's son had enjoyed visiting as a child so much that he moved to Ireland to live when he was eighteen. The rural five women described in detail their long annual visits to parents and relatives, associated for the children with many positive features including a break from school-work, a warm welcome, a 're-placed' mother, many cousins to play with, freedom to roam and summer weather. For some this frequent physical association with Ireland has continued into adulthood.

The extent to which adult children continued to visit Ireland varied between families and also between siblings in one family. Eileen said; 'My children love Ireland. They go back to Ireland quite a lot and they love it'. Nora described her two of her five children as 'very Irish' and that 'they like to feel that they can go back. . . . they keep up the relationship with their cousins and all, so that they will'. Another son, Tom, stopped going for some years but had recently taken it up again so enthusiastically that he had been back three or four times in the past year: 'now that he has started going back he's going back even more than I do'. Tom went to the family home area, but was also exploring other parts of Ireland. These connections were not necessarily severed by lack of use, but could be reactivated at different points in people's lives. However Bridie feared there was a trend towards 'falling away' with age and post-secondary education, as there had been to date in her own family. She knew of only a 'few families' who had maintained in Bolton their Irish cultural activities such as music and dancing.

Senses of Irish identities were also being passed to grandchildren, again casting doubt on the assimilation thesis with its assumption of the rapid loss of cultural difference. This was mentioned especially by the rural women. Bridie took her grandchildren to visit the family in Ireland on her own because her own children had lost interest. Eileen's daughter took her son to an Irish music club in Bolton where he was learning the piano accordian. Mary's son talked about using Irish language expressions with his own wife and children. Thus third-generation identities retain strong Irish elements. Despite pressures from the centre to deny continuing difference, diasporic identities are not contained within one or even two generations.

The stories the women told about their lives illustrate both diversity within the category of 'Irish women' in Britain and the specificity of their experiences in this particular town. The notion of a steady movement towards assimilation over time did not fit the accounts they gave of their own or their children's lives. Instead they had no difficulty in seeing themselves as simultaneously 'placed' in Bolton and 'displaced' by close, continuing ties with Ireland. They were 'at home' in Bolton, while Ireland remained the strongest source of their sense of self in all but one case. But these are not fixed identities; like those of their children and grandchildren, they are constantly 'producing and reproducing themselves anew, through transformation and difference' (Hall 1990: 235).

Conclusion

Can Irish women be described as outsiders in the United States and Britain? This analysis has provided ample evidence of the ambivalence with which they are placed in these categories. In the United States Irish women's location has changed since the nineteenth century, so that they are often now apparently placed at the heart of the nation, yet in certain contexts they retain traces of earlier exclusions. In Britain there is striking evidence of the simultaneous construction of Irish women as *both* outside and inside with remarkable persistence over time.

These findings thoroughly problematise binary classifications of identities. They expose the inventedness of bounded categories. Locating Irish women within the duality of outside/inside constructions privileges the hegemonic centre which sees itself as filling the space 'inside', and defines itself in opposition to 'outside' groups. Thus outsideness and insideness describe the states which the centre allocates to social groups. This power of the centre to define group identities, which is reflected in both political and popular discourses, has material effects on groups such as Irish women in Britain. Moreover it is underpinned and legitimised by binary theorisations. The discourse of migration, for example, supports a static view of places as bounded 'insides' by representing migrants as travelling between them along linear spatial, social and chronological trajectories. Places of destination need to protect their constructed homogeneity by incorporating migrants through marking their ongoing difference or by 'assimilation'. Both of these processes can be identified in the case of the Irish in Britain. On the one hand longstanding negative stereotypes continue to have purchase, while on the other difference is strenuously denied.

I have argued that diaspora provides an alternative framework for conceptualising the location of emigrant Irish women, one which does not trap them into the paradox of simultaneous inclusion and exclusion. Binary categories are not the only way in which societies can be represented. If places are imagined instead as meeting places, 'always unfixed, contested and multiple' and always and continuously being reproduced, then the 'outside is part of the inside' (Massey 1994: 5). The alternative view of Britain as a 'diaspora space' thus provides another way of imagining the relationship and reformulates issues of difference. Instead of focussing on boundaries between groups, it recognises the interconnections between them. In this conceptualisation Irish people become part of a much larger picture of the 'entanglements of dispersion with those of staying put'. Avtar Brah's (1996) choice of 'entanglement' as a metaphor vividly captures the complexity of the connections involved and the impossibility of, as well as the likely damage following from, attempts to unravel them. In fact, entanglements describe the creolisation of diaspora space, whether this is acknowledged or not.

My analysis provides a framework within which the specificity of Irish diasporic positionings and experiences can be examined. I have used an interdisciplinary approach to draw attention to the complex texturing of diaspora spaces. A particular concern has been to make connections between spatial and social positionings. The two key concepts of place and whiteness have threaded through the account and I shall reflect here both on their wider contribution to the narrative and on the directions for further research which they highlight.

Place, in its variety of spatial and social meanings, has been a central theme running through the book. The notions of 'outside' and 'inside' are notions of place, both geographically and socially. Diaspora references both simultaneously in its dual constitution as displacement and placement. The movement from a specific, named place to a settlement in another, and the ongoing links between the two, crucially define the lives of diasporic peoples. They continue to be labelled, and to label themselves, by the geographical name of their place of origin, which may then become hyphenated with the name of the destination at one scale or another.

Place gives specificity to diasporic experiences, grounding them in particular relations of power which can be brought into view more readily than by abstract theorising alone. I have argued that a comparative approach is particularly useful in situations where racialisation has become normalised, as in the case of the Irish in Britain. Comparisons can be made not only at the national scale, but also within national formations. I have identified marked regional and local variations in Irish women's experience of settlement in Britain in which, for example, their relationships with Englishness in London and Lancashire are sharply different. There are further distinctive aspects of Irish women's lives in Bolton which relate to the history of women's work in the town, the long time period over which contacts have been maintained and proximity to Irish Sea ports.

One of the strengths of the diaspora framework is the open-endedness of the analysis. Specificities can be stretched forward and back over time, and over larger and smaller geographic locations. The intersection of cross-cutting social positionings can also be complicated, for example, by foregrounding a range of social locations in addition to gender, such as class, age, generation, sexuality, ability, religion and parenthood. Each of these complications will reveal new facets of the entanglement and strengthen the evidence for multiple rather than binary relationalities. As Brah argues, within diaspora space,

> Axes of differentiation and division such as class, gender and sexuality articulate a myriad of economic, political and cultural practices through which power is exercised. Each axis signifies a *specific modality of power relation*. What is of interest is how these fields of power collide, enmesh and configure; and *with what effects*. What kinds of inclusions or exclusions does a *specific articulation of power* produce?
>
> (Brah 1996: 248, author's emphasis)

Ways in which the diaspora framework could fruitfully be extended in the study of Irish women's specific case are multiple and varied. For example, many other diasporic locations could be added to the analysis. Particularly interesting ones would be those with different political relationships with Britain, including Australia, Canada, New Zealand and South Africa. In Australia, for example, more than a third of the present population has Irish connections from the past. It has been suggested that the distinctive form of masculinity which has developed in Australia has origins in gendered relationships in nineteenth-century Ireland.

Thus the 'sheilas' of popular discourse derive from representations of disempowered women in Ireland (Dixson 1976).

At home, geographical variation within the diaspora space of Britain needs fuller attention. A location which is largely absent from my analysis is Scotland, one of the most important areas of settlement in the nineteenth century (Figure 4.2) and where the relationship to the British 'core' is mediated by national differences (Bradley 1995). What have been the experiences of Irish-born women and women of Irish descent in Scotland, given the centrality of Protestantism to the national identity? How has anti-Catholicism, widely recognised in the past but carrying contemporary resonances, affected their paid working and unpaid caring lives? What criss-crossings have there been in the lives of women of Irish and other non-Scottish backgrounds? The third component of the United Kingdom, Wales is even more invisible as a site of ethnic entanglements. Are there shared identities peripheral to the English centre in both these locations, despite the evidence I have cited of anti-Irish attitudes? The 1994 survey of attitudes between ethnic groups in Britain identifying themselves, and identified by others as, English, Scottish, Welsh and Irish, suggested unexpected similarities which could be carefully deconstructed with qualitative research (*Irish Post* 17 December 1994). This would provide a specific instance of Brah's proposal that 'border crossings do not occur only across the dominant/dominated dichotomy, but that, equally, there is traffic within cultural formations of the subordinated groups, and that these journeys are not always mediated through the dominant culture(s)' (Brah 1996: 209).

Places are also social positionings, the cross-cutting intersections between social categories within diaspora spaces. The homogenisation of particular groups of outsiders, which follows from the foregrounding of imagined ethnic or race boundaries, render such multiple identities invisible. I have chosen to highlight gender as a particularly significant omission. Gendered imagery suffuses the national constructions which rely on the boundary between outside and inside for their maintenance, and in turn this has significant effects on the day-to-day experiences of Irish people. Irish women have been differentially included in the national narratives of the United States and Britain. Their low visibility in Britain has not reflected their economic or social importance, but their own lives have been fundamentally affected by the unspoken place constructed for them by changing definitions of Englishness.

However, my focus on the majority experience of Catholic working-class women, predominantly from the Irish Republic, has also produced further homogenisations which need to be deconstructed. Protestant women are absent from most analyses. In the nineteenth century, the Catholic 'Famine Irish' came to dominate the emigration flow and have largely squeezed out Protestant identities from view in the United States (Akenson 1993). This is more explicable in the later twentieth century when Protestants form a very small proportion of women in the Republic, less than 5 per cent of the total. However their 'difference' in Ireland means that they have a distinctive experience after migration, not part of the majority yet treated identically by British people. The story of Rachel Harbron, told in *Across the Water* and subtitled 'Other people's worlds', illuminates this experience (Lennon, McAdam and O'Brien 1988). Larger numbers of Protestant women have left Northern Ireland, where they are in a majority, forming about 58 per cent of the female population in the 1990s. Many of these may be middle-class women who experience a double distancing from the majority positioning. Anne's story in Bolton, for example, is an extreme version of dislocation from an Irish past of a Protestant woman from Northern Ireland. The complexities of identification for young middle-class Protestant women settling in London are explored in detail by Mary Kells (1995a, 1995b), but other narratives about Protestant working-class women and those settling elsewhere in Britain remain to be told.

Middle-class Irish women have made relatively few appearances in my book although they form a significant proportion of the total number of Irish-born women in Britain. At least a third of all Irish-born women are in the Registrar General's Social Classes I and II, mainly in the 'professional' categories of nurses and teachers. Among women aged eighteen to twenty-nine the proportion is almost half and includes managers, administrators and financial advisers. They are not referenced in dominant constructions of Irishness but may be subjected to the negative consequences of association, as the accounts of Irish nurses in London illustrate. Those who have entered the middle classes in the second generation may carry with them memories of their childhoods, which can only gradually be named because of the enforced loss of identities in the socialisation process of school and the wider British society (Maguire 1997). Indeed the experiences and identification of girls and women born and brought up in Britain with one or two Irish-born parents is a critical area for future research.

More completely excluded are Traveller women. Even the numbers are not accurately known. There are also acute tensions in shared Irish identifications, replicating racist attitudes in both parts of Ireland towards Travelling people (McCann, O Siochain and Ruane 1994; Mac Laughlin 1995). As Nellie Power, born in Ireland in 1951 and now living in London, explained:

> Really and truly, most of the Irish people over here are more against the travellers than English people. I've never been to the Irish Centre for a drink, because a lot of travellers are barred, so we don't bother going up there. I think what it is, they're ashamed of travellers. It really hurts to describe. I think of myself as Irish. My five children were born in England, yet they call themselves Irish travellers. That's what they say, 'Irish travellers'. But when people know that you're a traveller, they don't think of you as Irish, they just say you're a traveller. A lot of pubs put up a sign that says 'No Travellers' – that means that even though you've never been in the pub, just because you're a traveller you can't go in them. It gets you when you're walking down the street and you look and see that written there. You're written off just because you're a traveller.
>
> (Lennon, McAdam and O'Brien 1988: 181–2)

Research has uncovered a wealth of information about the circumstances and experiences of Traveller women, especially those living mainly in London, but these have yet to be brought inside the space allocated to the remainder of the Irish population in Britain (Southwark Traveller Women's Group 1992; London Irish Women's Centre 1995). Nellie Power's comments highlight the need for dialogue within that space as well as between the traveller and settled populations more generally. The extreme exclusion of Travellers, arising out of fundamental anxieties about threats to hegemonic identities posed by mobility, touches on meanings of diaspora at a yet more deep-seated level (Sibley 1981, 1995).

One of the major obstacles to relocating Irish women conceptually within a diaspora framework is the strength of the black/white binary in popular, political and academic discourse. This is where the construction of the binary of outside/inside has been at its most powerful and it remains barely recognised. Whiteness shores up the outside/inside duality in unspoken ways. Academic discourse continues to underpin this binary in theorisations of blackness and whiteness. Blackness is now being subjected to detailed deconstruction and information about the widely varying socio-economic trajectories of different 'non-white' ethnic groups in Britain has been meticulously amassed, with substantial support from state funding. But the researchers in the widely-acclaimed Fourth National Report on Ethnic Minorities, *Ethnic Minorities in Britain: Diversity and Disadvantage*, contrasted each group with a monolithic white category, thus emphasising the divide which their evidence was undermining (Modood *et al.* 1997).

Whiteness has become a popular area of study in the 1990s (see Bonnett 1996). However the directions taken by 'White Studies' have reinforced rather than deconstructed the homogeneity of the category. There has been little recognition to date of the heterogeneity of its constituent parts. Many critiques, from different perspectives, while attempting to dislodge the power of the 'absent centre' by exposing its mechanisms to examination, continue to enforce inclusion of subordinate groups within it. For example, Vron Ware (1992) discusses 'the white woman's burden' and, in his review of 'White Studies', Alistair Bonnett (1996) makes reference to 'white identity', apparently a singular condition. Similarly Ruth Frankenberg (1993), while examining in detail the contexts of interracial encounters of her interviewees, does not consider the ethnic backgrounds of the white women in the United States whose attitudes she explores. Even Richard Dyer (1997), who recognises 'gradations of whiteness', chooses 'non-white' instead of 'black' in his discussion of naming. He argues that black excludes a range of people who are neither white nor black and reinforces the negative connotations of black in racial imagery. But the formulation makes white even more monolithic when it is part of a zero-sum binary in which there are no further groupings.

Another problem is the further conflation of whiteness with particular national formations. Diane Jeater (1992) unambiguously links whiteness with Englishness, entitling her article 'Roast Beef and Reggae Music: the Passing of Whiteness' and noting the association of 'white' with a supposed 'English cultural heritage'. In a different set of formulations from a black feminist perspective, Heidi Safia Mirza describes 'Black British feminism as a body of scholarship [which] is located in that space of *British* whiteness, that unchallenged hegemonic patriarchal discourse of *colonial and now postcolonial* times which quietly embraces our common-sense and academic ways of thinking' (Mirza 1999: 3 my emphasis).

Although Mirza may have intended by her formulation to specify a particular form of whiteness, this was not signalled and readers could assume an indissoluble link with Britishness. It appears to deny the experience of colonisation to white people, most notably the Irish. These conflations arise from, and confirm, the British strategy of drawing racial boundaries around the coast-line of the 'British Isles'.

However Magdalene Ang-Lydgate recognises the neglect of transnational diasporic experiences within black British feminism, which has marginalised important issues of diversity and differ-ence arguing that

> It is a mistake to fall prey to a racist/sexist mythology that insists that our experience of 'blackness' as non-Caucasian women puts us all in the same category as victims of racism, or that social inequality and injustice is ultimately reducible to 'race' or colour differences, without also drawing attention to the specific histories and experiences of racism.
>
> (Ang-Lydgate 1999: 171)

She points out that this reinforces the very principle of binary dualism through which exclusions are constructed:

> Accordingly, the possibility of theorising difference is confined to difference-as-opposition rather than difference-as-diversity. For example, translated into anti-racist discourse, there is no room in this particular schema for peoples of mixed parentage nor is there any space available for admitting the possibility of 'black'–'black' or 'white'–'white' racism, for example between South Asian and African-Caribbean or between English and Irish peoples. In retaining the current terminology of anti-racism in Britain that is based on this black/white rationale, the actual realities of many immigrant experiences of inter-ethnic racism is denied and the structures which feminists seek to change become reproduced.
>
> (ibid.: 172)

Resistance on the part of the British state to thinking in these more fluid ways about identities is illustrated by the categories selected for the 'ethnic question' in the Census. As Ang-Lydgate (1999: 177) argues 'the administrative technologies of the state construct the categories they then proceed to regulate'. They have perceived a particular 'problem' about classifying peoples of mixed parentage, which 'betrays hidden assumptions about racial purity'. The struggle by Irish community and welfare groups to have an 'Irish' category included in the 2001 Census illustrates the difficulty of admitting that white may also be less 'pure'. But the change has been made and a new form of the question has been agreed, creating a space for examining the social positioning of people of Irish descent in Britain whose existence has not previously been acknowledged. This will include women who have become especially invisible when their Irish names are lost through marriage.

I have argued that constructions of the Irish as white have resulted in forcible inclusion within an undifferentiated white category which causes invisibility. This has complex and contradictory consequences for Irish women. On the one hand it has protected Irish women from the negative aspects of gendered stereotyping directed against African-Caribbean and Asian women in Britain, for example. Sander Gilman (1992) argues that gender and race are combined in black women to produce a 'polar opposite' to the European male making them the most highly marked objects of his need for control over his inner fears. These representations are reproduced by cinematic discourse, for example, which subordinates and fetishizes both 'woman' and 'black' (Young 1996). Black women's sexuality is thus highly visible. Brah points out that

> It is important to stress that notions of female sexuality in Britain are racialised concepts. Asian women's sexuality is categorised broadly in three ways. First, there is the image of the exotic oriental women – sensuous, seductive, full of Eastern promise. Her sexuality is projected as suitably controlled but vulnerable. This image is most explicitly available in the portrayal of airline 'hostesses' in advertisements. The second type of representation is almost an antithesis of the first. Here, Asian women are characterised as 'ugly', 'smelly', 'oily-haired', etc. . . . In the third construction, Asian women's sexuality is portrayed as licentious.

> (Brah 1996: 78)

What are the equivalent representations of Irish women in Britain? Work needs to done on the deconstruction of these images, but at first sight they appear to be much more shadowy. They connect with longstanding representations of women in Ireland. Most common are desexualised figures, including mothers, nurses and nuns, echoing images of the Virgin Mary which have had such a powerful hold over women's lives in Ireland. Some association between young Irish women and innocent rural simplicity is also apparent, as it was in the late nineteenth century (Tebbutt 1983). There is a countering trace of the wild, beautiful, black-haired colleen of Celtic mythology but this is a romantic, untouchable image inspiring chivalrous protection. While these representations may leave Irish women less exposed to view and freer to construct their own identities, they are also limiting.

On the other hand more is now known about the profound material consequences of invisibility for Irish women. The CRE report on *Discrimination and the Irish Community in Britain* (Hickman and Walter 1997) brought together for the first time evidence of levels of material deprivation, partly as a result of discrimination. Many of these disadvantages were shown to have a particularly strong impact on women, especially those with prime responsibility for children. For example, substantially poorer than average housing conditions are recorded for those in private rented accommodation. This is a necessity for low-income migrants but accorded little priority now that Britain is no longer seen as a country of immigration, after the passage of the Immigration Acts from the early 1960s. Because they fill labour shortages, the occupations of Irish women are much more heavily weighted towards low-paid, insecure manual work than any other ethnic group originating inside or outside England. Access to social security benefits is also impeded by the anti-Irish prejudices of officials at benefits offices who regularly cast doubt on Irish people's rights and credentials, applying the stereotypes of 'scrounging' and 'fecklessness' which reproduce with startling precision the negative nineteenth-century representations outlined in Chapter 3.

Finally, perhaps most tellingly, there is now detailed evidence of substantially poorer than average health among the Irish in Britain (Greenslade 1992; Kelleher and Hillier 1996). This can be seen as an index of the range of social and economic exclusions faced by Irish people in Britain (Williams and Ecob 1998). There are gendered patterns to these health findings. For example, for reasons which still need clarification, second-generation Irish women have significantly higher rates of mortality in the middle-aged groups, even when social class is standardised (Harding and Balarajan 1996).

Many of these disadvantages and discriminatory practices have distinct parallels with the experiences of black groups in Britain, especially in the in housing, employment and health circumstances of African-Caribbean people. But whereas racism may be accepted as part of the explanation for the inequalities experienced by black people, it is strenuously resisted in the case of the Irish. Moreover, as Webster (1998) pointed out, the shared circumstances of migrancy are never acknowledged because blackness overrides all other positionings. Irish people are therefore overlooked in resource allocations aimed at ameliorating ethnic disadvantage. This has been signalled by the absence of an 'Irish' category from many ethnic monitoring procedures and the huge efforts which Irish welfare groups have to make to get their voices heard.

What all these theorisations and practices demonstrate is that

> Whiteness has been enormously, often terrifyingly effective in unifying coalitions of disparate groups of people. It has generally been much more successful than class in uniting people across national cultural differences and against their best interests. This has been strengthened by two instabilities that such a coalition produces. On the one hand, it creates a category of maybe, sometime whites, peoples who may be let in to whiteness under particular historical circumstances. The Irish, Mexicans, Jews and people of mixed race provide striking instances. . . . On the other hand, whiteness as a coalition also incites the notion that some whites are whiter than others. . . . A shifting border and internal hierarchies of whiteness suggests that the category of whiteness is unclear and unstable, yet this has proved its strength. Because whiteness carries such rewards and privileges, the sense of a border that might be crossed and a hierarchy that might be climbed has produced a dynamic that has enthralled people who have had any chance of participating in it.
>
> (Dyer 1997: 19)

There are very strong pressures on Irish people to remain within the powerful white category, even though this results in a failure to have their needs addressed. Whiteness is therefore 'enforced' not only by the refusal of hegemonic white Britishness to recognise Irish difference, but also by Irish anxieties about the consequences of becoming detached from its apparent 'safety'. Debates about inclusion of a separate 'Irish' category in the Census raised this fundamental dilemma. What appeared to administrative authorities as a mixed and rather inconclusive response from the Irish population to test questions was in fact a struggle between two irreconcilable positions in which the community as a whole was placed simultaneously outside and inside the white British nation.

Binary relationships do not adequately describe the reality of Irish people's lives in Britain and make it difficult to challenge disadvantage. The Irish position brings out especially strongly the need to replace either/or with both/and, that is to recognise that there are multiple identities which do not simply hinge around the black/white divide. A crucial advantage of the diaspora framework of analysis therefore is that it brings into relationship a much wider group of ethnicities, problematising those 'at home' as well as those 'from elsewhere'. Instead of a fixed, unchanging black/white boundary there is a much more complex intersection between these groups.

> In the post-war period this Englishness is continually reconstituted via a multitude of border crossings in and through other diasporic formations. These border crossings are territorial, political, economic, cultural and psychological. This Englishness is a new ensemble that both appropriates and is in turn appropriated by British-based African-Caribbeanness, Asianness, Irishness and so on. Each of these formations has its own specificity, but it is an ever-changing specificity that adds to as well as imbues elements of the other.
>
> (Brah 1996: 209)

I have hardly begun to explore ways in which Englishness has appropriated Irishness, another huge lacuna in academic study. My own biography suggested the embeddedness of an Irish presence in an apparently thoroughly English location over a long time period. I opened up the possibility that Irish servants may have played a significant role in the formative years of upper-middle-class boys in the nineteenth century and later. Irish ancestry may also be located much closer to the centre of power in the present day. In a throwaway line at a time of tension in the Northern Ireland Peace Process in 1994 a journalist noted that every member of the Conservative cabinet in Britain had at least one Irish grandmother. A more direct connection between Irish identity and political practice was suggested in Prime Minister Tony Blair's address to the Dail in 1998 on the issue of closer East West relations between Britain and the Irish Republic, when he revealed that his mother was born in Donegal and that he spent his summer holidays there as a child. These tantalising pointers to ways in which those 'staying put' are so much more creolised than are ever acknowledged, and possible the consequences of this, await much fuller deconstruction.

I argue that the framework of diaspora, despite some drawbacks, opens up very fruitful ways of 'thinking against the grain'. Reconceptualisations may not produce political change directly, but they feed into a climate where different configurations can be imagined and debated. Such arguments must be grounded in specific cases if they are to gain political purchase. Recasting Irish women's identities and experiences within a framework of diaspora brings together specific collective and individual histories over an extended time period in a wide variety of places. It also places them within a larger political context of the colonial relationship between Britain and Ireland and global labour migration flows. This framework chimes with Doreen Massey's call for a re-imagining of 'space as a sphere of the possibility of multiplicity; space as the sphere in which distinct narratives co-exist; space as the sphere of the possibility of the existence of more than one voice' (Massey 1999: 279).

Although 'maps of power' must still be recognised (Butler 1993: 114), Irish women need not be trapped into a binary of the 'same old story'. Bringing into view new intersections within diaspora spaces emphasises the possibility of change.

Bibliography

Akenson, D. (1995) *The Irish Diaspora: A Primer*, Toronto: P. D. Meany.

Allen, T. (1994) *The Invention of the White Race*, vol. 1, *Racial Oppression and Social Control*, London: Verso.

Anderson, J. (1989) 'Nationalisms in a Disunited Kingdom', in J. Mohan (ed.) *The Political Geography of Contemporary Britain*, London: Macmillan.

Anderson, M. (1971) *Family Structure in Nineteenth Century Lancashire*, Cambridge: Cambridge University Press.

Ang-Lydgate, M. (1999) 'Charting the Spaces of (Un)location: on Theorizing Diaspora', in H. S. Mirza (ed.) *Black British Feminism: A Reader*, London: Routledge.

Anthias, F. and Yuval-Davis, N. (1992) *Racialised Boundaries: Race, Nation, Gender, Colour and Class and the Anti-racist Struggle*, London: Routledge.

Arensberg, C. and Kimball, S. (1968) *Family and Community in Ireland*, second edition, Cambridge, Mass.: Harvard University Press.

Babcock, B. (1978) *The Reversible World: Symbolic Inversion in Art and Society*, Ithica, N.Y.: Cornell University Press.

Barrington, C. (1997) *Irish Women in England: An Annotated Bibliography*, Dublin: Women's Education Research and Resource Centre, University College.

Bayor, R. and Meagher, T. (eds) (1996) *The New York Irish*, Baltimore, Md.: Johns Hopkins University Press.

Beale, J. (1986) *Women in Ireland: Voices of Change*, London: Macmillan.

Bhabha, H. (1994) *The Location of Culture*, London: Routledge.

Birmingham Sunday Mercury (1997) 'Irish Joke's on Us', 29 June: 14.

Black, J. (1837) *A Medico-topographical, Geological and Statistical Sketch of Bolton and its Neighbourhood*, Bolton.

Bonnett, A. (1996) '"White studies": The Problems and Projects of a New Research Agenda', *Theory, Culture and Society* 13, 2: 145–55.

Bourke, J. (1993) *Husbandry to Housewifery; Women, Economic Change and Housework in Ireland 1890–1914*, Oxford: Clarendon.

—— (1987) 'Women and Poultry in Ireland', *Irish Historical Studies* 25: 293–310.

—— (1990) 'Dairywomen and Affectionate Wives: Women in the Irish Dairy Industry 1890–1914', *Agricultural History Review* 38: 149–64.

Bradley, A. and Valiulis, M. (eds) (1997) *Gender and Sexuality in Modern Ireland*, Amherst: University of Massachusetts Press.

Bradley, J. (1995) *Ethnic and Religious Identity in Modern Scotland: Culture, Politics and Football*, Aldershot: Avebury.

Brady, A. (1988) *Women in Ireland: An Annotated Bibliography*, New York: Greenwood.

Brah, A. (1996) *Cartographies of Diaspora: Contesting Identities*, London: Routledge.

Brody, H. (1973) *Inishkillane: Change and Decline in the West of Ireland*, London: Allen Lane.

Buckley, M. (1997) 'Sitting on your Politics: the Irish among the British and the Women among the Irish', in J. Mac Laughlin (ed.) (1997) *Location and Dislocation in Contemporary Irish Society*, Cork: Cork University Press.

Bunreacht na hEireann (Constitution of Ireland) (1980), Dublin: Stationary Office.

Burchell, R. (1979) *The San Francisco Irish 1848–1880*, Manchester: Manchester University Press.

Busteed, M., Hodgson, R. and Kennedy, T. (1992) 'The Myth and Reality of Irish Migrants in Mid-Nineteenth Century Manchester: A Preliminary Study', in P. O'Sullivan (ed.) *The Irish in the New Communities*, vol. 2, *The Irish World Wide: History, Heritage, Identity*, Leicester: Leicester University Press.

Butler, J. (1993) *Bodies that Matter: On the Discursive Limits of 'Sex'*, London: Routledge.

Byrne, A. (1997) 'Single Women in Ireland: A Re-examination of the Sociological Evidence', in A. Byrne and M. Leonard (eds) *Women and Irish Society: A Sociological Reader*, Belfast: Beyond the Pale.

Byrne, A. and Leonard, M. (eds) (1997) *Women and Irish Society: A Sociological Reader*, Belfast: Beyond the Pale.

Cairns, D. and Richards, S. (1988) *Writing Ireland*, Manchester: Manchester University Press

Carter, E., Donald, J. and Squires, J. (eds) (1993) *Space and Place: Theories of Identity and Location*, London: Lawrence and Wishart.

Casey, Maud. (1987) *Over the Water*, London: Livewire.

Casey, Marion (1996) '"From the East Side to the Seaside": Irish Americans on the Move in New York City', in R. Bayor and T. Meagher (eds) *The New York Irish*, Baltimore: Johns Hopkins University Press.

Chaliand, G. and Rageau, J-P. (1995) *The Penguin Atlas of Diasporas*, Harmondsworth, Middlesex: Penguin.

Clarke, C., Ley, D. and Peach, C. (eds) (1984) *Geography and Ethnic Pluralism*, London: George Allen and Unwin.

Clark, D. (1973) *The Irish in Philadelphia: Ten Generations of Urban Experience*, Philadelphia: Temple University Press.

—— (1986) *Hibernia America: The Irish and Regional Cultures*, New York: Greenwood.

—— (1991) *Erin's Heirs*. Lexington, Ky.: University of Kentucky Press.

Clifford, J. (1994) 'Diasporas', *Cultural Anthropology* 9: 302–38.

Cohen, P. (1988) 'The Perversions of Inheritance: Studies in the Making of Multi-racist Britain', in P. Cohen and H. Bains (eds) *Multi-racist Britain*, London: Macmillan.

Cohen, P. and Bains, H. (eds) (1988) *Multi-racist Britain*, London: Macmillan.

Colley, L. (1992) *Britons: Forging the Nation 1707–1837*, New Haven and London: Yale University Press.

Collins, B. (1981) 'Irish Emigration to Dundee and Paisley during the First Half of the Nineteenth Century', in J. Goldstrom and L. Clarkson (eds) *Irish Population, Economy and Society*, Oxford: Oxford University Press.

Commission on Emigration and Other Population Problems 1948–1954 (1956) *Reports*, Dublin: Government Stationery Office.

Compton, P. (1976) 'Religious Affiliation and Demographic Variability in Northern Ireland', *Transactions of the Institute of British Geographers* 1, 4: 433–52.

—— (1992) 'Migration Trends for Northern Ireland; Links with Great Britain', in J. Stillwell, P. Rees and P. Boden (eds) *Migration Processes and Patterns*, vol. 2, *Population Redistribution in the United Kingdom*, London: Belhaven.

Conway, S. (1992) *The Faraway Hills are Green: Voices of Irish Women in Canada*, Toronto: Women's Press.

Coombes, M. and Charlton, M. (1992) 'Flows to and from London: A Decade of Change?' in J. Stillwell, P. Rees and P. Boden (eds) *Migration Processes and Patterns*, vol. 2, *Population Redistribution in the United Kingdom*, London: Belhaven.

Cooter, R. (1973) 'The Irish in Co. Durham and Newcastle c. 1840–1880', unpublished M.A. thesis, University of Durham.

Corcoran, M. (1993) *Irish Illegals: Transients between Two Societies*, Westport, Conn.: Greenwood.

—— (1996) 'Emigrants, Eirepreneurs and Opportunists: A Social Profile of Recent Irish Immigration in New York City', in R. Bayor and T. Meagher (eds) *The New York Irish*, Baltimore: Johns Hopkins University Press.

Cullen, K. (1996) 'Beyond Class and Clan', *The Boston Globe* 4 October: B1: 9.

Curtis, L. (1984) *Nothing but the Same Old Story: The Roots of Anti-Irish Racism*, London: Information on Ireland.

Curtis, L. P. (1968) *Anglo-Saxons and Celts: A Study of Anti-Irish Prejudice in Victorian England*, Bridgeport, Conn.: University of Connecticut Press.

—— (1971) *Apes and Angels: The Irishman in Victorian Caricature*, Newton Abbot: David and Charles.

Daily Mail (1994) 'Who's taking the Mickey?' 8 June: 1.

—— (1997) 'Heard the One About the Latest Ethnic Minority?' 26 June: 1.

Daily Telegraph (1994) 'Question: Why Can't They Make Icecubes in Ireland?' 9 June: 17

Daniels, M. (1993) 'Exile or Opportunity? Irish Nurses and Wirral Midwives', *Irish Studies Review* 5: 4–8.

Davidoff, L. (1974) 'Mastered for Life: Servant and Wife in Victorian and Edwardian England', *Journal of Social History* 7, 4: 406–59.

—— (1995) *Worlds Between: Historical Perspectives on Gender and Class*, Cambridge: Polity.

Davis, G. (1991) *The Irish in Britain 1815–1914*, Dublin: Gill and Macmillan.

Davis, J. (1996) 'Race and the Residuum: The Irish Origins of the English Underclass', paper to King's College Social History Seminar, Cambridge, UK.

Derry Film and Video (1988) *Mother Ireland*, film directed by Anne Crilly.

Diner, H. (1983) *Erin's Daughters in America*, Baltimore: Johns Hopkins University Press.

Dixson, M. (1976) *The Real Matilda*, Ringwood, Victoria: Penguin.

Dodd, P. (1986) 'Englishness and the National Culture', in R. Colls and P. Dodd (eds) *Englishness: Politics and Culture 1880–1920*, London: Croom Helm.

Donald, J. and Rattansi, A. (eds) (1992) *'Race', Culture and Difference*, London: Sage.

Doyal, L., Gee, F., Hunt, G., Mellor, J. and Pennell, I. (1980, 1984) *Migrant Workers in the National Health Service*, Part I (1980), Part II (1984), Social Science Research Council.

Dublin, T. (1979) *Women at Work: The Transformation of Work and Community in Lowell, Massachusetts 1826–1860*, New York: Columbia University Press.

Dudden, F. (1983) *Serving Women: Household Service in Nineteenth Century America*, Middletown, Conn.: Wesleyan University Press.

Dyer, R. (1997) *White*, London: Routledge.

Eastern Daily Press (1997) 'Race Board is the Worst Joke of All', 28 June: 9.

Emmons, D. (1992) 'Faction Fights: The Irish Worlds of Butte, Montana 1875–1917', in P. O'Sullivan (ed.) *The Irish in the New Communities*, vol. 2, *The Irish World Wide: History, Heritage, Identity*, Leicester: Leicester University Press.

Engels, F. (1971) *The Condition of the Working Class in England 1845*; trans. W. Chaloner, Oxford: Blackwell.

Fanning, C. (1996) 'The Heart's Speech No Longer Stifled: New York Irish Writing since the 1960s', in R. Bayor and T. Meagher (eds) *The New York Irish*, Baltimore: Johns Hopkins University Press.

Fielding, S. (1993) *Class and Ethnicity: Irish Catholics in England 1880–1939*, Buckingham: Open University Press.

Fitzpatrick, D. (1986) '"A Share of the Honeycomb": Education, Emigration and Irish Women', *Continuity and Change* 1, 2: 217–34.

—— (1989) 'A Curious Middle Place: The Irish in Britain, in 1815–1939', in R. Swift and S. Gilley (eds) *The Irish in Britain 1871–1921* London: Pinter: 10–59.

Flynn, E. (1955) *The Rebel Girl: An Autobiography*, New York: International.

Foley, A. (1973) *A Bolton Childhood*. Manchester: Manchester University Extra-mural Department and Northwestern District of the Workers' Educational Association.

Foster, J. (1967) 'Capitalism and Class Consciousness in Earlier Nineteenth-Century Oldham', unpublished Ph.D. thesis, University of Cambridge.

Frankenberg, R. (1993) *White Women, Race Matters: The Social Construction of Whiteness*, London: Routledge.

Gilman, S. (1992) 'Black Bodies, White Bodies: Towards an Iconography of Female Sexuality in Late Nineteenth Century Art, Medicine and Literature', in J. Donald and A. Rattansi (eds) *'Race', culture and difference*, London: Sage.

Gilroy P. (1987) *'There ain't no Black in the Union Jack': The Cultural Politics of Race and Nation*, London: Hutchinson.

—— (1993a) *The Black Atlantic: Modernity and Double Consciousness.* London: Verso.

—— (1993b) *Small Acts: Thoughts on the Politics of Black Cultures*, London: Serpent's Tail.

Glynn, S. (1981) 'Irish Immigration to Britain 1911–1951: Patterns and Policy', *Irish Economic and Social History* 8: 50–69.

Gray B. (1996a) '"The Home of our Mothers and our Birthright for Ages"? Nation, Diaspora and Irish Women', in M. Maynard and J. Purvis (eds) *New Frontiers in Women's Studies; Knowledge, Identity and Nationalism*, London: Taylor and Francis.

—— (1996b) 'Irishness: A Global and Gendered Identity?', *Irish Studies Review* 16: 24–8.

—— (1996c) 'Accounts of Displacement: Irish Migrant Women in London', *Youth and Policy* 52: 22–9.

—— (1997) 'Unmasking Irishness: Irish Women, the Irish Nation and the Irish Diaspora', in J. Mac Laughlin (ed.) *Location and Dislocation in Contemporary Irish Society*, Cork: Cork University Press.

—— (1999) 'Longings and Belongings – Gendered Spatialities of Irishness', *Irish Studies Review* 7, 2: 193–210.

Greater London Council (1984) *Report on Consultation with the Irish Community*, London: Greater London Council.

Greenslade, L. (1992) 'White Skins, White Masks: Psychological Distress among the Irish in Britain', in P. O'Sullivan (ed.) *The Irish in the New Communities*, vol. 2, *The Irish World Wide: History, Heritage, Identity*, Leicester: Leicester University Press.

Grossberg, L. (1989) 'The Formation of Cultural Studies: An American in Birmingham', *Strategies* 2: 114–49.

Guardian (1986) 'Scots of the Second City Suffer an Ethnic Setback' 15 March: 3.

—— (1998) 'Blair Denies Intention to Convert to Catholicism', 5 March 1: 3..

—— (1999) 'Scotland's Shame' 10 August.

Hall, C. (1998) 'A Family for Nation and Empire', in G. Lewis (ed.) *Forming Nation, Framing Welfare*, London: Routledge.

Hall, S. (1990) 'Cultural Identity and Diaspora', in J. Rutherford (ed.) *Identity: Community, Culture, Difference*, London: Lawrence and Wishart.

—— (1995) 'New Cultures for Old', in D. Massey and P. Jess (eds) *A Place in the World? Places, Cultures and Globalization*, Oxford: Oxford University Press.

—— (1997) 'The Spectacle of the "Other"', in S. Hall (ed.) *Representation: Cultural Representations and Signifying Practices*, London: Sage.

Handley, J. (1947) *The Irish in Modern Scotland*, Cork: Cork University Press.

Handlin, O. (1941) *Boston's Immigrants*, Cambridge, Mass.: Harvard University Press.

Harding, S. and Balarajan, R. (1996) 'Patterns of Mortality in Second Generation Irish Living in England and Wales: Longitudinal Study', *British Medical Journal* 312: 1389–92.

Harper's New Monthly Magazine (1856) 'Valentines Delivered in our Street' 14 February.

Harris, R. and O'Keeffe, E. (eds) (1993) *The Search for Missing Friends: Irish Immigrant Advertisements Placed in the Boston Pilot*, Boston: New England Historic Genealogical Society.

Harrison, P. (1973) 'Culture and Migration: The Irish English', *New Society* 20 September.

Hartsock, N. (1983) 'The Feminist Standpoint: Developing the Ground for a Specifically Feminist Historical Materialism', in S. Harding and M. Hintinnka (eds) *Discovering Reality: Feminist Perspectives on Epistemology, Metaphysics, Methodology and Philosophy of Science*, Dordrecht: Reidel.

Harvie, C. (1977) *Scotland and Nationalism*, London: George Allen and Unwin.

Hearn, M. (1989) 'Life for Domestic Servants in Dublin 1880–1920', in M. Luddy and C. Murphy (eds) *Women Surviving: Studies in Irish Women's History in the Nineteenth and Twentieth Centuries*, Dublin: Poolbeg.

Heath, A. and Ridge, J. (1983) 'Social Mobility of Ethnic Minorities', *Journal of Biosocial Sciences* Supplement 8.

Hickey, J. (1967) *Urban Catholics in England and Wales from 1829 to the Present Day*, London: Geoffrey Chapman.

Hickman, M. (1990) 'A Study of the Incorporation of the Irish in Britain with Special Reference to Catholic State Education: Involving a Comparison of the Attitudes of Pupils and Teachers in Selected Secondary Schools in London and Liverpool', unpublished Ph.D. thesis, University of London Institute of Education, London.

—— (1995) *Religion, Class and Identity: The State, the Catholic Church and the Education of the Irish in Britain*, London: Avebury.

Hickman, M. and Walter, B. (1995) 'Deconstructing Whiteness: Irish Women in Britain', *Feminist Review* 50: 5–19.

——. (1997) *Discrimination and the Irish Community in Britain*, London: Commission for Racial Equality.

Hillyard, P. (1993) *Suspect Community: People's Experience of the Prevention of Terrorism Act in Britain*, London: Pluto.

Hiro, D. (1971) *Black British, White British*, London: Eyre and Spottiswoode.

Hodges, G. (1996) '"Desirable Companions and Lovers": Irish and African Americans in the Sixth Ward 1830–1870', in R. Bayor and T. Meagher (eds) *The New York Irish*, Baltimore: Johns Hopkins University Press.

Hoff, J. and Coulter, M. (eds) (1995) *Irish Women's Voices: Past and Present, Journal of Women's History* 6, 4 and 7, 1.

Hoggart, R. (1988) *A Local Habitation*, London: Chatto and Windus.

hooks, b. (1991) *Yearning: Race, Gender and Cultural Politics*, London: Turnaround.

Hornsby-Smith, M. and Dale, A. (1988) 'The Assimilation of Irish Immigrants in Britain', *British Journal of Sociology* 36: 519–43.

Hornsby-Smith, M. and Lee, R. (1979) *Roman Catholic Opinion*, Guildford: University of Surrey.

Ignatiev, N. (1995) *How the Irish Became White: Race and the Making of the American Working Class*, London: Routledge.

Independent (1996) 'If you're hip, you must be Irish' 1 July: 14.

Irish Post (1994) 'Irish in Britain: A Formidable Presence', November 26: 7.

—— (1994) 'How Close are the British to the Irish?' 17 December: 7.

Irish Times (1990) 'We Have Passed the Threshold of a New Pluralist Ireland', 4 December: 3.

—— (1992) 'The President's address to the Houses of the Oireachtas', 9 July: 8.

Jackson, J. (1963) *The Irish in Britain*, London: Routledge and Kegan Paul.

Jackson, P. and Penrose, J. (eds) (1993) *Constructions of Race, Place and Nation*, London: UCL.

Jeater, D. (1992) 'Roast Beef and Reggae Music: The Passing of Whiteness', *New Formations* 18: 107–21.

John, A. (ed.) (1991) *Our Mother's Land*, Cardiff: University of Wales Press.

Johnson, N. (1992) 'Nation-building, Language and Education: The Geography of Teacher Recruitment in Ireland 1925–55', *Political Geography* 11: 170–89.

—— (1995) 'Cast in Stone: Monuments, Geography and Nationalism', *Environment and Planning D: Society and Space* 13: 51–65.

—— (1996) 'Where Geography and History Meet: Heritage Tourism and the Big House in Ireland', *Annals of the Association of American Geographers* 86, 3: 551–66.

Jones, P. (1967) 'The Segregation of Immigrant Communities in the City of Birmingham 1961', *University of Hull Occasional Papers* 7.

Kanya-Forstner, M. (1997) 'The Politics of Survival: Irish Women in Outcast Liverpool 1850–1890', unpublished Ph.D. thesis, University of Liverpool.

Kearney, M. (1991) 'Borders and Boundaries of State and Self at the End of Empire', *Journal of Historical Sociology* 4, 1: 52–74.

Kelleher, D. and Hillier, S. (1996) 'The Health of the Irish in England', in D. Kelleher and S. Hillier (eds) *Researching Cultural Differences in Health*, London: Routledge.

Kells, M. (1995a) *Ethnic Identity amongst Young Irish Middle Class Migrants in London*, Irish Studies Centre Occasional Papers Series 4, University of North London.

—— (1995b) '"I'm Myself and Nobody Else": Gender and Ethnicity among Young Irish Middle-class Women in London', in P. O'Sullivan (ed.) *Irish Women and Irish Migration*, vol. 4, *The Irish World Wide: History, Heritage, Identity*, Leicester: Leicester University Press.

Kelly, K. and Nic Giolla Choille, T. (1990) *Emigration Matters for Women*, Dublin: Attic Press.

—— 'Listening and Learning: Experiences in an Emigrant Advice Agency', in P. O'Sullivan (ed.) Irish Women and Irish Migration *vol. 4 The Irish World Wide: History, Heritage, Identity*, Leicester: Leicester University Press.

Kennedy, R. (1973) *The Irish: Emigration, Marriage, and Fertility*, Berkeley, Calif.: University of California Press.

Kerr, B. (1958) *The People of Ship Street*, London: Routledge and Kegan Paul.

Kerr, M. (1938) 'Irish Immigration into Great Britain 1798–1838', unpublished B.Litt. thesis, University of Oxford.

King, R. and O'Connor, H. (1996) 'Migration and Gender: Irish Women in Leicester', *Geography* 81, 4: 311–25.

Kirkaldy, J. (1979) 'English Newspaper Images of Northern Ireland 1968–73: An Historical Study in Stereotypes and Prejudices', unpublished Ph.D. thesis, University of New South Wales.

Knight, J. (1965) 'Recruitment and Wastage of Nursing Staff: Who Comes, Stays or Goes?' *Nursing Times* 12 November: 1540–2.

Knobel, D. (1986) *Paddy and the Republic: Ethnicity and Nationality in Antebellum America*, Middletown, Conn.: Wesleyan University Press.

Lappin, E. (1995) 'At Home in Exile: A Conversation between Eva Hoffman and Elena Lappin', *Jewish Quarterly* 160, winter.

Lavie, S. and Swedenburg, T. (eds) (1996) *Displacement, Diaspora and Geographies of Identity*, Durham, S.C.: Duke University Press.

Lawrence, D. (1974) *Black Migrants, White Natives: A Study of Race Relations in Nottingham*, Cambridge: Cambridge University Press.

Leach, E. (1979) 'The Official Irish Jokesters', *New Society* 20/27 December: vii–ix.

Lee, J. (1978) 'Women and the Church since the Famine', in M.

MacCurtain and D. O'Corrain (eds) *Women in Irish Society: The Historical Dimension*, Dublin: Arlen House.

Lees, L. (1979) *Exiles of Erin: Irish Migrants in Victorian London*, Manchester: Manchester University Press.

Lennon, M. (1982) '"A Haemorrhaging from the Land": a History of Irish Women's Emigration to Britain', *Spare Rib* 118: 38–9.

Lennon, M., McAdam, M. and O'Brien, J. (1988) *Across the Water: Irish Women's Lives in Britain*, London: Virago.

Lennon, S. and Lennon, M. (1980) '"Off the boat": Irish Women Talk about their Experiences of Living in England', *Spare Rib*, May: 52–5.

Letford, L. (1997) 'Irish and Non-Irish Women Living in their Households in Nineteenth Century Liverpool: Issues of Class, Gender, Religion and Birthplace', unpublished Ph.D. thesis, University of Lancaster.

Lewis, J. (1984) *Women in England 1870–1950*, Sussex: Wheatsheaf.

Liddington, J. and Norris, J. (1978) *One Hand Tied Behind Us: The Rise of the Women's Suffrage Movement*, London: Virago.

Limerick Rural Survey (1962) *Third Interim Report: Social Structure*, Tipperary: Muintir na Tire.

Lloyd, D. (1994) 'Making Sense of the Dispersal', *Irish Reporter* 13: 3–4.

Loftus, B. (1990) *Mirrors: William III and Mother Ireland*, Dundrum: Picture.

London Evening Standard (1998) 'Family from Hell Ruin £180,000 Home', 4 March: 1.

London Irish Women's Centre (1984) 'Report of First London Irish Women's Conference: Our Experiences of Emigration', London: London Irish Women's Centre.

—— (1995) *Rights for Travellers*, London: London Irish Women's Centre.

Luddy, M. (1995) *Women in Ireland 1800–1918*, Cork: Cork University Press.

Luddy, M. and Murphy, C. (eds) *Women Surviving: Studies in Irish Women's History*, Swords: Poolbeg.

Luibheid, E. (1997) 'Irish Immigrants in the United States' Racial System', in J. Mac Laughlin (ed.) *Location and Dislocation in Contemporary Irish Society*, Cork: Cork University Press.

Mackenzie, S. and Rose, D. (1983) 'Industrial Change, the Domestic Economy and Home Life', in J. Anderson, S. Duncan and R. Hudson (eds) *Redundant Spaces in Cities and Regions*, London: Academic.

Mac Laughlin, J. (1994) *Ireland: the Emigrant Nursery and the World Economy*, Cork: Cork University Press.

—— (1995) *Travellers and Ireland: Whose Country, Whose History?* Cork: Cork University Press.

—— (ed.) (1997) *Location and Dislocation in Contemporary Irish Society*, Cork: Cork University Press.

Maguire, M. (1997) 'Missing Links: Working-class Women of Irish Descent', in P. Mahony and C. Zmroczek (eds) *Class matters: 'Working-class' Women's Perspectives on Social Class*, London: Taylor and Francis.

Marston, S. (1986) 'Adopted Citizens: Community and the Development of Consciousness among the Irish of Lowell, Massachusetts 1839–1885', unpublished Ph.D. thesis, University of Colorado.

—— (1990) 'Who are "The People"?: Gender, Citizenship, and the Making of the American Nation', *Environment and Planning D: Society and Space* 20: 449–58.

Massey, D. (1994) *Space, Place and Gender*, Cambridge: Polity.

—— (1995) 'The Conceptualization of Place', in D. Massey and P. Jess (eds) A Place in the World? *Places, Cultures and Globalization*, Oxford: Oxford University Press.

—— (1999) 'Spaces of Politics' in D. Massey, J. Allen and P. Sarre (eds) *Human Geography Today*, Cambridge: Polity.

Massey, D., Allen, J. and Sarre, P. (eds) (1999) *Human Geography Today*, Cambridge: Polity.

Massey, D. and Jess, P. (1995) 'Places and Cultures in an Uneven World', in D. Massey and P. Jess (eds) *A Place in the World? Places, Cultures and Globalization*, Oxford: Oxford University Press.

McAdam, M. (1994) 'Hidden from History: Women's Experience of Emigration', *Irish Reporter* 13: 12–13.

McCaffrey, L.(1976) *The Irish Diaspora in America*, Bloomington: Indiana University Press.

—— (1980) 'A Profile of Irish America', in D. Doyle, and O. D. Edwards (eds) *America and Ireland 1776–1976*, London: Greenwood.

—— (1996) 'Forging Forward and Looking Backward', in R. Bayor and T. Meagher (eds) *The New York Irish*, Baltimore: Johns Hopkins University Press.

McCaffrey, L., Skerrett, E., Funchion, M. and Fanning, C. (1987) *The Irish in Chicago*, Urbana Ill.: Urbana University Press.

McCann, M., O Siochain, S. and Ruane, J. (1994) *Irish Travellers: Culture and Ethnicity*, Belfast: Institute of Irish Studies.

McClintock, A. (1995) *Imperial Leather: Race, Gender and Sexuality in the Colonial Contest*, London: Routledge.

McCourt, F. (1996) *Angela's Ashes: A Memoir of Childhood*, London: Harper Collins.

McCrone, D. (1992) *Understanding Scotland: The Sociology of a Stateless Nation*, London: Routledge.

McCullough, C. (1991) 'A Tie that Blinds: Family and Ideology in Ireland', *Economic and Social Review* 22: 199–211.

McDannell, C. (1986) *The Christian Home in Victorian America, 1840–1900*, Bloomington: Indiana University Press.

McDannell, C. (1996) 'Going to the Ladies' Fair: Irish Catholics in New York City 1870–1900', in R. Bayor and T. Meagher (eds) *The New York Irish*, Baltimore: Johns Hopkins University Press.

McDowell, L. and Massey, D. (1984) 'A Woman's Place?', in D. Massey and J. Allen (eds) *Geography Matters!*, Cambridge: Cambridge University Press.

McKivigan, J. and Robertson, T. (1996) 'The Irish American Worker in Transition 1877–1914: New York as a Test Case', in R. Bayor and T. Meagher (eds) *The New York Irish*, Baltimore: Johns Hopkins University Press.

McKiernan, J. and McWilliams, M. (1997) 'Women, Religion and Violence in the Family', in A. Byrne and M. Leonard (eds) *Women and Irish society: A Sociological Reader*, Belfast: Beyond the Pale.

McNickle, C. (1996) 'When New York was Irish, and After', in R. Bayor and T. Meagher (eds) *The New York Irish*, Baltimore: Johns Hopkins University Press.

Meade, R. (1997) 'Domestic Violence: An Analysis and Response from Community Activists', in A. Byrne and M. Leonard (eds) *Women and Irish Society: A Sociological Reader*, Belfast: Beyond the Pale.

Meagher, T. (1986) 'Irish, American, Catholic: Irish-American Identity in Worcester, Massachusetts 1880–1920', in T. Meagher (ed.) *From Paddy to Studs: Irish-American Communities in the Turn of the Century Era 1880–1920*, New York: Greenwood.

Meaney, G. (1993) 'Sex and Nation: Women in Irish Culture and Politics', in A. Smyth (ed.) *Irish Women's Studies Reader*, Dublin: Attic.

Miles, R. (1982) *Racism and Migrant Labour*, London: Routledge and Kegan Paul.

—— (1993) *Racism after 'Race Relations'*, London: Routledge.

Miles, R. and Dunlop, A. (1987) 'Racism in Britain: The Scottish Dimension', in P. Jackson (ed.) *Race and Racism: Essays in Social Geography*, London: Allen and Unwin.

Miller, K. (1985) *Emigrants and Exiles: Ireland and the Irish Exodus to North America*, Oxford: Oxford University Press.

—— (1990) 'Class, Culture and Immigrant Group Identity in the United States: The case of Irish-American Ethnicity', in V. Yans-McLaughlin (ed.) *Immigration Re-considered: History, Sociology and Politics*, Oxford: Oxford University Press.

Miller, K. with Doyle, D. and Kellegher, P. (1995) '"For Love and Liberty": Irish women, migration and domesticity in Ireland and America, 1815–1920', in P. O'Sullivan (ed) *Irish Women and Irish migration*, vol. 4, *The Irish World Wide: history, heritage, identity*, Leicester: Leicester University Press.

Mirza, H. S. (1992) *Young, Female and Black*, London: Routledge.

—— (ed.) (1999) *Black British Feminism: A Reader*, London: Routledge.

Mitchell, B. (1986) '"They do not Differ Greatly": The Pattern of Community Development among the Irish in Late Nineteenth Century Lowell, Massachusetts', in T. Meagher (ed.) *From Paddy to Studs: Irish-American Communities in the Turn of the Century Era 1880–1920*, New York: Greenwood.

Mitchell, K. (1997) 'Different Diasporas and the Hype of Hybridity', *Environment and Planning D: Society and Space* 15, 5: 533–53.

Modood, T., Berthoud, R., Lakey, J., Nazroo, J., Smith, P., Virdee, S. and Beishon, S. (1997) *Ethnic Minorities in Britain: Diversity and Difference*, London: Policy Studies Institute.

Morgan, S. (1997) 'The Contemporary Racialization of the Irish in Britain: An Investigation into Media Representations and the Everyday Experience of Being Irish in Britain', unpublished Ph.D. thesis, University of North London.

Nairn, T. (1977) *The Break-up of Britain: Crisis and neo-nationalism*, London: NLB.

—— (1988) *The Enchanted Glass: Britain and its Monarchy*, London: Radius.

Nandy, A. (1983) *The Intimate Enemy: Loss and Recovery of Self under Colonialism*, Oxford: Oxford University Press.

Nash, C. (1993) 'Remapping and Renaming: New Cartographies of Identity, Gender and Landscape in Ireland', *Feminist Review* 44: 39–57.

—— (1996) 'Men again: Irish masculinity, nature and nationhood in the early twentieth century', *Ecumene* 3.4: 427–53.

—— (1999) 'Genealogies of Irishness: Ancestor Searching and Diasporic Identities', paper to Institute of British Geographers Annual Conference, Leicester.

Neal, F. (1988) *Sectarian Violence: The Liverpool Experience 1819–1914, as Aspect of Anglo-Irish history*, Manchester: Manchester University Press.

Ni Laoire, C. (1999) 'Gender Issues in Rural Out-migration', in P. Boyle and K. Halfacree (eds) *Migration and Gender in the Developed World*, London: Routledge.

Nolan, J. (1989) *Ourselves Alone: Women's Emigration from Ireland 1885–1920*, Lexington: University Press of Kentucky.

—— (1995) 'A Patrick Henry in the Classroom: Margaret Haley and the Chicago Teachers' Federation', *Eire-Ireland* 30, 2: 104–17.

O'Carroll, I. (1990) *Models for Movers: Irish Women's Emigration to America*, Dublin: Attic.

—— (1995) 'Breaking the Silence from a Distance: Irish Women Speak on Sexual Abuse', in P. O'Sullivan (ed.) *Irish Women and Irish Migration*, vol. 4, *The Irish World Wide: History, Heritage, Identity*, Leicester: Leicester University Press.

O'Connor, H. (1993) 'Women Abroad: The Life Experiences of Irish Women in Leicester', unpublished M.litt. thesis, Trinity College, University of Dublin.

O'Connor, P. (1998) *Emerging Voices: Women in Contemporary Irish Society*, Dublin: Institute of Public Administration.

O'Connor, T. (1988) *South Boston: The History of an Ethnic Neighbourhood*, Boston: Northeastern University Press.

—— (1995) *The Boston Irish: A Political History*, Boston: Northeastern University Press.

Office of Population Censuses and Surveys (1993a) Census, Britain.

Ethnic Group and Country of Birth Tables, London: HMSO.

Office of Population Censuses and Surveys (1993b) 1991 Census, Britain. County Report: Greater Manchester (Part 1), London: HMSO.

O'Flynn, J. (1993) *Identity Crisis: Access to Social Security and ID Checks*, London: Action Group for Irish Youth.

O'Grada, C. (1973) 'A note on nineteenth-century Irish emigration statistics', *Population Studies* 29: 143–9.

O'Grady, A. (1988) *Irish Migration to London in the 1940s and 1950s*, Irish in Britain Research Forum Occasional Papers.

O'Leary, P. (1991) 'Anti-Irish riots in Wales', *Llafur: Journal of the Welsh Labour History Society* 5: 27–36

Omi, M. and Winant, H. (1986) *Racial formations in the United States from the 1960s to the 1980s*, New York and London: Routledge and Kegan Paul.

Osmond, J. (1988) *The Divided Kingdom*, London: Constable.

O'Sullivan, P. (ed.) (1995) *Irish Women and Irish Migration*, vol. 4, *The Irish World Wide: History, Heritage, Identity*, Leicester: Leicester University Press.

Pajaczkowska, C. and Young, L. (1992) 'Racism, Representation, Psychoanalysis', in J. Donald and A. Rattansi (eds) *'Race', Culture and Difference*, London: Sage.

Panayi, P. (1996) 'The Historiography of Immigrants and Ethnic Minorities: Britain Compared with the USA', *Ethnic and Racial Studies* 19, 4: 823–40.

Parliamentary Papers (1836) Royal Commission on the Condition of the Poorer Classes in Ireland. XXXIV. Appendix G. State of the Irish Poor in Great Britain.

Peach, C. (1968) *West Indian Migration to Britain*, Oxford: Oxford University Press.

—— (ed.) (1975) *Urban Social Segregation*, London: Longman.

Perlmann, J. (1988) *Ethnic Differences: Schooling and Social Structure among the Irish, Italians, Jews and Blacks in an American City 1880–1935*, Cambridge: Cambridge University Press.

Prandy, K. (1990) The Revised Cambridge Scale of Occupations, *Sociology* 4: 24.

Prendiville, P. (1988) 'Divorce in Ireland: An Analysis of the Referendum to Amend the Constitution, June 1986', *Women's Studies International Forum* 11: 355–63.

Redford, A. (1926) *Labour Migration in England 1800–1850*, Manchester: Manchester University Press.

Reimers, D. (1996) 'An End and a Beginning', in R. Bayor and T. Meagher (eds) *The New York Irish*, Baltimore: Johns Hopkins University Press.

Rex, J. and Moore, R. (1967) *Race, Community and Conflict: A Study of Sparkbrook*, Oxford: Oxford University Press.

Roberts, R. (1971) *The Classic Slum*, Manchester: Manchester University Press.

Roche, C. (1997) 'Home from Home? Irish Women in Birmingham', unpublished M.Sc. thesis, University of Birmingham.

Roediger, D. (1991) *The Wages of Whiteness: Race and the Making of the American Working Class*, London: Verso.

—— (1994) *Towards the Abolition of Whiteness; Essays on Race, Politics and Working Class History*, London: Verso.

Rossiter, A. (1992) '"Between the Devil and the Deep Blue Sea": Irish Women, Catholicism and Colonialism', in G. Saghal and N. Yuval-Davis (eds) *Refusing Holy Orders: Women And Fundamentalism in Britain*, London: Virago.

—— (1996) 'In Search of Mary's Past: Placing Nineteenth Century Immigrant Women in British Feminist History', in J. Grant (ed.) *Women, Migration and Empire*, Stoke-on-Trent: Trentham.

Saghal, G. and Yuval-Davis, N. (1992) *Refusing Holy Orders: Women and Fundamentalism in Britain*, London: Virago.

Sales, R. (1997) *Women Divided: Gender, Religion and Politics*, London: Routledge.

Sarbaugh, T. (1986) 'Exiles of Confidence: The Irish-American Community of San Francisco', in T. Meagher (ed.) *From Paddy to Studs: Irish-American Communities in the Turn of the Century Era 1880–1920*, New York: Greenwood.

Sharkey, S. (1993) 'Frontier Issues: Irish Women's Texts and Contexts', *Women: A Cultural Review* 4: 125–35.

Short, J. (1991) *Imagined Country: Society, Culture and Environment*, London: Routledge.

Sibley, D. (1981) *Outsiders in Urban Society*, Oxford: Blackwell.

—— (1995) *Geographies of Exclusion: Society and Difference in the West*, London: Routledge.

Simms, K. (1989) 'The Norman Invasion and the Gaelic Recovery', in R. Foster (ed.) *The Oxford Illustrated History of Ireland*, Oxford: Oxford University Press.

Skerrett, E. (1986) 'The Development of Catholic Identity among Irish Americans in Chicago 1880 to 1920', in T. Meagher (ed.) *From Paddy to Studs: Irish-American Communities in the Turn of the Century Era 1880–1920*, New York: Greenwood.

Smyth A. (ed.) (1993) *Irish Women's Studies Reader*, Dublin: Attic Press.

Snyder, R. (1996) 'The Neighbourhood Changed: The Irish in Washington Heights and Inwood Since 1945', in R. Bayor and T. Meagher (eds) *The New York Irish*, Baltimore: Johns Hopkins University Press.

Southwark Travellers Women's Group (1992) *Moving Stories: Traveller Women Write*, London: Traveller Education Team.

Sowell, T. (ed.) (1978) *Essays and Data on American Ethnic Groups* n.p.: The Urban Institute.

Spender, D. (1980) *Man-made Language*, London: Routledge and Kegan Paul.

Spinley, B. (1953) *The Deprived and the Privileged*, London: Routledge and Kegan Paul.

Storkey, M. (1994) *London's Ethnic Minorities: One City, Many Communities – an Analysis of 1991 Census Results*, London: London Research Centre.

Summerfield, P. (1984) *Women Workers in the Second World War; Production and Patriarchy in Conflict*, London: Routledge.

Sun (1994) 'The All-time Greatest Irish Jokes' 22 January: 9.

—— (1995) 'Prat's Life' 23 September: 6.

Swift, R. and Gilley, S. (eds) (1985) *The Irish in the Victorian City*, London: Croom Helm.

—— (eds) (1989) *The Irish in Britain 1815–1939*, London: Pinter.

Swirsky, R. (1999) 'Migration and Dislocation: Echoes of Loss within Jewish Women's Narratives', in A. Brah, M. Hickman and M. Mac an Ghaill (eds) *Thinking Identities: Ethnicity, Racism and Culture*, Basingstoke: Macmillan.

Tchen, J. K. W. (1996) 'Quimbo Appo's Fear of Fenians: Chinese-Irish-Anglo Relations in New York City', in R. Bayor and T. Meagher (eds) *The New York Irish*, Baltimore: Johns Hopkins University Press.

Tebbutt, M. (1983) 'The Evolution of Ethnic Stereotypes: An Examination of Stereotyping, with Particular Reference to the Irish (and to a Lesser Extent the Scots) in Manchester during the Late Nineteenth And Early Twentieth Centuries', unpublished M.Phil. thesis, University of Manchester.

Thernstrom, S. (1973) *The Other Bostonians: Poverty and Progress in the American Metropolis 1880–1970*, Cambridge, Mass.: Harvard University Press.

Times (1990) '"Cricket test" is defended by Tebbit', 21 April: 1.

Tololyan, K. (1991) 'The Nation State and its Others; in Lieu of a Preface', *Diaspora* 1: 3–7.

Towey, M. (1986) 'Kerry Patch Revisited: Irish Americans in St. Louis in the Turn of the Century Era', in T. Meagher (ed.) *From Paddy to Studs: Irish-American Communities in the Turn of the Century Era 1880–1920*, New York: Greenwood.

Travers, P. (1995) '"There Was Nothing For Me There": Irish Female Emigration, 1922–71', in P. O'Sullivan (ed) *Irish Women and Irish Migration*, vol. 4, *The Irish World Wide: history, heritage, identity*, Leicester: Leicester University Press.

Trudgill, P. (1983) *On Dialect: Social and Geographical Perspectives*, Oxford: Blackwell.

Ullah, P. (1983) 'Second Generation Irish Youth: A Social Psychological Investigation of a Hidden Minority', unpublished Ph.D. thesis, University of Birmingham.

—— (1985) 'Second-generation Irish Youth: Identity and Ethnicity', *New Community* XII: 310–20.

Walker, W. (1979) *Juteopolis: Dundee and its Textile Workers 1885–1923*, Edinburgh: Scottish Academic Press.

Wall, R. (1991) *Leading Lives: Irish Women in Britain*, Dublin: Attic.

Walshaw, R. (1941) *Migration to and from the British Isles: Problems and Policies*, London: Jonathan Cape.

Walter, B. (1979) 'The Geography of Irish Migration to Britain with Special Reference to Luton and Bolton', unpublished Ph.D. thesis, University of Oxford.

—— (1980) 'Time–space Patterns of Second Wave Irish Settlement in British Towns', *Transactions Institute of British Geographers*, New Series 5: 297–317.

—— (1984) 'Tradition and Ethnic Interaction: Second Wave Irish Settlement in Luton and Bolton', in C. Clarke, D. Ley and C. Peach (eds) *Geography and Ethnic Pluralism*, London: George Allen and Unwin.

—— (1986) 'Ethnicity and Irish Residential Segregation', *Transactions of the Institute of British Geographers* 11: 131–46.

—— (1988) *Irish Women in London*, London: London Strategic Policy Unit.

—— (1989a) *Irish Women in London: The Ealing Dimension*, London Borough of Ealing Women's Unit.

—— (1989b) *Gender and Irish Migration to Britain*, Cambridge: Anglia Working Paper 4.

—— (1991) 'Gender and Recent Irish Migration to Britain', in R. King (ed.) *Contemporary Irish Migration*, Dublin: Geographical Society of Ireland Special Publications.

—— (1995) 'Irishness, Gender and Place', *Environment and Planning D: Society and Place* 13: 35–50.

—— (1997) 'Contemporary Irish settlement in London: Women's Worlds, Men's Worlds', in J. Mac Laughlin (ed.) *Location and Dislocation in Contemporary Irish Society*, Cork: Cork University Press.

—— (1998) 'Challenging the Black/White Binary: The Need for an Irish Category in the 2001 Census', *Patterns of Prejudice* 32, 2: 73–86.

—— (1999) 'Inside and Outside the Pale: Diaspora Experiences of Irish Women', in P. Boyle and K. Halfacree (eds) *Migration and Gender in the Developed World*, London: Routledge.

—— (2000) '"Shamrocks Growing out of their Mouths"; Language and the Racialisation of the Irish in Britain', in A. Kershen (ed.) *Language, Labour and Migration*, Abingdon: Ashgate.

Ware, V. (1992) *Beyond the Pale: White Women, Racism and History*, London: Verso.

Webster, W. (1998) *Imagining Home: Gender, 'Race' and National Identity 1945–64*, London: UCL.

White, R. (1998) *Remembering Ahanagran: Storytelling in a Family's Past*, New York: Hill and Wang.

Williams, R. (1990) *Hierarchical Structures and Social Value; the Creation of Black and Irish Identities in the United States*, Cambridge: Cambridge University Press.

Williams, R. and Ecob, R. (1999) 'Regional Mortality and the Irish in Britain: Findings from the ONS Longitudinal Study', *Sociology of Health and Illness* 21, 3: 344–67.

Wilson, F. (1946) 'The Irish in Britain during the First Half of the Nineteenth Century', unpublished M.A. thesis, University of Manchester.

Woodward, K. (ed.) (1997) *Identity and Difference*, Milton Keynes: Open University Press.

Wright, P. (1985) *On Living in an Old Country*, London: Verso.

Young, I. M. (1990) *Justice and the Politics of Difference*, Princeton, N.J.: Princeton University Press.

Young, R. (1995) *Colonial Desire: Hybridity in Theory, Culture and Race*, London: Routledge.

Index

Stowe, Harriet Beecher 55
strategies of avoidance 171–7
Strokestown Famine Museum 40
suffrage 136–7, 139
Summerfield, Penny 88
Sun 114, 115
Sunday Times 85
Swedenburg, T. 6, 8, 9, 10, 118,
   162, 195, 213, 214
Swift, R. 3
Swirsky, R. 260, 264

Tchen, John Kuo Wei 70
teachers *see* Irish migrant women's
   work, second generation
Tebbutt, M. 90, 135, 146, 275
textile industry *see* Irish migrant
   women's work
Thatcher, Margaret 107
Thernstrom, S. 48
Tipperary, County 228, 229
Toloyan, K. 11
Towey, M. 48
trade unionism 52, 56, 67, 110,
   133, 137, 139, 140
Travellers 25, 188, 259, 271
Travers, P.
Trudgill, P. 164
tuberculosis 218

Ullah, Philip 176, 212
unemployment 121, 135, 146
United Kingdom, definitions of
   77–8
United Nations: Commissioner
   for Human Rights 11
United States Catholic
   Conference 36
United States of America 1, 5,
   8–9, 23, 25, 31, 32, 103, 105,
   106, 109, 110, 119, 144, 165,
   198, 203, 209, 218, 253:
   economy of 51; 'illegals' in 2,
   36, 38; 57, 71; immigration
   restrictions of 35, 119; missing
   persons in 37; concepts of
   'whiteness' in 24–6, 40, 188; *see
   also* Irish in the United States
   of America

Valiulis, M. 2
Virgin Mary, The 18, 26, 200, 275
voice 95, 163–7

Wales 86, 95, 96, 127, 128, 144,
   159; *see also* Welshness
Walker, W. 132
Wall, Rita 3–4
Walshaw, R. 91
Walter, B. 2, 5, 17, 23, 25, 85, 88,
   93, 95, 96, 128, 133, 155, 161,
   163, 166–9 *passim*, 172–7
   passim, 181, 182, 184, 189, 190,
   192, 199, 216, 275
Ware, V. 272
Washington, George 43
WASPs (White Anglo-Saxon
   Protestants) 40, 42, 44, 45, 48,
   56
Weavers' Association 137, 140, 141
Webster, Wendy 96, 106, 108, 109,
   149, 168, 256, 276
Welsh Nationalist Party 30
Welshness 30, 31, 32
West Coast of America 49
'white blouse' work 56, 146
'White Studies' 272
White, Richard 37
White, Sara 37
whiteness 1–2, 5–6, 24–5, 65–71,
   79, 80, 109–11, 160, 231, 272,
   277
Williams, Richard 39, 51, 53, 60,
   61, 65, 66, 276
Wilson, F. 145
Winant, H. 69
Winchester, Simon 85
Wirral 185–7, 193
Woodward, Katherine 197
Worcester, Massachusetts 48, 49,
   131
Workers' Education Association 141
Wright, P. 95

Young, Iris Marion 26, 165
Young, L. 24
Young, R. 94, 275
Yuval-Davis, Nira 97, 111